A Political Life

A Political Life

Norberto Bobbio

Edited by Alberto Papuzzi

Translated by Allan Cameron

polity

This translation copyright © Polity Press 2002. First published as Norberto Bobbio, *Autobiografia*, a cura di Alberto Papuzzi © 1997. Gius Laterza & Figli Spa, Roma–Bari. English language edition arranged through the mediation of Eulama Literary Agency.

First published in 2002 by Polity Press in association with Blackwell Publishers Ltd, a Blackwell Publishing Company.

Published with the financial assistance of the Italian Ministry of Foreign Affairs.

Editorial office:
Polity Press
65 Bridge Street
Cambridge CB2 1UR, UK

Marketing and production:
Blackwell Publishers Ltd
108 Cowley Road
Oxford OX4 1JF, UK

Published in the USA by
Blackwell Publishers Inc.
350 Main Street
Malden, MA 02148, USA

ISBN 0-7456-2215-1
ISBN 0-7456-2216-X (pbk)

A catalogue record for this book is available from the British Library and has been applied for from the Library of Congress.

Typeset in 10.5 on 12pt Sabon
by Graphicraft Limited, Hong Kong
Printed in Great Britain by TJ International, Padstow, Cornwall

This book is printed on acid-free paper.

Contents

The plates will be found between pages 120 and 121.

Cartoon of Norberto Bobbio by his schoolfriend Ugo Borgogno (1927).

Introduction
Teresa Chataway

Norberto Bobbio is the most important legal and political philosopher of post-war Italy. Emeritus professor of the University of Turin
since 1984, he is one of the foremost theorists of democracy in the
twentieth century and has devoted a lifetime of research to thinking
about the theory and practice of democratic politics. His scholarly
endeavour, spanning a period of more than sixty years, is concerned
almost entirely with the moral sciences, in particular law, ethics and
politics. His principal intellectual aim has been an extended search
for a synthesis of the liberal concern with individual liberty, human
rights and the rule of law in a democracy underpinned by what is
known in Italy as 'liberalsocialist' philosophy. Norberto Bobbio participated in the anti-fascist struggle during the Resistance, and his life
experience is interwoven with the complex history of Italy's First
Republic and the equally challenging transition to the Second Republic. A thinker of the left as well as an objective commentator on
Italian politics from the 1950s to the present, Bobbio defends the
rights of liberty in various spheres by highlighting the aspirations and
expectations of citizens in changing democracies. During the many
vicissitudes and transformations of Italian democracy, Bobbio has
upheld the democratic ideal of building a society that is more free,
more civilized and more just.

A *Political Life* is Bobbio's account of his multifaceted experience
under the impact of fascism and other major political events in Italy.
The book includes previously unpublished documents and other
material gleaned by its editor, Alberto Papuzzi, in conversation with
Bobbio. The resulting narrative offers a new perspective on the life of

this remarkable man, revealing how the early phases of Bobbio's intellectual development and political involvement (which took place under an authoritarian regime) were critical for his scholarly achievement and public contribution. It becomes clear that Bobbio is one of the very few individuals in Italy who was both a protagonist and an analyst of the country's intellectual, cultural and democratic transformations. What is more, Bobbio's story highlights the way in which a 'normal' life (as Bobbio is apt to describe his own) can also reflect all the themes, doubts and contradictions that marked the twentieth century.

Intellectual and political development

Norberto Bobbio was born in 1909 in Turin, at a time when Italy was a parliamentary monarchy. Ten years later, Mussolini founded the Fascist Movement, and, following his rise to power, Italy underwent a process of *fascistizzazione* [fascistization]. Bobbio's early experience of dictatorship helped shape his role as a 'mediating or engaged intellectual', dedicated to defending the primacy of liberty. Throughout his life, Bobbio has been concerned with the question of intellectuals and their different attitudes towards political power and culture.[1] In his view, intellectuals must be 'independent but not indifferent' in defending the fundamental principles of democracy and in drawing attention to what needs to be under continual review. In choosing to employ this approach of rational dialogue and tolerance (as opposed to a more direct political method), Bobbio differentiated himself from other liberal thinkers.

Bobbio has long been convinced of the importance of dialogue in free and open societies. His interest in, and vocation for, dialogue originated during the Cold War when he participated in the Société Européenne de Culture [European Society of Culture]. In the face of the military and political obstacles represented by the Iron Curtain, the society aimed to unite intellectuals from both sides of a divided Europe; under the banner of the 'politics of culture', it hoped to overcome the restraints of the 'politics of politicians'. Bobbio's 'Invito al colloquio' ['Invitation to dialogue'], addressed to the Communist Party leader, Palmiro Togliatti, promoted a series of debates on liberty, power, the role of intellectuals in an open society and the meaning of democracy. The open discussion of the fundamental problems in Italy's democratic development sought to address the relation between the liberal tradition (which needed renewal) and the socialist tradition (which in the Italy of that time was principally represented by the Communist Party). This public experience identified Bobbio as an engaged intellectual, as well as establishing an important precedent for the Italian left.

In his work, Bobbio has striven to convey to the general public exactly what the struggle for liberty and justice entailed during the fascist years. This emphasis is clear in all his writings, including his journalistic pieces, most of which appeared in the Turinese daily paper *La Stampa* from 1976 to the present. In these articles, Bobbio's appeal is usually twofold: first, to civil society for a more active democratic participation, and second, to the Italian political class for transparency and responsibility. Bobbio's emphasis on participation and transparency has deep roots. During Bobbio's formative years, Turin was a barometer for intellectual activity and change in northern Italy and Europe. The cultural and intellectual initiatives that flourished between the 1920s and 1950s constituted an extended phase of urgent political action, which generated the so-called *cultura militante* [militant culture]. In Bobbio's view, militant culture does not translate into immediate political action, even if it is deeply inspired by it and even if it may, under certain conditions, acquire a political dimension. A militant culture is a culture based on firm moral premisses. It is also a culture engaged in constant debate. It is this combination that enables a cultural tradition to survive and to perpetuate itself.

Militant culture thrived in the academic environment of the University of Turin, and Bobbio's time there exerted an enormous influence on his political and intellectual direction. Indeed, three figures who played a key role in shaping his intellectual life were the legal philosopher, Gioele Solari (who was also Bobbio's mentor), the leading professor of ecclesiastical and canon law, Francesco Ruffini, and the liberal economist and journalist Luigi Einaudi (who later became the first Italian president, 1948–55). Like many of his generation, Bobbio was also inspired by the Italian philosopher Benedetto Croce (1866–1952). Bobbio engaged critically with Croce's work, especially during his political involvement with the Partito d'Azione [Action Party, or Pd'A].[2] From Croce's example and work Bobbio derived the following orientations: first, a way in which to theorize the relation between politics and culture; and second, the conviction of the superiority of liberalism for the foundation of any form of civilized state and as the necessary, if not sufficient, condition for any democratic government. Above all, the defence of liberty and democratic institutions for the realization of justice and equality is crucial for Bobbio, because through them democracy becomes the substance of life and the basis for behaviour and choices.

Bobbio's breadth of knowledge encompasses the work of German and other European theorists, and he employs them in his search for a healthy realism that is often otherwise absent in the Italian tradition. Indelible, too, is the influence of English philosophers such as Thomas Hobbes, John Locke and John Stuart Mill, whose philosophical and methodological rigour helped Bobbio to define directions, clarify concepts, and combat prejudices or myths from the Italian context. Indeed, a key characteristic of his intellectual development is this ability to synthesize the legal and political heritage of continental and English philosophers.

Bobbio's early post-war writing included the seminal essay, 'Legal science and linguistic analysis',[3] in which he introduced analytical linguistic philosophy into Italian legal culture. By establishing the logical-positivist basis of Italian legal theory, he influenced a generation of Italian jurists. Bobbio criticized natural law theory and shifted towards legal positivism. During the 1950s, this led to his 'conversion' to Kelsenism. His attraction to the jurist Hans Kelsen (1881–1973) resulted from his study of Kelsen's writings on 'the pure theory of law'.[4] The Kelsenian influence is discernible in Bobbio's own theories of the state, democracy and peace. However, in light of the developments in the welfare state, Kelsen's legal structuralism seemed somewhat anachronistic, and in the 1970s Bobbio went beyond this to elaborate 'a functional theory of law'.[5] This theory takes into account both the structure and aims of law, thus linking neo-positivism and the sociological orientation.

The period between 1935 and 1948 was crucial for Bobbio's political formation, including his attraction to 'liberalsocialism'. Liberalsocialism emphasizes the need to combine the claims of liberalism (liberty) with those of socialism (justice) in a concrete political project. In the Italian tradition, the term 'liberalsocialism' was coined as a single word [*liberalsocialismo*] by Guido Calogero and Aldo Capitini. Calogero was professor of philosophy at the University of Pisa and the author of an anti-fascist book on ethics and education.[6] Capitini was a free thinker and the author of a book that promoted the use of non-violence and civil disobedience as a means of opposing all unjust laws.[7] In 1937, Calogero and Capitini founded a clandestine political group in Pisa identified as the Liberal-Socialist Movement. Bobbio joined the movement, thus shifting from an idealist attitude towards anti-fascism to one of conscious and active participation in the Action Party. As a party of intellectuals, the Action Party did not interpret the War of Liberation as a class war, but as an ideological precursor to a democratic revolution. Bobbio became involved in the Resistance in Padua and then in Turin. While teaching at university, he contributed to the ongoing political debate, in particular through his incisive pieces for the daily paper *Giustizia e Libertà* [*Justice and Freedom*], the representative organ of the Action Party. A close reading of his democratic writings from the 1950s to the present reveals the relevance of the liberalsocialist perspective to his analyses of the diverse moral and political issues in Italy's pluralist society. In fact, liberalsocialism is a leitmotif that runs throughout Bobbio's work.

During 1968–9, Italy's economy experienced a severe structural crisis. This was a result of the pressure generated by the accelerated economic growth and the consequent political transformations. The so-called *autunno caldo* ['hot autumn'] with its strong winds of student protest and worker militancy, dramatically changed Italy's cultural and political climate. The prevailing mood was threatening and reactionary. At the time, Bobbio observed that the turmoil meant putting aside his studies on legal theory, for these were no longer of any interest to his students, who were instead engaged in revolutionary ferment. Whilst Bobbio's emphasis on legal teaching abated, he began to devote greater attention to the ensuing political questions of reform, terrorism, law and order, state responsibility and the role of political parties in democratic states. This experience was a turning point in his legal career, for much of his legal reasoning was then incorporated into his political philosophy. These different strands of Bobbio's philosophical development lead to a better comprehension of some of the reasons that underpinned his persistent search for a more effective and a stronger democracy. Besides the issues of peace and human rights, democracy has been 'the magnet for his lifetime of study'.[8]

Democracy: the rules of the game

In the contemporary liberal-democratic tradition, definitions of democracy revolve around the 'rules of the game', or 'universal rules of procedure'. However, in Bobbio's view, such rules only establish *how* one must arrive at political decisions, not *what* must be decided.[9] The rules that are always needed are those that serve to prevent the abuse of power. As such, they can assert and strengthen the rule of law, outside which even democracy becomes autocracy. Amongst the various definitions of democracy that appear in Bobbio's writings, the two that best summarize the main themes are the *legal* (or *procedural*) and the *political* definitions. According to the legal definition, the democratic form of government is characterized by the 'institutionalization of opposition', popular election of leaders through a free vote, the separation of powers and the observance of the 'rule of law'. Fundamentally, the rule of law is a system of governmental behaviour and authority that is constrained by law and which respects the law. This formulation represents the legal-political nexus that is inherent to the liberal-democratic state and which also draws on Kelsen's argument that law and power are two sides of the same coin (that is to say, only power can create law and only law can limit power).[10] These procedural rules are closely connected to – and indeed become operational through – institutions. Bobbio insists that institutions are essential for a working democracy. He also appeals for transparency in the modalities and instruments employed to monitor power.

According to its political definition, democracy is characterized by the fact that leadership emerges from the competition for votes by parties, which can alternate peacefully. With regard to the question of competition, Bobbio's theorization appears indebted to the Austrian economist Joseph Schumpeter (1883–1950), who maintains that democracy is best understood as a representative government in which competitive political parties are authorized to act as intermediaries between individuals and government. Bobbio's political definition of democracy was influenced by Karl Popper (1902–94) who also described democracy as a form of government characterized by a system of rules that facilitates the changeover of leaders without the need to resort to violence. In this view, non-violence represents the ideal, which humanity, riven by increasingly destructive internal conflicts, should aspire to achieve.

Over the years, Bobbio has consistently advocated an end to the persisting Italian anomaly of the multi-party system, which is considered to be the major cause of frequent government changes. In the elections of April 1996, l'Ulivo ['the Olive Tree'], consisting of the centre-left coalition led by Romano Prodi, won convincingly. This victory, Bobbio stated in *Le Monde*, 'marks the end of the Italian anomaly'.[11] Finally, the long-awaited change in Italian politics was to a certain extent historically realized, but 'the real novelty, which is much more important and decisive for the evolution of democracy, is alternation'.[12]

Another distinguishing aspect of Bobbio's concept of democracy is his analysis of the 'unkept, or broken, promises' and of unforeseen obstacles, which persistently undermine the efficacy of democratic processes. If democracy is defined first as the widest participation by citizens in collective decision-making, and second as a peaceful method for the resolution of conflicts, it becomes evident that the unkept promises concern above all the first definition. This relative lack of fulfilment also supports Bobbio's contention that democracy is 'difficult' due to its incompleteness.[13] Bobbio's understanding of democracy includes the wider areas of civil society, both within and between states. In this respect, he observes that – although the number of democratic states is increasing and the international system is becoming more democratized – new challenges are continually emerging as a result of both globalizing and localizing pressures. Among those challenges, there is still the pressing concern for human rights.

Human rights

Bobbio contends that the recognition and protection of rights (the *conditio sine qua non* for the survival of democracy) must be placed at the centre of contemporary world problems. Drawing on Immanuel Kant (1724–1804), Bobbio interprets the growing attention to the question of human dignity as a premonitory sign of the moral progress of humanity. His theory of rights is also influenced by Rousseau and *The Social Contract*, as well as by Hobbes, Locke and other natural law theorists. According to Bobbio, natural rights are historical rights. They emerge in different times, and are subject to transformation and expansion. After the Second World War, human rights theory advanced mainly in two directions: the universality and multiplication of rights.

In international law, universality is considered the point of departure for the transformation of the traditional right of 'peoples' into that of 'individuals'. Such transformation potentially endows individuals with the right to question their state on any issue that concerns their rights. Thus they are theoretically citizens not only of one state but also of the world. The multiplication aspect is seen as a social phenomenon. This accounts for the origin of rights and their relationship with society, as well as for the close nexus between social change and the emergence of new rights. Classical rights of liberty have been extended to include political, social and other rights, the ultimate aim of which is the defence of humanity's three great assets: life, liberty and economic security. Bobbio perceives such an extension of human rights as providing historical evidence of the compatibility of liberalism and socialism. He refers optimistically to the 'fact that today more so than in the past, we live and work in a universe of shared values, which are those of liberal democracy construed as a set of rules for living together. These rules are based on the acknowledgement of human rights, and are aimed at eliminating the use of force as a solution to social conflict.'[14] When we pause to consider the struggle for rights historically, we realize that this was fought on different fronts and, in particular with three opponents: religious power (the Church), political power (wars of conquest) and economic power (capitalism). Today, threats to life, liberty and security emerge from the power of science and its manifold technical applications. Modern societies are now characterized by enormous, rapid and irreversible progress, and by technological and technocratic transformation of the globe. As a result of these advances, additional new rights (which Bobbio terms of the third and fourth generation) feature prominently in the continuing debate within states and on an international level.

In summary, Bobbio sees the nexus between rights, democracy and peace as the basis for the survival of democratic states and for the continuation of international democratization. In *The Age of Rights* that nexus is elaborated as follows: 'Recognition and protection of rights rest at the foundation of modern democratic constitutions. Peace, in turn, is the necessary precondition for the recognition and effective protection of rights within individual states and the international system.'[15] However, Bobbio is also aware that, due to the principle of non-intervention, human rights protection is not at present guaranteed within the international system, since that stops at the threshold of individual sovereign states. Moreover, the global extension of human rights can only become effective when individuals have the right of recourse to courts higher than those of their state. Breaking with the tradition of *jus publicum Europaeum* implies that not only states, or collective entities, but also persons are considered subjects of the international system. As Bobbio recently emphasized: 'I am especially in favour of the fact that we are moving towards an international law whose subjects are no longer just states, but also, and especially, individuals.'[16] He further remarks that Kant's idea of a 'cosmopolis', where everyone is potentially a citizen not only of an individual state but also of the world, has not received due attention within legal theory. Accordingly, to theorize the cosmopolitical dimension of rights, citizenship and democracy, Bobbio draws on Kant's notion of *jus cosmopoliticum* [cosmopolitical right].[17]

Cosmopolitical democracy and peace

In his writings on democracy among nations, Bobbio restates his argument that in the twentieth century (and, by extension, the twenty-first), the real challenge to democracy within states comes from the outside. This is due to the uneven democratization of the international system. In his view, the democracy of the future must encompass the cosmopolitical dimension. In 'Democracy and the international system', Bobbio presents cosmopolitical democracy as a way of extending, or strengthening, peace outside the boundaries of individual states.[18] Briefly, 'cosmopolitical' relates to all states and polities, and concerns the issue of a universal polity.[19] In general, this principle indicates the need for a law capable of governing relations at the supranational level. It is also part of the discourse of cosmopolitical theory, which rejects territorial and political divisions (homeland, nation or state), and asserts the right of individuals to define themselves as citizens of the world. Drawing on Kant's *Perpetual Peace*, Bobbio advances the notion of this cosmopolitical right that potentially exists alongside internal and international rights.

Bobbio's concept of peace originates from Hobbes's theory and draws on Kant's thinking.[20] Bobbio interprets Hobbes's contractualism in a Kantian sense, attributing to it a universalist and cosmopolitical value. At the same time, he synthesizes Kantian thought from a Hobbesian viewpoint, assigning to Kantian federalism the meaning of a real project for overcoming the sovereignty of national states, thus leading to the constitution of a global federal state. By adopting the domestic analogy model, Bobbio borrows from the central philosophical and political categories used by Hobbes to depict the passage of individuals from the state of nature to a secure and peaceful civil (or political) society. For example, within a state, the foundations of democratic society rest on the pact of non-aggression. This leads to a permanent association (*pactum societatis*) and to the obligation to comply with the collective decisions previously established by common consent (*pactum subjectionis*). However, for both the negative pact of non-aggression and the positive pact of obedience to be valid and efficacious, they must be guaranteed by a legitimate power under the rule of law. Such pacts are understood metaphorically by Bobbio as consensual procedures through which states also confer to a 'third party' the power to regulate, even by coercion, their relations. Above all, the remedy is sought in the concentration of power in a democratically organized supreme entity, as the holder of the legitimate monopoly of international force. The question is whether such an imperfect construct, which, although successful within the state, has the potential to become operational in the global context and to guarantee stable peace in the international system.

Conclusion

Since the 1960s, Bobbio's writings on law and on democracy have stimulated increasing interest throughout the world. Over time, the broad range and diversity of his work has prompted both academic and public acknowledgements. In July 1984, Bobbio was made a life senator of the Italian Republic by President Sandro Pertini. This was Bobbio's only political appointment since his earlier involvement in the Action Party. More recently, he has been awarded the Balzan International Prize (1994), the Agnelli International Prize (1995) and the Hegel Prize (2000). The growing interest in Bobbio's work is in part a result of his commitment to unravelling some of the major issues that confront contemporary societies. It can also be attributed to the wide-ranging nature of his work, which is inspired by particular ideals and which clearly reflects the social and political conditions of post-war Italy. But the most important reason for reading and revisiting Bobbio's writings lies in his intellectual and moral convictions: his belief in the primacy of freedom and in the relevance of justice to democracy.

1

Before the Conflagration

The twenty months between 8 September 1943 and 25 April 1945 formed a period in our lives that involved us in events far bigger than ourselves. Fascism had forced us to disregard politics, and then suddenly we found ourselves compelled to take part in politics in the exceptional circumstances provided by German occupation and the War of Liberation, for what might be called moral reasons. Our lives were turned upside down. We all encountered painful incidents: fear, flight, arrest, imprisonment and the loss of people dear to us. *Afterwards* we were no longer what we had been *before*. Our lives had been cut into two parts: a 'before' and an 'after', which in my case were almost symmetrical, because when fascism fell on 25 July 1943, I had, at the age of thirty-four, almost reached what Dante termed 'the middle of life's course'. In the twenty months between September 1943 and April 1945, I was born into a new existence, completely different from the previous one, which I came to regard simply as an apprenticeship to the real life I commenced in the Resistance as a member of the Action Party.

When I talk about 'us', I mean a generation of intellectuals who, like me, lived through that transition from one Italian reality to an opposing one. It was to this generation that I dedicated my collection of portraits and personal accounts which were published in 1964 by the youthful publishing house Lacaita di Manduria as *Italia civile* [*Civilized Italy*]. Curzio Malaparte's *Italia barbara* [*Barbarian Italy*], which was published by Gobetti in 1925, had suggested the title to me by way of contrast. As I explained in the new edition (Passigli: Florence, 1986), the characters that appear in *Civilized Italy* – and the other two collections of portraits published by Passigli: *Maestri e compagni* [*Mentors and Comrades*] (1984) and *Italia fedele* [*Loyal Italy*] (1986) – belong to an ideal country, another Italy, which is free from the traditional vices of the old Italy. We always believe that we have left the reality of that old Italy behind, but then we suddenly find ourselves up against it again. I wrote that it was an Italy characterized by arrogance and self-importance at the top, and servility and idleness at the bottom. It was an Italy in which astuteness and intrigue were considered the ultimate art of government, and cunning and petty deceit the meagre art of survival. The people whose lives I have experienced and written about represent another Italy and a wholly different history.

Norberto Bobbio was born in Turin on 18 October 1909. A wave of protests, demonstrations, public meetings and parliamentary motions, appeals by intellectuals, trade union activities and diplomatic incidents had been rocking Europe for a week, following the shooting in Barcelona of the Catalan revolutionary Francisco Ferrer, who had been accused by the Spanish government of inciting revolt and found guilty in a trial in which no evidence was produced. In Italy, the Trade Union Confederation had declared a general strike in Rome and Turin. The political tension was further heightened by the socialist and anarchist hostility to the arrival of Tsar Nicholas II of Russia in Reggia di Racconigi.

On Monday 18 October, the registrar of births and deaths in Turin recorded twenty-two births – twelve boys and ten girls. The day was damp and cloudy. Emma Gramatica's theatre company was at the Teatro Carignano. Fiat, which had been founded in 1899, was producing about 1,800 cars a year. Aviation was so much in vogue that the Turin daily newspaper La Stampa *published an advert under 'Situations wanted': 'A distinguished young man with a passion for aviation wishes to pilot aircraft.' Piero Gobetti, who Bobbio was never to meet, was eight years old and attended Pacchiotti Primary School. Cesare Lombroso, who had been a lecturer in medical law and public health at Turin University since 1876, died on Tuesday 19th, the day after Bobbio's birth.*

My father, Luigi Bobbio, came from the province of Alessandria and worked as a consultant surgeon at the San Giovanni Hospital, one of the most prestigious in the city. My paternal grandfather, Antonio, was a primary school teacher, and later a director of education. He was a Catholic liberal, who worked on the Alessandria newspaper *La Lega*, and took an interest in philosophy. He published two critical works on the positivists Roberto Ardigò and Herbert Spencer, as well as a book on Manzoni whose title would now make us smile: *Truth, Beauty and Goodness in 'The Betrothed'*.[1] Quite recently, the young historian from Alessandria, Cesare Manganelli, edited a selection from the unpublished diaries that my grandfather wrote throughout his life, under the title of *Memoirs*.[2] In the preface, I wrote: 'We youngsters always saw our grandfather as a venerable and venerated old man of whom we were slightly fearful, and about whom even his children spoke with admiration and reverence.'

My mother was called Rosa Caviglia, and she came from Rivalta Bormida, a village 8 kilometres from Acqui, which I still visit and to which I have always felt a strong emotional attachment. Giuseppe Baretti's family came from there, and I recall that the first magazine I subscribed to when I was at university was *Il Baretti*, founded by Gobetti. Croce, Cecchi, Montale and Saba were all contributors.

In *De senectute*, I indulged in a curious and light-hearted digression to illustrate aspects of my Piedmontese culture, whose strengths and limitations I am only too aware of:

> I will start with the name: nomen omen, as once used to be said. Or to parody a famous title 'The importance of being Norberto'. I inherited this strange name of a German bishop who lived in the eleventh and twelfth centuries from my maternal grandfather, who was born in 1847 in a small village on the right bank of the Bormida between Acqui and Alessandria. Family legend has it that when my grandfather was born the last of a numerous family which had exhausted his parents' stock of the usual seven or eight family names, they decided to give him the name of a Piedmontese poet who was very fashionable at the time: Norberto Rosa. It has always been a mystery to me that this unexceptional poet from Val di Susa could have been so popular in Val Bormida, especially as I have attempted many times to read his poetry in deference to this name, but I have never got past the first fifty pages. The same family tradition has passed down the inaccurate story that Norberto Rosa was famous in the Alessandria area because he campaigned to collect the funds for the purchase of the Hundred Cannons which were supposed to defend the city's so-called 'external forts'. He did in fact do this, but not until 1857, when my grandfather was ten years old. The truth is that Norberto Rosa was made famous by his poetry. I leave to literary scholars the question of how and why he was so famous that he caused an unsuspecting child born in 1847 and his even more unsuspecting grandchild born 70 years later to carry a name so foreign to the Monferrato Region.[3]

I had a happy childhood and adolescence. My family was affluent, I lived in a nice house with two people in service, a private chauffeur working for my father during the more prosperous years from 1925 to 1940, and two cars. My brother Antonio was two years older than me and somewhat different: extrovert, highly intelligent, always top of the class. He managed to get through the second and third year of senior secondary school[4] by studying through the summer. He chose to follow our father into a medical career. He became the professor of surgery at Parma University. Unfortunately he became very ill before reaching the age of sixty, and died a few years later.

However there was a source of melancholy that ran through my conventional adolescence. I was a sick child and that illness has affected the whole of my life. Even though my father was a doctor, I never discovered the exact nature of my ailment. I can never forget that I went through the whole of the first year of junior secondary school[5] with my arm in a sling, as though I had fallen and broken it. I started to write poetry very young, and I recently tore it all up. I wrote my first poems in 1923 when I was in the fourth year of junior secondary school, and they were a mixture of Leopardian pessimism and the *crepuscolarismo*[6] of Gozzano. I can still remember the last verse of Gozzano's *Colloqui*:

> I will be the tender timeworn son,
> The one who sighed at starry rays
> Whose mind did to Friedrich and Arthur run,
> But abandoned the page of rebel displays
> To bury unburied swallows
> And offer grass blades to legs that craze
> On desperate overturned beetles.

Arthur is Schopenhauer and Friedrich is Nietzsche. I remember that poetry now, because ultimately it reflects a state of mind I can identify with.

My passion for reading started late, but immediately became intense and all consuming. An idea of this obsession can be found in the lists of books I read each month, carefully written down on my father's prescription pads. For instance in December 1928, during my first year at university, I read eighteen titles, ranging from religious and political works to biographies, poetry and plays.[7] I had clearly taken advantage of the Christmas holidays and one of the works, Géraldy's love poetry, was evidence of the dispersive interests that are typical of a voracious reader. While I read French in the original (as I had studied French at school), I read English works in translations, as testified by Shelley's poetry in Italian, which also appeared in the list. I did not start to learn English until I went to university, which was generally the rule in that period.

One of my friends at the time was Cesare Pavese, who had attended the modern senior secondary school rather than the classical senior secondary school. The 'modernity' of these schools resided precisely in the fact that they taught English instead of Greek. When he heard that I was learning English on my own, he suggested that we should read some of the best-known texts together. For a period of time, we met at my house in the morning. In order to avoid being disturbed, we would shut ourselves in the waiting room of my father's office where he saw his patients in the afternoon. Pavese was the teacher, and I was the student. He would read the text, translate it and comment upon it. I can remember Shelley's 'To a Skylark' very well, because I attempted to do my own translation, as can be seen from a note in the same prescription pad on a slightly later page.[8]

I was never a great novel reader. I read a lot of Balzac, because we had a book series, which included many of his novels. Of course I read all the great nineteenth-century novelists, such as Stendhal, Flaubert, Dostoyevsky and Tolstoy, who were considered essential reading at the time, but apparently no longer are. The writer, whose works I have read almost in their entirety during various periods of my life, is Thomas Mann. How could I ever forget the famous conversation between Settembrini and Naphta in *The Magic Mountain*? Or the parting from John Castor, 'the honest Benjamin of life', on the last page. Or the final words: 'Out of this universal feast of death, out of this extremity of fever, kindling the rain-washed evening sky to a fiery glow, may it be that Love one day shall mount?'

In my family, I was never made aware of the class conflict between the bourgeoisie and the proletariat. We were brought up to look on all men as equal, and to think that there was no difference between the educated and uneducated, or between the rich and the poor. I referred to this upbringing to a democratic way of life in *Left and Right*, and confessed to always being uncomfortable with the spectacle of differences in wealth between those at the top and at the bottom of the social scale, while fascist populism was attempting to regiment Italians in a social organization that wanted those inequalities to be set in stone:

These differences were particularly evident during the summer holidays in the countryside where we city lads played with the sons of peasants. To tell the truth, our friendship was based on a perfect understanding, and the class differences were completely irrelevant, but we could not help noticing the contrast between our houses and theirs, our food and theirs, and our clothes and theirs (in the summer they were barefoot). Every year when we started our holidays, we learnt that one of our playmates had died the previous winter from tuberculosis. I do not remember a single death amongst my schoolfriends in the city.[9]

However, it was not at the family hearth that I developed my aversion to Mussolini's regime. I belonged to a family that supported fascism, as did the majority of the middle class. I remember very well the conversation we had in our home, when the fascists came to power in October 1922 at the time of the March on Rome. I was thirteen years old. I have vivid memories of the last democratic elections held in 1921, because the daily newspaper in Turin, *La Gazzetta del Popolo*, had organized a competition with prizes to be won by whoever managed the closest forecast to the real results. My brother and I took part in the competition and followed all the events in the electoral campaign with enthusiasm. At that time there was no television or even radio campaigning, so the poster campaigns were hard-fought affairs. Via Sacchi, where we lived, was covered with election posters all the way along. The War Veterans' Party supported two lawyers, Bardanzellu and Villabruna, and the Peasants' Party presented just one candidate, a sitting member of parliament called Stella. We may not have won the competition, but because of it we became very interested in elections, as though they were football matches or cycle races.

I can remember very well the great strike of the summer of 1922: the hotly debated 'Legalitarian Strike' which lasted from 1 to 3 August. It was the last act of popular resistance to fascist violence. We were coming home by train with our parents after our holidays at the seaside in Spotorno on the Ligurian riviera, but we had to interrupt our journey at Novi Ligure. I can still see clearly the station surrounded by darkness, the train stationary along the platform, the fascist Blackshirts securing the railway. I feel as though I can still hear the reactions of the upright middle-class people like my father: they were saying that if we did not defend ourselves, we would be taken over by 'subversives' or 'Bolsheviks', as socialists and communists were called without distinction. My family, like many other bourgeois families, greeted the March on Rome with approval, partly because it was widely believed that fascism was just a passing phase. It was considered useful for stopping those who wanted to be 'like Russia'. There can be no doubt that the Russian Revolution represented a danger to the middle classes, a 'terrible fright'. The fascist gangs were frightening too, but the attitude towards them tended to be more benign.

From 1919 to 1927, I was fortunate enough to study at Massimo D'Azeglio School, where the majority of our teachers were antifascists. I will mention two of them: Umberto Cosmo had been the literary critic for *La Stampa* when it was run by Frassati and took a neutralist position during the First World War in support of Giolitti.

He was a great Dante scholar and the author of well-known critical works such as *Vita di Dante* (1930) and *L'ultima ascesa* (1936), both published by Laterza. He was accused of defeatism and anti-nationalism, and attacked in Parliament on May 1926 by the prominent nationalist and fascist professor of Italian literature at Turin University, Vittorio Cian, for 'opposing the directives of the national government'. After having been asked to explain himself to the then minister Pietro Fedele, he was suspended from teaching in October and deprived of his university post the following year.[10]

The other anti-fascist teacher was the professor of philosophy, Zino Zini, who was first a socialist, and then a communist. He wrote for *Ordine Nuovo* and was a friend of Antonio Gramsci.[11] He was loathed by the Fascists because he wrote a book considered outrageous at the time, *Congresso dei morti*, in which he had famous warlords and criminals from the past meet in the next world to justify war and crime. By contrast, he praised the 'soldier of Lambessa' who threw away his weapons and declared himself a Christian.[12] I was often at Zini's home, even after leaving D'Azeglio School, as I was a friend of his daughter, who was a few years older than me, and his cousin, Carlo Zini, a young lawyer: both were among my closest companions during my youth.

I learned about politics at school rather than at home. Augusto Monti, who taught the B stream, was later to become an author who wrote partially autobiographical novels set in Piedmont. At the time, he was known as a friend of Piero Gobetti and a dedicated contributor to Gobetti's magazine *La Rivoluzione Liberale*. But some of my friends were also important, particularly Leone Ginzburg. He was like a man from another world. He was a Russian Jew from Odessa, whose family left Russia following the Revolution and moved to Berlin. They had been in the habit of visiting the Italian seaside for their holidays. When the First World War broke out, they decided to leave the then five-year-old Leone behind with a very close Italian friend, thinking that the war would be over in a year. Thus he stayed on in Viareggio by himself, and spoke Italian better than us, because he had a Tuscan accent. When the war ended, he joined his family in Germany, but in 1924 his mother returned to Italy with her children, so that the eldest, Nicola, could study at Turin Polytechnic. So we ended up as school companions in the first year at senior secondary school. He had an extraordinary brain: the recently published writings of his youth are more than sufficient to demonstrate his precocious mind.[13] He was even then an out-and-out anti-fascist. I do not remember many political discussions amongst my other fellow pupils, so it was the time I spent with Leone Ginzburg and Vittorio

Foa during my university days that gradually drew me away from the pro-fascism of my family. Foa, who was in Monti's stream, was also extremely intelligent and an anti-fascist from the very beginning.

You can get an idea of what kind of school Massimo d'Azeglio Secondary School was, if you read the chapter on how it resisted the first decade of fascism in Augusto Monti's account of his teaching career. It refers to many people who were close to Bobbio: Cesare Pavese, 'sharp-featured, you never knew if he was paying attention or dreaming'; Giulio Einaudi, nicknamed Giulietta because of 'his tendency to blush and burst into tears'; Massimo Mila, 'a fair-haired youth with eyes that were still dreamy but already unflinching'; Renzo Giua, killed in 1938 in the Spanish Civil War; Emanuele Artom, partisan in Giustizia e Libertà *['Justice and Freedom'],[14] murdered by the Fascists; Gian Carlo Pajetta, who was expelled from all the secondary schools in the kingdom for having distributed 'Marxist' leaflets; Vittorio Foa, ' "a rocket" that "took off" in the second year, entering the third year in July with an average of eight points in his results, and he then took his final exams in October and achieved one of the highest results'; Felice Balbo, 'a prim and proper youth, clearly much cared for by his mother'; and Tullio Pinelli, with whom 'we had arguments over the beast in the first canto of the* Divine Comedy *and Dante's use of allegory which were not at all bad'. Monti also wrote: 'Massimo D'Azeglio School was truly a breeding ground for anti-fascism, but not because of any faults or merits amongst the staff. It was just something in the air or in the soil of that Turin and Piedmontese "environment" '. That school was like one of those houses in which "you can feel something", where its subsequent occupants are visited by spirits and souls in their sleep, or even when they are awake.'[15]*

Although I was in the A stream, and Monti taught the B stream, as soon as I went to university, I joined a group that he had set up with his most loyal students. It used to be called the 'gang', or 'confraternity' as Mila renamed it. During its meetings, Monti would on occasions read aloud, chapter by chapter, from his autobiographical novel *Sansôssi*, in which a father was reborn through his son, just as the generation of democrats defeated by fascism was being reborn in the generation that was to fight anew against fascism. Those readings left a strong impression in my memory:

When I read Monti, it is as though I can still hear him speaking. Every word contains his lively character whose voice captivated us. He was austere and tolerant but never easy-going. He could appear melancholic, yet he also knew how to be cheerful. He liked to tell stories about everyday things in a light-hearted almost jaunty manner, while at the same time imparting a lesson without appearing to do so. That lesson was always meaningful, and concerned respect for oneself through respect for others, a question of resoluteness and dignity.

When asked what Monti's secret was, Carlo Mussa Ivaldi, one of his pupils who was never to forget him, replied that it was the ability to translate literary values into inner qualities and civic virtues. He remembers an incident in which Monti was arrested. Referring to the other persons arrested who were nearly all his students, the OVRA[16] official asked: 'What do you teach at school?' And Monti replied: 'To have respect for ideas.' 'But what ideas?' The succinct response was: 'Their own.'[17]

As I have already said, Leone Ginzburg's powerful personality represented the model of political education within that circle of friends. He was top of the class at school, and he read everything from the classics to the latest novel. He bought two newspapers every day, *La Stampa* and *Corriere della Sera*, and read them with extreme thoroughness. He often visited our home, and launched into lengthy discussions with my father and brother about current affairs and books that had enthused him. While we were still at school, he translated Gogol's *Taras Bulba* for Alfredo Polledro's newly established Turin publishing house, Slavia. Immediately afterwards, he started on Tolstoy's *Anna Karenina*. He was also often a guest at our country home in Rivalta Bormida. Leone was passionate about his friendships:

His nature was well-balanced, and this was demonstrated by the fact that his intellectual rigour had nothing to do with moralistic pedantry or the punctilious adherence to personal responsibilities, but was concerned with self-improvement solely as the means for better relationships with other people. The customary scrupulousness with which he fulfilled his duties might have led you to believe he followed an ethic of perfectionism. However, in his treatment of others, particularly within our circle of friends, it became clear that he had a much greater, more inclusive and more human ideal, and that was the ethic of companionship. He loved conversation, company and the world at large. He was sociable and could not be alone. He needed to be expansive, to communicate and to know a lot of people in order to exchange ideas and impressions on events, books and other people, and current news (thus he was always very well informed about all manner of things). His network of relationships was vast and complex. He always liked to meet new people, whom he analysed, assessed, catalogued and added to his collection of character types. Fundamentally, human beings were the thing that most interested him, with their virtues, vices and oddities (his secret ambition was to be a writer of psychological stories). He loved the company of his contemporaries, but also of older people, who generally admired him and held him in esteem for his wisdom and his balanced judgement and opinions. He was happy in the company of girls of our own age, whom he met at school, on holiday or in society. He treated them as equals, without shyness or conceit, without an inferiority complex or a constant desire for conquests. He entered into their confidence, and they into his. He admired their grace and kindness, and that feminine sensitivity for matters of the heart which makes teenage life less savage, arduous and truculent. He was extremely warm with his friends: the continuous pursuit of friendship was an important part of his life.[18]

On finishing school in 1927, I went to Turin University to study law. The university environment also contributed to my slow political education, through the teachings of lecturers such as Francesco Ruffini, Luigi Einaudi and Gioele Solari, and through the disputes with the regime which involved both teachers and students. I will just refer to a couple of the better-known incidents. In 1928, a demonstration in support of Ruffini, who had opposed the anti-democratic electoral law in the Senate, turned into a brawl with fascist students. In 1929, a letter in support of Benedetto Croce, whom Mussolini had called a 'malingerer from history' because of his opposition to the Lateran Pacts, led to the arrest of Antonicelli, Mila and other friends of mine. I had not taken part.

While sitting my exams, I tried my luck in a competition organized by the Turin University Association for student revues, together with some friends I had met on holiday. These included Riccardo Morbelli, who a few years later was to come to prominence for co-writing a serialized radio dramatization of *The Three Musketeers* with Angelo Nizza. To my great surprise, the competition was won by our revue *Fra gonne e colonne*, the music for which had been written by my cousin Norberto Caviglia. The jury was chaired by the conductor Blanc, the author of the song 'Giovinezza', which later, following changes to the words, was to become the fascist anthem. The revue was put on by a student company (which also did the female parts, with the exception of the prima donna who played the title role in *La Madone des sleepings*, the famous novel by Maurice Dekobra).

In reality, fascism was by then a part of the daily lives of most Italians. I myself was a member of the Fascist University Groups. It is thought that there were personal conflicts over politics, but this was not the case. Sitting next to Leone Ginzburg through secondary school was Ludovico Barattieri, the most fascist of us all. We often met at his home to discuss things.

I was published for the first time while at university: an anonymous review, little more than a summary, of Monti's *Sansôssi*. It was published by Ceschini, and appeared in *Giornale di Acqui* on 16–17 November 1929. In 1931, I graduated in law with a thesis on the philosophy of law. My supervisor was Gioele Solari, who in 1922 had filled the same role for Gobetti, and then for several other figures who became involved in Piedmontese anti-fascism: Mario Andreis, Dante Livio Bianco, Aldo Garosci and Renato Treves. Sandro Galante Garrone, Giorgio Agosti and Franco Antonicelli (who took an arts degree) all graduated at the same time as myself. Solari's teaching was inspired by the civic role of the philosophy of law:

> The civic nature of that teaching was precisely that it kept the attention of young people on the general problems of the state and law, which were much more complex and profound than orthodox interpretations would lead you to believe. It consisted of elevating political questions into philosophical ones, and therefore ultimately into matters of conscience, or in other words, it turned that which in average behaviour had become complacent conformism into something highly dramatic. In that lecture hall on the ground floor of the old university building where he spoke from a lectern which looked like a pulpit, authority, obedience and power were no longer dogmas but questions to be analysed, politics was no longer an oracle but a science, and the state was no longer a fetish but a concept. Thus we observed the propriety and continuity of an open-minded cultural tradition.[19]

I had never had any real political vocation, unlike Vittorio Foa who had a very powerful one, and so I decided to continue my studies. With my father's approval, I started the third year of philosophy with the intention of obtaining a second degree. In 1933, I graduated with a thesis on Husserl's phenomenology. My supervisor was Annibale Pastore who had given a series of lectures on Husserl's philosophy, which I had attended assiduously. It was my intention to study the early writings, published at the time, of jurists who were guided by phenomenology. In truth, my passion for the philosophy of law represents the only link between the *before* and *after* of my life.

In 1932, I went to Germany with Renato Treves and Ludovico Geymonat, after having had a few German lessons from Barbara Allason,[20] the eminent writer and German scholar. At the beginning, we were in different cities: Treves was in Cologne where he met Hans Kelsen, Geymonat was in Göttingen where the university was famous for its teaching of mathematics, and I was in Heidelberg where Gustav Radbruch, previously minister of Justice in the Weimar Republic, was well known at the time for his teaching of philosophy of law. Jaspers was also in Heidelberg, and I saw him at one of his lectures. I remember that distant sojourn in Heidelberg, which lasted about a month, as a wonderful time. I met up with Treves and Geymonat again in August at a summer course at the University of Marburg. In the dining room at the house where we lodged, there was a large photograph of a young man who had died in the First World War, and I never knew whether it was the landlady's husband or son. At the end of the stay, we had learnt to converse a little in German.

Following the second degree, I wrote my first academic article.[21] In 1934, Treves and I both qualified to teach at university level. My studies on Husserl, the subject of my first article for *Rivista di Filosofia*,[22] for which I have been writing now for sixty years, led to my very close friendship with Antonio Banfi, who had been the first to become involved in the applied phenomenology of law and whom I used to visit at his home in Milan.

At that time, the first half the thirties, I was a frequent visitor to Barbara Allason's palatial house on the Po riverfront. It was one of the salons where opponents of the regime used to meet in Turin. Barbara Allason herself recalled these encounters in her memoirs.

Because of my contacts with anti-fascist circles, I was arrested during a police round-up in May 1935, which the regime hoped would destroy the core of the Justice and Freedom organization. I was not an activist. I had not taken part in the kind of anti-fascist activity in Turin which Leone Ginzburg, Vittorio Foa and Massimo Mila had been involved in. What did it mean to take an active part? Mila explained it very well in his *Scritti civili*:[23] it meant for example taking news of the movement to the exiles in France, bringing clandestine material such as anti-fascist books, pamphlets and posters to Italy, and getting articles by activists in Italy to Paris for publication by Justice and Freedom. They therefore needed people like Mila who were capable of taking the mountain routes and passing the border in secret. Of course, they knew everything about everyone at the police headquarters: they knew who was really involved. Indeed, I was given the lightest punishment, a caution. Only a few of us ended up before the special tribunal. I was one of a group of friends who used to meet outside on the corner of Corso Sommeiller in front of Caffè Strocco (later Varesio). The police would listen to our telephone conversations and put our walks under surveillance, even when they had nothing to do with politics. I remember that we were all fascinated by Giorgina Lattes, who was a few years younger than us and lived in Corso Sommeiller in the same block as Antoncelli. Giorgina was a student of Casorati and has left us a beautiful portrait of Leone Ginzburg. The police spied on our comings and goings, but never managed to understand which political activist was animating our group. It was Giorgina, but not for political reasons. It was her beauty and good nature that attracted us, and she and her youthful parents were always very welcoming.[24]

I found a passage devoted to this circle in a report by the fascist police on myself in 1935, which, in spite of the bureaucratic style, gave a fairly lively picture. Apart from the bad grammar, there were several errors in the information: Vittorio Foa became Foà, and Guido Solari instead of Gioele. More amusingly, my nickname Bindi which was used by old friends, appears in this statement as a different person from Bobbio. As can be seen, the fascist police were not known for their efficiency.

It has been ascertained that in 1933–34 Bobbio frequently visited the well-known anti-fascist circle of the well-known Prof. Barbara Allason, where well-known opponents of the regime would meet, including Dr Mario Levi, now abroad, Dr Leone Ginzburg and Dr Sion Segre who have been found guilty by a Special Tribunal of activities against the regime, as well as the lawyer Vittorio Foà and Dr Giulio Muggia, supporters of the Justice and Freedom movement in Turin. It has been shown that Dr Bobbio belongs to this movement not only through his frequent visits to Allason's circle, but also because of the persistence with which he has frequented supporters of the said movement, such as the aforementioned Vittorio Foà, Dr Giulio Muggia, etc. Indeed, informant 282 has confirmed the frequent contacts between Bobbio, Vittorio Foà, Alberto Levi, Prof. Franco Antonicelli, Carlo Luigi Zini and Piero Luzzatti, in his reports of 4 and 24 February 1935. These reports are backed up by wire-tap no. 1166 of 3 March 1935, from which we detected the following statement by Vittorio Foà to a person unknown (possibly Alberto Levi, see wire-tap no. 1167 of the same day): 'I'm going out to get a little sun with Bobbio, Antonicelli and Muggia – (Where am I going) . . . I don't know, I cannot tell you. I will let you know later.'

He writes for the well-known magazine *La Cultura*. The report on Justice and Freedom of February 1935 from the Police Headquarters of Turin, states that: 'Dr BOBBIO . . . identified as: Norberto BOBBIO, son of Luigi and Rosa Caviglia, born in Turin on 18.10.1909, resident there at Via Sacchi no. 66. Contacts with Prof. Antonicelli have not yet been ascertained. An examination of the correspondence shows that on 23 February, he received, through Solari (Guido) a letter from a Piero Martinetti, resident in Castellamonte (Aosta), which states:

'Those of us who are getting on in years must find some satisfaction in seeing new and promising forces rising up after us, who will perpetuate the values of our generation, perhaps better than we did. We thought we were doing a service by keeping the magazine going as an expression of unbiased and independent thought. I hope that the group of young people who are working with us will soon be able to take on all of this work, which, whatever its effects on the outside world, is a worthy end in itself and can, in some circumstances, be a moral duty.'

And Solari added, in sending on Martinetti's letter: 'I am increasingly certain that you are doing the right thing by entering into the company of persons capable of disinterested love for their duty.'

The report on Justice and Freedom of March 1935 from the Police Headquarters of Turin, states that: 'Norberto Bobbio: on 3 March, he took part in a meeting with Vittorio Foà, Antonicelli, Muggia and a fourth individual who has not been identified. On the 19th, at a meeting with Zini, Martinetti, Bindi and Foà at the home of Vittorio Foà. On the 24th, at the home of the notary Annibale Germano, with the same people and another person who has not been identified.

From wire-tap no. 1530 on 19 March 1935, we discovered:

From telephone no. 51244 (Vittorio Foà) the said person phoning. id. no. X phoning Mr Carlo Zini.
F. – We have decided to go to Barovero's at 21.30.
Z. – In my current state of health, I cannot go out. Come to my house, and as Bobbio is coming, I'll keep him here.
F. – Alright.

This meeting was confirmed in a later wire-tap on the same day 19 March no. 1529:[25]
From telephone no. 51244 (Vittorio Foà) the said person phoning. id. no. X phoning an unidentified person.
F. – I'm free this evening, so we can meet up with Bindi, Carlo Zini and Bobbio at Barovero's (down below) at 21.30.
X. – Have you mentioned anything to Bindi?
F. – No. He'll have worked it out himself.'[26]

The Justice and Freedom group in Turin was the one that suffered the most police repression, but it always managed to rebuild an embryonic organization. The first serious blow was suffered in December 1931 and January 1932, when the original leader, Mario Andreis, was arrested, beaten and tortured in order to get him to talk. The Special Tribunal gave him an eight-year prison sentence, along with a young university teacher, Luigi Scala, while Aldo Garosci managed to escape to Paris. Franco Venturi and his father, Lionello (the art historian who had refused to take the oath of allegiance to fascism), were already in exile in the French capital. Several students were picked up with Andreis and Scala, and these included Renzo Giua, one of Monti's pupils: the tribunal found them 'unstable', but not beyond reform, so it discharged them. Monti recalled in account of his teaching how Renzo Giua, suffering from a fever, stood up and protested: 'But there's a Dante lesson this afternoon.' This Dante enthusiast was also to reappear in France, and then died at

Estremadura on 17 February 1938, leading a battalion of the XII Garibaldi Brigade. In the meantime, however, he had also involved his father, Michele, in the Justice and Freedom movement.

Two years later, the police struck again: Sion Segre and Mario Levi, brother of the novelist Natalia Ginzburg and an official representative of Justice and Freedom, were surprised by the authorities on 11 March 1934 while returning across the border from Switzerland with a bundle of anti-fascist pamphlets. The police in Turin then carried out a series of arrests which led to the imprisonment of Leone Ginzburg, the central link with the exiles in Paris, Barbara Allason, the young physicist Carlo Mussa Ivaldi, and the famous professor of anatomy and father of Mario, Giuseppe Levi. The press release with the list of persons arrested called them 'anti-fascist Jews in the pay of exiles'. As Luigi Salvatorelli has pointed out, it was one of the first cases in which the repression of an anti-fascist conspiracy was used to foster anti-Semitism.[27] The Special Tribunal, in a ruling that declared Justice and Freedom to be a revolutionary and subversive association, found only Ginzburg and Segre guilty, and sentenced them to four and three years of imprisonment respectively. These sentences were reduced by two years as part of an amnesty which gave out remissions. On completing his sentence, Ginzburg remained on probation from 1936 to 1940, when, at the outbreak of war, he was condemned to enforced residence in a remote village in the Abruzzi until the fall of fascism. He was to die on 5 February 1944 in the Regina Coeli prison hospital in Rome.

The file on Bobbio does not have a date, but it is very probable that it was opened just before the police operation on 15 May 1935. Wire-taps, tailing and opening post were used in the investigations into Justice and Freedom, as well as inside information from Dino Segre, code name Pitigrilli, who was an OVRA agent. Franco Antonicelli, Norberto Bobbio, Giulio Einaudi, Vittorio Foa, Michele Giua, Carlo Levi, Piero Martinetti, Massimo Mila, Augusto Monti, Cesare Pavese and Carlo Zini were all arrested, as were two of the 'unstable' students discharged in 1932, Vindice Cavallera and Alfredo Perelli. The latter's father, Giannotto, worked for the provincial authorities in Cuneo.

The police had struck somewhat randomly, as they locked up both real activists like Foa and Mila, who liaised with the anti-fascist exiles, and intellectuals who had only put up a kind of moral Resistance to the regime, such as the philosopher Piero Martinetti. In 1931, at the age of fifty-nine, he and Lionello Venturi were among the eleven Italian academics out of 1,200, who refused to take the oath of allegiance to fascism. He had to abandon his teaching of theoretical philosophy and moral philosophy at Milan University and withdraw to his books and the family home in Castellamonte to the north of Turin, a house that was always crawling with cats. His bluff manner, typical of country people in Piedmont, disguised a good heart. He was the editor of *Rivista di Filosofia* in all but name, as it was considered more opportune to have his loyal friend Luigi Fossati appear as such. He gave his consent to my article on Husserl, although he found it 'a little obscure'. He was the Martinetti whose letter was quoted in the police report about me as proof of anti-fascist involvement. In reality, it was just a postcard congratulating me on becoming a member of the editorial committee of *Rivista di Filosofia*.

The commitment to maintain the independence of *Rivista di Filosofia* was taken as evidence, if not conclusive proof, of conspiratorial activity. I heard a wonderful account of Martinetti's arrest from Solari's widow. The philosopher was expected for breakfast at the Solari home on the morning of 15 May. The circumstances of the arrest are like something out of a film:

> That morning police officers arrived at the Solari home (at around six o'clock) and started to search the house. Amongst other things, they found some 'stones' in Mrs Solari's chest of drawers. They were a handful of earth from Gobetti's tomb which had been brought there by a friend from Paris. At ten, Martinetti arrived from the country with some asparagus. He did not notice the uproar. Solari went up to him and greeted him loudly and, as they were passing the detective in charge of the search of the premises, said: 'Let me introduce my dear friend, Professor Piero Martinetti.' 'Well, precisely the man we were looking for,' replied the detective with obvious satisfaction. According to Mrs Solari, Martinetti suddenly poured abuse on them, saying amongst other things a line that I have heard many times: 'I am a European citizen who has, by chance, been born in Italy.' Mrs Solari was adamant that the detective could not arrest Martinetti in their home. By agreement, Martinetti was taken back to Castellamonte where he was officially arrested.[28]

Martinetti, the amiable author of *Introduzione alla metafisica* (1904) and *La libertà* (1928), published under fascist rule, spent a few days in prison in Turin, without knowing the reason for his imprisonment. Like all intellectuals who became acquainted with the inside of a cell for political reasons and were confronted with something outside their experience, Martinetti analysed his imprisonment and what prison represents with moral candour in a brief note to Gioele Solari:

> During my brief imprisonment I had the opportunity to make several observations. The first is that in general the prison staff are more

human than is often imagined: I did not see any signs of mistreatment and the governor seemed to me to be a very understanding person. The second is that there are just as many decent men in prison as there are on the outside. I saw some evil-looking faces, especially amongst the old lags, but I also saw many faces that expressed humanity and goodness, especially amongst the young. First offenders should carry out their sentence in special institutions, separated from re-offenders. I believe that in this way half those who have committed crimes could be saved.

. . . The regulations are the main cause of cruelty, they are a fetish that insensitively dominates and often obstructs decency. Only those who have spent at least a month in prison should be allowed to draw up such regulations. But the truth is that in many areas they are not applied.

. . . The removal of freedom is itself a cruel punishment. In prison, you feel life passing as something useless and empty: you live like a dead person in a cement coffin. Imprisonment should be imposed as a punishment much less often. But above all, they should remove one of the major causes of suffering: the isolation from the outside world.[29]

Martinetti was released after a few days, while Bobbio got away with a caution and a curfew, which required him to stay at home from nine in the evening to six the following morning. A few were forcibly removed to remote areas (Antonicelli, Pavese and Carlo Levi). In the trial of 27–8 February 1936, the Special Tribunal handed down prison sentences on Vittorio Foa (15 years), Vindice Cavallera (8 years), Alfredo Perelli (8 years), Massimo Mila (7 years), Augusto Monti (5 years) and Giannotto Perelli (5 years). The harshness of the punishments was attributed to Mussolini's anger that they had 'to try unrepentant anti-fascist intellectuals' during the critical period of the Ethiopian enterprise.[30] In any event, fascist repression had effectively destroyed Justice and Freedom's organization in Turin: the leaders and activists were mainly in prison or exile. There remained a few, including the magistrate Giorgio Agosti and the lawyer Dante Livio Bianco, who were left to 'weave together the threads of a debilitated movement'.[31] An era was coming to an end, even though anti-fascism survived as an intellectual and moral viewpoint.

Perhaps the truest and most touching picture of the inextricable mix of private lives, public commitments, personal relationships and political positions that typified middle-class anti-fascism in Turin in the early thirties was given by Franco Antonicelli. He was a supply teacher at D'Azeglio School, who remained a friend with Bobbio throughout his life. In a brief work written in memory of an old friend, Gustavo Colonnetti, the professor of construction engineering at the Polytechnic, he wrote: 'There was an unforgettable period in which a small group of trusted friends would meet with spontaneous desire to liberate their souls from the distasteful burden of suspicion, discreet silences, anxiety and sudden dangers. This happened in many houses and many cities. The period I am referring to was the period of fascism.'[32] *One of the houses that offered such hospitality belonged to the notary public Annibale Germano, who became Franco Antonicelli's father-in-law. Indeed, Germano's daughter Renata married the elegant man of letters when he was forced to live in the remote town of Agropoli in the province of Salerno. Some amusing photographs of that marriage survive: the bridegroom wearing an impeccable morning suit and top hat, and the bride in a white dress with a train, standing in a scene of poverty amongst bemused youngsters from the village. The notary's house in Corso Galileo Ferraris and his villa in Sordevolo near Biella were familiar and even fashionable meeting places for intellectuals of different generations and different educational backgrounds, but united in their hostility towards the regime. They included Benedetto Croce, who had a holiday home in Pollone, a few kilometres from Sordevolo. The picture which Antonicelli paints is of a middle-class circle living as outcasts, who distanced themselves from the viciousness of fascist life and nurtured a current of opposition that was to swell with the introduction of the race laws and entry into the war.*

After securing the qualification to teach philosophy of law at university level, I obtained a teaching post in 1935 at the University of Camerino. It was in this period that I wrote a letter that was fished out of the archives nearly sixty years later, stirring up controversy in the newspapers that lasted for several days. It was a registered letter sent directly to 'His Excellency Sir Benito Mussolini, head of the government, Villa Torlonia':[33]

Turin, 8 July 1935 XIII

Excellency!
I hope Your Excellency will excuse me if I am so bold as to contact you directly, but the matter with which I am concerned is of such great importance that I do not believe that there is any better and more certain way of finding a solution.

I, Norberto Bobbio, son of Luigi, born in Turin in 1909, graduate in law and philosophy, am currently a teacher in philosophy of law at this university. I am a member of the Fascist National Party and the Fascist University Group since 1928, when I went to university. I became a member of the Youth Vanguard in 1927, when the first group of the Vanguard was set up at D'Azeglio Senior Secondary School as the result of an assignment entrusted to comrade Barattieri of San Pietro and myself. Because of a childhood illness that left me with ankylosis in the left shoulder, I was rejected at the medical check-up for military service, and was unable to join the Militia. I grew up in a patriotic and fascist family (my father, consultant surgeon at the San Giovanni Hospital in this city, has been a member of the Fascist National Party since 1923, one of my two uncles on my father's side is a general in the Armoured Corps in Verona, and the other is a brigade general at the Military School). During my time at university, I took an active part in the life and work of the Turin Fascist University Group, organizing student magazines, single issues and student trips, to the extent that I was given the task of giving commemorative lectures on the March on Rome and the Victory to secondary-school students. Finally, in recent years, after having completed my degrees in law and philosophy, I have devoted myself entirely to studying philosophy of law and publishing the articles and papers that have earned me the qualifications to teach at university level. The theoretical basis of these studies has helped me to consolidate my political opinions and deepen my fascist convictions.

On 15 May of this year, I was searched by the political police (a search that was extended to my mother and father), and even though nothing of any significance was found during the search, I was arrested and held in prison for seven days awaiting interrogation. Following an interrogation lasting a few minutes, for which a statement was drawn up, I was immediately released. All this occurred without my being told the reasons that had led to these measures being taken against me, given that during the interrogation I was not confronted with any specific accusations, but was merely asked for information about my acquaintance with persons who are not fascists. I answered these questions, as written in the statement, by stating that 'I could not help knowing them, as they were at school with me and of my own age'. I was then asked why I had written for *La Coltura*, something that I have already justified in a letter dated 27 June, as required of me by His Excellency Starace, through the Fascist Provincial Headquarters in Turin.

I had good reason to believe that the unfortunate incident had been resolved, but today I received an instruction to appear on the 12th of this month before the Commission of the Provincial Magistrature in order to submit my defence. I was informed that 'having examined the report on your caution, . . . and the related documents, it appears that you have become a danger to the lawful order of the state through your activities carried out in consort with persons recently committed for trial by the Special Tribunal for membership of the Justice and Freedom sect'.

I do not know what documents could possibly be the basis for this series of accusations, given that neither the search nor the interrogation were able to come up with anything against me. Equally, I do not consider that the discovery of a photograph of Dr Leone Ginzburg dated 1928 in my possession constitutes grounds for prosecution (as we were both nineteen years old at the time and schoolfriends). Still less can the same be said of my writing for *La Coltura* (which was only a review published in the March issue of this year), as this is one of the oldest and most renowned Italian literary magazines. This article, for obvious reasons, could not have disguised any political insinuation either by myself or by those who asked me to write the article, and simply demonstrates my desire to make a modest and honest contribution to a cultural activity that is valued by the public and subject to control.

I declare in good faith that the above-mentioned accusation, which is not only curious and unexpected, but also unjustified, given the results of the search and interrogation, deeply hurts me and offends against my consciousness as a fascist, about which you can obtain valid evidence from the opinions of those persons who have known me and kept my company as friends in the Fascist University Groups and the Fascist Provincial Branch.

I renew my apologies to Your Excellency for having been so presumptuous as to write directly to you, but I was moved by the certainty that, with your elevated sense of justice, you will wish to release me from the burden of this charge, which can have no basis in my activities as a citizen and scholar, and contradicts the oath that I loyally gave.

With devotion,

Norberto Bobbio
Via Sacchi 66, Turin

This letter brought me face to face with another self who I thought I had defeated forever. I was not disturbed so much by the controversies that surrounded my character, as the letter itself and the fact that I had written it, in spite of its being, in a sense, part of a bureaucratic practice whereby the fascist police themselves asked you to humiliate yourself: 'Now, if you were to write to the Duce . . .'.

Almost sixty years later, Bobbio's letter came out of the archive and appeared in a weekly magazine. The journalist Giorgio Fabre published it in Panorama *on 21 June 1992, as part of the documentary evidence for an article on collusion by anti-fascist intellectuals. He demonstrated that Cesare Pavese had written two of these letters of 'submission' and that Giulio Einaudi gave information on the anti-fascism of some of those arrested during the interrogations of 1935. He cited letters to Mussolini from Antonicelli and Mila. The magazine also published a brief interview of Bobbio by Fabre, in which the philosopher declared:*

Anyone who has lived under a dictatorship knows that it is a state different from all other states. Even this letter, which now appears shameful to me, demonstrates this. Why did a person like me, who was an academic and of a middle-class family, have to write a letter of this kind? A dictatorship corrupts people's souls. It forces hypocrisy, lies and servility upon you. This is a servile letter. Although I acknowledge that what I wrote was true, I exaggerated my fascist credentials in order to gain advantage. This is by no means a justification. In order to save yourself under a dictatorship, you need strength of character, generosity and courage, and I recognize that at the time, having written this letter, I did not have these. I have no difficulty in examining my own conscience, as I have already done many many times.

The letter to Mussolini, following advance warning from Panorama, *became an issue for the national press. Most commentators felt that the letter had little sense if not put in the context in which it was written. 'Especially amongst the young', explained the philosopher Eugenio Garin in* La Repubblica:

those who had decided to stay in Italy were obliged to accept the consequences of that decision. Even if they were privately opposed to the regime, and even if they took part in clandestine activities aimed at overturning it, they had to maintain an outward appearance that would allow them to continue with their own business. Croce used to say that the important thing was to write a good comment on a Petrarchan sonnet. It was not a matter of a heroic attitude, it was an attempt at self-defence; this was the room for manoeuvre left in the difficult daily business of living under a dictatorship. If you didn't opt for exile, you had to operate in a situation that was conspicuously ambivalent. You had to lie and you had to wear a mask. Descartes said '*Larvatus prodeo*' – I go forward behind a mask.[34]

Typically, the journalist Giorgio Bocca attacked the publication of the letter:

These people do not know what a dictatorship is. They don't understand that they sent you to prison and took away your means to earn a living. In the same situation, I would have written not one letter to Mussolini, but ten! In 1935, even communists in exile wrote a letter to their 'Comrades in black shirts', because it was the year in which the [Italian] Empire was founded, and Togliatti felt that there was no longer anything they could do against fascism. We should not forget that only thirteen professors refused to take the oath. Now they're taking it out on Bobbio: there is no respect for one of the few decent people around today.[35]

Vittorio Foa was interviewed in La Stampa. *What did this old friend think about the fact that Bobbio claimed to be a good fascist in the letter?*

We shouldn't get confused over this. It was one thing to be a fascist, and quite another to be a member of a fascist organization. Many of my friends, including my brother, were members of the Fascist Party, even though they weren't fascists, and were often clearly anti-fascists. The fascist membership card was in many cases a requirement for being able to do a job commensurate with your own abilities, and sometimes just to have a job at all.

Foa also looked on the letter as justifiable self-defence:

Let me say straight away that that letter is completely irrelevant from a political, moral or any other point of view. The caution was a violence against him. It was a punitive measure that put restrictions on his personal freedom and his ability to travel and work. It was an act of violence against which Bobbio was entitled to defend himself: I would call it justifiable self-defence. He defended himself as he was fully entitled with shrewdness by extending his previous fascist sympathies up to the present. That letter should be read as an appeal against a bureaucratic procedure.[36]

The historian of the Action Party, Giovanni De Luna questioned the use to which the letter was put in the context of the political struggle that was taking place during the last two years of Cossiga's presidency, following the demise of the Communist Party.

It can also be read as part of the attempt to take away the First Republic's legitimacy, by challenging the constituent DNA which it inherited from anti-fascism. With the communist tradition out of the picture, there remained the 'respectable' democratic anti-fascism of Justice and Freedom, and the Action Party. Once this had been destroyed, there would not be anything left of anti-fascism, thus removing an inconvenient package of moral values and civic commitment.[37]

The affair went beyond Norberto Bobbio's reputation. It concerned 'abolition of the distinction between past and present', as the historian from Turin, Marco Revelli, pointed out in an article in Il Manifesto, *where he distanced himself from the wave of emotion that had overtaken it and analysed its more general significance. 'The organic nature of the past is broken up and reduced to individual "exhibits" or items of evidence susceptible to consumption by an insatiable but inattentive public: at any time splinters of history can leap out of an archive.' This procedure reduces the whole of the past to the present, cancels out the hiatus that divides them and confuses the language of today with that of yesterday 'in an indistinct and misleading murmur'. The context is everything. But this use of history also cancels another fundamental distinction. Revelli wrote:*

> The most typical and disturbing aspect of the use of history for the purpose of scandal, is the abolition of any differentiation between the public and private spheres. It is the attribution, without making any allowances, of public significance to even the most intimate acts, those that are most directly linked to the inner person. This is the real 'scandal', the subjection of essentially private matters to public judgement. This is the violent and contrived manner in which the darkness of the unfathomable centre of the private world with its contradictions, uncertainties, ambivalence and weaknesses, is brought together with the clearly defined and glossy public world.[38]

In 1935, Bobbio succeeded in getting his caution removed. However, he was still considered an 'anti-fascist element', in spite of the letter, as can be seen from a report sent to Turin Police Headquarters by the Ministry of Internal Affairs on 27 June 1936:

> Some elements who have already drawn attention because of their close relations with suspect or arrested persons belonging to the Culture Group, have turned up in the university with various duties and all wear the party badge. Example: Bobbio (resident in Via Sacchi, brother of the surgeon, previously close friend of Antonicelli) currently secretary on the Examinations Committee at the Faculty of Law; Artom, also living in Via Sacchi, arts student. They meet up with Guaita, who has returned from enforced residence in a remote place (subject of a recent report).
>
> The party badge allows these meetings to appear normal, but there is no logical reason to believe that these meetings are normal or free from political content, if you take into account their previous form. Naturally prudence makes it difficult to get more than superficially close to these conversations between elements who have become extremely circumspect.
>
> But we can report a general impression amongst students and others: their . . . 'conversion to the party, expressed by the badge' is not convincing and can only be an appearance.[39]

I taught at Camerino for three years. I had moved to that small town from a large northern city. The journey had been very long and uncomfortable. I taught the philosophy course and had very few students, not more than ten. The majority of my colleagues, mainly of my own age, were not fascists. I recall with affection the pharmacologist Luigi Scremin, who died many years ago now. From Verona, he was a very principled Catholic and an implacable anti-fascist. There was also the future President Giovanni Leone, a lecturer in criminal law, with whom I entered into a good-natured friendship. We had full board in a hotel also called Leone, whose owner, a Mr Tirabasso, had written a cookery book called *Il cuoco classico*. In November of 1935, I gave my first lecture at Camerino University. The day of my first lecture was tense, and the anxiety was increased at the last moment before entering the lecture hall when Leone shouted out to the other colleagues 'Let's go and listen to Bobbio!' I can remember that the small and elegant lecture hall and the presence of my colleagues so unnerved me that I only managed to speak for half an hour.

At the same time, I was studying for the exam to obtain a permanent teaching post. The notification of the exam came in 1938, the year of race laws. As a result, Renato Treves was not allowed to take part, and he decided to leave Italy for Argentina. However, shortly before the examination committee met, I received a brief letter from the education minister Bottai, no more than three or four lines of official language, which, coming straight to the point, informed me that my certificates were being returned. I decided to resist what I considered an enormous injustice, namely that I was not to be allowed to take part in the promotion procedure simply because somebody had revealed that I had been arrested for anti-fascism. I had an uncle who was a general in the army and a friend of the leading fascist Emilio De Bono.[40] He drew De Bono's attention to my situation, and De Bono took the matter up with Mussolini. A couple of months later I received another equally bureaucratic letter, inviting me to resubmit my certificates.

Inevitably this incident was also used to stir up controversy. The newspaper *Il Tempo* published De Bono's letter to Mussolini asking for me to be readmitted to the selection procedure on two different occasions, in 1986 and again in 1992. This same letter was referred to by a right-wing intellectual, Marcello Veneziani, the author of a pamphlet *Sinistra e destra* written in response to my book *Left and Right*:[41] 'If an anti-fascist like Bobbio could have a successful career under fascism, then that means either that fascism was not the totalitarian and oppressive regime that Bobbio claims it was, or that Bobbio was a supporter of the regime.'[42] In reality, De Bono's letter to Mussolini is just an insight into the behaviour and phraseology of the fascist nomenclature:

> Dear Head of Government,
>
> I'm going to have to bother you again, but it really isn't my fault.

The last time I came to see you, I mentioned among other things a favour that General Bobbio had asked of me. You'll remember that it concerned his nephew, the son of Professor Bobbio, the consultant surgeon in Turin, who was not admitted to the promotion procedure for the professorship of philosophy of law, and it would appear that this was for ill-founded political reasons. You kept the letter, the memorandum sent to you by Professor Bobbio the father, and you told me using these exact words: 'He's a member of the party, I deal with this.' 'How?' I asked. 'I'll tell Bottai.' You said 'I'll tell', not 'I'll talk about it'. I therefore thought that the matter was settled, so I asked if I could pass on the news to General Bobbio. You answered in the affirmative and I told Bobbio: 'Rest assured.' Now, I get another letter from the same Bobbio in which he tells me that his nephew still *hasn't* received any invitation to resubmit his certificates for the promotion procedure, and the deadline will be passed in a few days. Listen, boss, you're entitled to do what you want, but for some time you have been happily taking me for a ride, much to my amusement. I would ask you to give me an unambiguous reply: one of those 'monosyllables' that you have asked of me in difficult times and which I have always telegraphed back to you without argument. You must understand that being able to say yes *in your name* and then having to say or write 'no' is humiliating for me, because people will end up thinking that I am *all mouth*, something I have never been in my whole life. Surely it can't be that you haven't understood me yet! I must be mistaken: you'll take me for a nuisance and positively understand me to be *a complete fool*. Thy will be done!

Yours truly,
E. De Bono[43]

This letter was published in order to imply that I had obtained a university chair because of my fascist credentials, whereas what happened was exactly the opposite. The fascist regime attempted to stop me from taking part in the university promotion procedure, in spite of my qualifications. They did not want to give me the chair, they wanted to take it away, as I explained to Veneziani in a letter which he published with my consent in *Corriere della Sera*:

Clearly the reason for my exclusion was political, and it was therefore an abuse of power. Why was I supposed to accept it? I resorted to the only available methods in a state where the rule of law does not exist . . . It appears that you do not realize that by attacking the expedients by which people defend themselves under dictatorships, you are taking the part of the dictatorship, which by definition is always right. You put yourself on the side of the dictator when you do not say a single word to condemn the arbitrary decision, but you are strident in denouncing someone who was trying to get by, using the only methods the dictatorship allowed.[44]

In the same letter, I asked whether it was worse that university professors took the oath of allegiance to fascism or that the minister forced them to take that oath? Who is more morally reprehensible: those who had to swear or those who made them?

However, I have to admit that the subterfuge to which I resorted (I wrote a servile letter to the minister Bottai) was repugnant, even though it was the only alternative to submission, particularly because it was a remedy only available to those who had the support of persons in high office, while other poor devils had put up with the abuses of power in silence. Anyone who uses such a stratagem was forced to lie in the most shameless manner. My protectors and myself were obliged to declare in bad faith that the supplicant, in spite of a few indiscretions attributable to his youth, was in reality a loyal subject to the regime. This was not true, particularly by the time of this incident, when I was close to the Liberal-Socialist Movement.

The book which Bobbio wrote for the promotion procedure, L'analogia nella logica del diritto, *was published in 1938 by the Law Institute of the University of Turin. The examination committee's report gave the following portrayal of the successful candidate:*

Norberto Bobbio, who graduated in law in 1931 and in philosophy in 1933, has been a qualified university teacher in philosophy of law since 1935, and has been employed since then by the University of Camerino. He has a sophisticated grasp of law and philosophy, and has carried out a wide-ranging study of institutionalist and social currents of legal thought in France and phenomenological currents in Germany. From the latter, he has inferred the need for new thinking in relation to questions of corporate franchise, concepts of society and its interpretation, as well as the discipline's general direction. Even for those of us who remain unconvinced by his conclusions or who find them unacceptable, we are happy to acknowledge that the candidate has unique critical abilities, excellent methodology and effective prose, so that all the examiners agree that he achieved the purpose of this selection procedure. We expect Bobbio to clarify his theoretical ideas, and also to extend his speculative interests beyond phenomenology, so that he can put his capacity for systematic analysis to better and greater use, with a more solid independence of thought.[45]

Having been successful in the selection procedure, Bobbio was then summoned to Siena University at the end of 1938. He stayed there for two years. In December of 1940, he obtained the chair of philosophy of law at the Faculty of Law at Padua University. It was at this stage that he entered the ranks of active anti-fascism.

2

The Resistance

My early contribution to militant anti-fascism was recorded in a drawing by Renato Guttuso. While I was living in Camerino, I started to attend meetings of the Liberal-Socialist Movement which had been set up by Guido Calogero, a young professor of philosophy at Pisa University, and Aldo Capitini, who was the secretary at the Scuola Normale, a college attached to Pisa University. These meetings took place in a beautiful villa near Cortona, which belonged to Umberto Morra di Lavriano who had always been an anti-fascist. He was also a friend of Piero Gobetti and a contributor to *Rivoluzione Liberale*. On one occasion, he introduced a young man, and added: 'He's a brilliant young painter, and he's going to go far.' By one of those tricks of fate, my brother happened to see a sketch he had done at that Cortona meeting in 1939 at one of his earliest exhibitions, and so I heard about it through my brother. I then wrote to Cesare Luporini, who got Guttuso to give it to him as a present, and he made copies for his friends. The drawing shows Guido Calogero, with a book in his hand and his finger raised, along with Morra, Capitini, Luporini and myself. The book that Capitini is holding is called 'Non-Violence' and the one that Calogero is holding is called 'Social Liberalism'. Thus, by sheer chance, we have a record of the Liberal-Socialist meetings: I believe that that was the time when I moved on from anti-fascism in the sense of an abstract belief to conscious and militant anti-fascism.

Although I formally belonged to fascist institutions, first the Fascist University Group and then the party, because of my family's fascist leanings, I did not frequent either fascist groups or circles. My personal relationships and friendships fell entirely within non-conformist circles, such as Augusto Monti's so-called 'gang', evening gatherings at the homes of Barbara Allason or Professor Zino Zini, my own academic field where I was guided by Gioele Solari, and my writings for Giulio Einaudi's newly created publishing firm and for *Rivista di Filosofia* which was edited by Piero Martinetti. As I have already said, my friends were Leone Ginzburg, Vittorio Foa, Franco Antonicelli, Carlo Zini, Ludovico Geymonat and Renato Treves. My involvement in militant anti-fascism was probably made easier by moving away from the family, as a result of my appointment at Camerino University. I do not remember on what occasion and at whose behest I met Aldo Capitini in Perugia when he was about to publish *Elementi di un'esperienza religiosa* (1937), which I have always considered one of liberal-socialism's two fundamental texts: along with Calogero's *La scuola dell'uomo* (1938). Aldo had already become a significant and effective reference point for ethical and religious opposition, and through his friendship with Calogero this led to the Liberal-Socialist clandestine movement, which later became one of the organizations which made up the Action Party. In order to maintain links between Perugia and Camerino, I would contact a young philosophy lecturer, a friend of Capitini called Agostino Buda, who came from Sicily. I lost all contact with him with the passing years.

The Liberal-Socialist Movement, which Bobbio joined at the end of the thirties, developed into a network of opposition groups which sprang up spontaneously in universities, clubs, religious associations and cultural organizations, often as a result of dissent amongst young intellectuals who were taking part in fascist institutions, or as a result of the 'reawakening of consciences', especially after the passing of the race laws. As Ruggero Zangrandi pointed out in Il lungo viaggio attraverso il fascismo, *'this manner of political involvement was very much based on chance'. From 1939 the Liberal-Socialist Movement developed on the fertile ground, with Capitini as its philosopher and Calogero its political leader. According to Zangrandi, there were two reasons for its success: 'it was the first cultural anti-fascist movement that was not inspired by Marxism and it was also outside the tradition that had built up around Croce whose influence was enormous, but led to inaction'. It was able to express 'both social and libertarian demands which reflected the most fundamental needs of young intel-lectuals'.[1] His book refers to Bobbio as one of the activists in the Liberal-Socialist front, working with other intellectuals such as Piero Calamandrei, Tristano Codignola, Enzo Enriquez Agnoletti, Carlo Ragghianti, Cesare Luporini, Guido Aristarco, Giorgio Bassani, Attilio Bertolucci, Tommaso Fiore and Enzo Paci. The links between the various groups in Pisa, Florence, Umbria, Rome, Emilia and Apulia were very loose, and only after the war broke out was a real network established. Even then, they were not comparable with organizational structures like that of the Communist Party. 'We would travel a long way to meet people who, we had been told, thought like us,' explained Mario Delle Piane, one of the first activists in contact with Siena University when Bobbio arrived there. 'We would approach other young people, suggesting that they should read certain books (for example Malraux's La Condition humaine).'[2] The main activity was proselytizing in the expectation that one day things would change, as well as some modest propaganda work, which became an apprenticeship for the struggle: putting up handwritten posters on the city walls or sticking gummed strips on cinema walls with pacifist slogans. 'In the spring of 1940, letters were sent out from Siena to generals, admirals and officers responsible for garrisons, urging them to refuse to enter the war on the side of Germany.'[3]*

I devoted two chapters in my *Maestri e compagni* to Aldo Capitini and in 1990 I wrote the preface to his *Elementi di un'esperienza religiosa*, which was published when fascism was at the peak of its power following the conquest of Ethiopia.

Even though he declared himself to be a liberal-socialist from the very beginning of the movement, he liked to make the distinction between his own liberal-socialism and that of the others, because his commitment was ethical and religious, and not just motivated by politics. He always fiercely rejected the primacy of politics (which was the result of totalitarianism), and the idea that all human conduct should be reduced to political activity. Liberal-socialism was not initially a party (and it should never have become one): it was 'an attitude of mind, a constant willingness to renew one's outlooks, convictions and hopes', and 'a disposition of one's conscience'. Of course it was an ideology as well as all this. But even as an ideology, Capitini's liberal-socialism was a minority tendency, almost a heresy, which referred back to Piero Gobetti's 'liberal revolution' rather than Carlo Rosselli's 'liberal socialism'.[4]

While it may have escaped the police's attention that, underneath the outward appearance of a work of religious edification, Capitini's book had a political message and was provocatively anti-fascist, this did not escape Croce's attention. He decided to publish it, even though, as a philosopher of immanence and a political realist, he disagreed with the author's ideas. Still less could this work escape the notice of young discontents in search of a way out from the regime, who were forming small opposition groups. Do not forget that *Elementi* was one of the first anti-fascist books coming from the new generation that had been brought up under the regime, as opposed to the generation of our teachers, such as Croce, Salvatorelli, De Ruggiero, Omodeo, Luigi Russo and those who lived in exile like Salvemini and Carlo Rosselli. There have been many accounts of the resonance that this book had amongst the young of the time.[5]

However Calogero was the creative, organizational and, above all, theoretical driving force behind liberal-socialism. He was a few years older than me (born in 1904), and taught philosophy at the Scuola Normale in Pisa. He was an expert in Greek philosophy and had been taught by Gentile.[6] His first book, written at the age of twenty-three, was on the fundamentals of Aristotelian logic. Following his studies into logic, he studied law and graduated with a book on the role of judges and how they should be controlled by the Court of Cassation,[7] which I analysed in my book *L'analogia nella logica del diritto* (1938). After that, we met on several occasions, and entered into a warm and lifelong friendship. His book *La scuola dell'uomo* was a work of secular ethics and a political controversy whose intentions were clearly educative. During that period, Calogero gave a series of lectures on Marxist critique, on which he based his book *La critica dell'economia e il marxismo* which was published in 1944.

He wrote the first manifesto of liberal-socialism, which was distributed in the summer of 1940. The second one, which constituted a fully-fledged political programme, was drafted a year later during the summer in Cortina d'Ampezzo by a small group of young university lecturers, including myself. It stated that: 'Liberalism and socialism, understood in their best sense, are not opposing ideals or dissimilar concepts, but parallel applications of a single ethical principle, which is the universal canon of all histories and all civilizations.'

When, a year later, the Action Party was founded and the Liberal-Socialist Movement became a part of it, Calogero summed up his thoughts at a conference in 1944, after liberation, on the theme 'Democracy at a crossroads and the third way' with the following words: 'On the right there is the error of agnostic or conservative liberalism which leads to freedom without justice. On the left there is the error of authoritarian collectivism which leads to justice without freedom. The Action Party does not take either path, because it knows the true way forward, the third way, the way which brings together both justice and freedom in an indissoluble union.'

This strand of liberal-socialism took up the themes of Carlo Rosselli's own version of liberal socialism, although it did not come under his direct influence. However it carried this formula to such a level of abstraction as to render it of little use in practical politics, and gave its opponents the pretext for accusing the whole of the Action Party of intellectual arrogance and sterile dogmatism. As I have said, my relationship with Calogero was always very friendly, and I once defined him as the youngest of my teachers. However, in both philosophical and political debates, we were more often in disagreement than in agreement.[8] I always interpreted liberal-socialism not as a philosophical formula, but as a programme of political compromise which could be only brought into effect, as Calamandrei well understood, through the recognition that the social rights demanded by the socialist tradition were a pre-condition for the full implementation of the libertarian rights demanded by the liberal tradition.

Curiously, liberal-socialism, which was a philosophical construct, was embodied in what was supposed to be a party of 'action'. In any case, its action proved to be very short-lived. The last time I had an opportunity to take up the question, I said 'both [Rosselli's] liberal socialism and [Capitini's and Calogero's] liberal-socialism were doctrinal and artificial formulations, armchair inventions that were more notional than real'. It was a combination whose historical significance was that it represented a reaction against an asocial liberalism on the one hand and an illiberal socialism on the other. I also went on to say that the theoretical assertion that liberalism and socialism are not incompatible, does not say anything about the form and the way in which they could be brought together. Would the emphasis be on liberalism or socialism? What degree of liberalism? What degree of socialism? These questions are sufficient to show the difficulties in transforming a philosophical doctrine into political practice. My conclusion was that:

> if we want to keep our feet more firmly on the ground, instead of the two isms we should be talking of freedom and equality. . . . We could perhaps add that the former question refers to liberal doctrine and the latter to socialist doctrine. But I am more at home, for reasons that are partly emotional, with the motto 'Justice and Freedom'.[9]

Things were radically different in Padua compared with what they had been in Camerino. Italy's entrance into the war was a decisive rift between us and the regime, causing us to enter into a more concrete form of opposition, although it was more a demonstration of opposition than effective opposition itself. Looking back on the past, I once said that my contacts with Capitini and Calogero were those of an amateur conspirator. It is true that I must have had some policeman on my tail, as Capitini was always under extensive surveillance, but we were really aspiring conspirators, or rather conspirators without a conspiracy.[10] When I took over the chair of philosophy of law at Padua University, however, the general situation had become much more dramatic. We had been at war for a few months as Hitler's allies. It was a dishonourable war, which was to lead us to catastrophe. The time had come to make the final choice.

The Action Party attracted members of Justice and Freedom and liberal-socialists, political anti-fascism and spontaneous anti-fascism. As Giovanni De Luna explained in his Storia del Partito d'Azione,

> the formation of the Action Party took place over the period 1940 to 1942, and accelerated with the increasingly clear prospect of fascism's imminent military defeat. This was immediately perceived by its activists, and, together with the other anti-fascist parties, it took on the specific nature of democratic-socialist constituent organization which, through various political and ideological developments, led to it's bringing together nearly all the non-communist anti-fascist conspiratorial elements within a single organization.[11]

The Institute of the Philosophy of Law in Padua, of which Bobbio was the director, became 'one of the major centres for gatherings and meetings of anti-fascists in the Veneto region'. In his book on fascist experience, Zangrandi recalls a meeting with Bobbio in early 1942 following the arrest of Guido Calogero. The conversation mainly concerned the matter of whether it would be appropriate to adopt more conspiratorial techniques in order to keep the identity of anti-fascist activists secret. Having introduced himself at the meeting with a false name, Zangrandi explained to Bobbio that this precaution gave him protection from the danger of betrayal, to which the philosopher, on the other hand, was exposed. Were not the Liberal-Socialists' lack of caution and their underestimation of the importance of conspiratorial techniques responsible for the loss of a leader like Calogero? To which Bobbio replied, according to Zangrandi in a Socratic manner, by asking him if he did not think that a 'useless' sacrifice could in fact be useful as an example and as incitement to others, and 'whether it was not, in the final analysis, a form of propaganda, a higher and more noble way of demonstrating one's beliefs beyond any contingent conspiratorial requirement?'[12] Following the apprenticeship in Turin with Justice and Freedom and then the first conspiratorial activities with the liberal-socialist groups, Bobbio publicly broke with the regime in Padua. It was still a form of bourgeois

*anti-fascism, which took advantage of family and professional priv-
ileges, but it was not limited to protest: he was actively preparing
for the changes to come.*

The two major figures in the Resistance in Padua were the Latin
scholar Concetto Marchesi and the pharmacologist Egidio Meneghetti,
who were teaching at the university when I arrived at the end of
1940.

Marchesi, whose books on Tacitus and Seneca had been read during
the period of the dictatorship as a kind of anti-conformist handbook,
was a man of almost embarrassing sincerity whose whole being was
governed by two emotions: compassion for the oppressed and contempt for the powerful. Not only was he one of the greatest scholars
in his field, he also had his tragic, although not hopeless, vision of the
world. He considered himself to have the mind of an oppressed person but unlike the oppressed he was not resigned to his fate. Since the
advent of socialism in the world, he had had no doubts over what his
role had to be: something to which he kept faith on an intellectual
level right up to his death. I would often meet him in the evening
at the ancestral home of the Counts Papafava dei Carraresi in Via
Marsala, where he lived. The landlord was Count Novello, a friend
of Gobetti, who had published three books, partly based on articles
that appeared in *Rivoluzione Liberale*.[13] Some time ago, I wrote this
portrait of Marchesi:

> He was short of stature, almost slightly built, with a penetrating and
> melancholy expression. He often frowned and his intelligent eyes would
> often half-shut when talking as though savouring his words which
> were always precise, clearly pronounced and to the point. His high
> cheekbones and small hooked nose suggested the image on an ancient
> medal, as Leonida Repaci observed in a lively portrayal. He had long
> narrow lips that ended with a sardonic twist. He gave the impression
> of great composure but it was composure achieved through domina-
> tion of a passionate nature, and unsettled by instinctive resentments,
> awe-inspiring outbursts and magnanimous fits of anger: behind the
> calm exterior there was a storm-lashed sea. In the few moments when
> he lost his self-control, his voice would become scathing, his gestures
> agitated, and the strength which emanated from his person irresistible:
> he was as solemn and terrible as an angered god. I was with him in the
> rector's office on the day when the Fascists and the police announced
> for the first time that they intended to search the university premises:
> he immediately stood up and proclaimed his refusal with such vehe-
> mence that no one dared open their mouth, and the Fascists stayed
> outside.[14]

Meneghetti, who was awarded four medals for bravery in the First World War – two of which he received on the battlefield – was a free spirit both morally and intellectually: a natural anti-fascist.[15] On 16 December 1943, his wife Maria and his only daughter Lina died when Padua was bombed. They were found in each other's arms buried under the debris of the explosion. After that, his life had no more meaning except in the struggle against fascism.

> He was able to give new meaning to his life by devoting himself tire-lessly and pitilessly to that struggle with a courage that bordered on foolhardiness. He kept control of the party in which he was active, and was the prime mover in the Veneto Committee of Liberation and the Military Command. There was not a partisan action, whether in the city or the countryside, that was not organized by him or his close associates.
>
> . . .
>
> He was arrested on 7 January 1945, shortly before the stunt he had prepared for the new anniversary of 8 February: a record placed on the university roof was supposed to broadcast a proclamation written by Meneghetti himself, whose main slogan was 'The university shall not yield'. After his arrest, he was taken to Palazzo Giusti and put before Commander Carità, who greeted him by slapping him twice and having him subjected to torture by his thugs over the following days. On arrival, he sees a pale Pighin dying on a stretcher. Carità shouted to him in triumph: 'Here's your friend Renato.' He spoke of his sufferings in a cold, detached and bureaucratic manner: 'I received many punches and kicks, and suffered a partially detached retina to my left eye.'
>
> [In the Bolzano concentration camp], he was not kept in the section for long-term prisoners, but in the narrow dark cells where 'no people could be seen' and 'which barely let a glimmer of light filter through', as he described in one of the most famous of his poems in dialect. The most terrifying room was the black cell or *schwarze Zelle*, where there was not even the smallest chink of light, and from which came the continuous agonizing screams of the victims of the brutal Ukrainian guards, Missa and Oto. They appear in Meneghetti's poetry throwing a small Jewish woman into a coffin, a victim of their torture, while they sing 'Heiliges Judenschwein / ora pro nobis'. After some time, he was freed from his cell and, as he was a doctor, he was sent to work in the infirmary.[16]

I took part in the establishment of the Veneto section of the Action Party in October of 1942. The clandestine meeting took place in Treviso at the law firm of Leopoldo Ramanzini, who came from an anti-fascist family and became the prefect of Treviso after the

Liberation. Ugo La Malfa was also there. He was not a liberal-socialist, but rather a radical democrat in the tradition of Giovanni Amendola, and the only one of us who had been active in politics before the advent of fascism. I represented the Paduan group, along with Luigi Cosattini (of whom I will speak later). With the birth of the Action Party, the decision to be an anti-fascist became a serious political commitment. La Malfa had come from Milan in order to explain the programme and give us instructions on the contacts that we were to keep with the other nuclei of the new party. We needed to tighten up security in order to create a clandestine organization, as only the communists had managed to do up to that time. On our return, Cosattini told me: 'I think we're beginning to do some things that really count.' We were aware that we had taken a decisive step and the time had come to face up to some crucial responsibilities. We had to move on from words to deeds.

The Institute of Philosophy of Law, where Enrico Opocher acted as my assistant, was considered a free zone. Every day, hundreds of students were entering the new university building next to the famous Palazzo del Bo. As people were coming and going continuously, it was easily possible to enter by one door and leave by another without arousing any suspicion. We had a friendly janitor who knew very well that not all the people who came to see us were lecturers and students. It is not easy to give an idea of the intensity of the meetings that took place during the period 1942–3 in order to establish an anti-fascist network. Of course, the police were aware of what was going on. I do not know what was written about me in the Paduan police archives, but I would like to. I was not yet married and I lived in lodgings at the Regina Hotel (which no longer exists). After the Liberation, the hotel porter would ask me: 'What were you getting up to, Professor? Every time you came in, someone from police headquarters would follow asking for information.' (I still have a cutting from *Bò*, the university newspaper; it is from a regular column called 'Campana del Bò' which made the following statement: 'Question: Is Prof. Norberto Bobbio of our Royal University enrolled in the party? If so, why doesn't he wear the fascist badge during lessons? Would you please let us know why he does not wear the badge?'). However our lessons were free: I divided my last course into three parts, one on the themes of justice, freedom and democracy, one on a brief history of liberalism, starting with the declarations of rights at the end of the eighteenth century, and one on a brief history of socialist doctrines. The course concluded with the idea that a perfect society would have to be inspired by an amalgamation of both ideologies and be implemented through democratic government, of which I then had a highly individual interpretation (as I will explain later). Indeed one of my students at the time, who later became a well-known politician, told me at a meeting many years later that the students used to say that I was teaching the programme of the Action Party.

In the spring of 1943, when it was already clear that we were close to disaster, I ran into some trouble. The provincial party secretary, a native of Parma and lecturer in agricultural law, had the idea, which I do not think was his but came down from above, to invite all the university lecturers to dedicate a votive lamp in the memorial chapel to those who fell in the fascist revolution who were buried in the city cemetery. It was a way of 'calling muster' as they liked to call it, a symbolic and propitiatory gesture in the hope of victory. Naturally, the move caused havoc. The fascist lecturers (who in truth were very few) tried to persuade the others to join, claiming that you had to support the country in time of war, the same argument of the nation in peril that Giovanni Gentile was to use in his 'Address to the Italians' at the Capitol on 24 June 1943. After days of argument, everyone agreed to take part in the ceremony, with the exception of Aldo Ferrabino, a well-known professor of ancient history, and myself. After that, there was a stream of colleagues coming to my study to dissuade me from my refusal. I can still remember the dean, a professor of statistics who was a dear and mild person, an old-fashioned gentleman: 'My dear Bobbio, do me a favour. A personal favour. In any case, it will all be over in a year.' My refusal was not without its consequences. The rector, an archaeologist of note and a fascist through and through, summoned me and told me that he would have to report me. I justified my actions to the provincial party secretary by arguing that as the ceremony was religious, it was not appropriate for a non-believer like me. However, I was reported. Fortunately for me, Bottai was no longer the minister of national education, and had been replaced by Carlo Alberto Biggini, a lecturer in constitutional law at the University of Pisa, who, although a staunch fascist, was a decent person and, being more or less of my generation, I had known him for some time. Clearly embarrassed by the predicament in which he found himself, he took all the formal procedures against me, but in the end did not proceed with my expulsion.

On 27 February 1943, he asked me for explanations in a perfunctory letter, to which I replied with a letter in which I tried to defend my untenable position and justify my refusal. He did not fall for it and answered point by point, threatening to suspend me from my university post. The correspondence was as follows:[17]

Rome, 27 February 1943, Year XXI

Prof. Norberto Bobbio
Royal University of Padua

Re: Padua University Initiative to dedicate a votive lamp.

It has come to my attention that, having being invited by the rector to support an initiative whereby Padua University dedicated a votive lamp for the Memorial Chapel to the dead of the Revolution and the Conquest of the Empire, you decided not to accept the invitation.

I would like you to explain to me the reasons for your absence. I await your prompt reply.

The Minister

Padua, 2.3.1943

Your Excellency,

You have asked me to explain my failure to attend the ceremony organized by the rector of our university in order to dedicate a votive lamp to the Memorial Chapel of the Fallen in the Revolution. When I notified the dean of my decision, I voluntarily offered to clarify the reasons for my attitude. I am therefore pleased that you have given me this opportunity to explain it to you directly.

In a moment such as this of great spiritual and moral tension for our citizens, who have been called upon to carry out their duties in accordance with their abilities and responsibilities, I was under the impression that a symbolic gesture, whose symbolism was purely rhetorical and banal, was not in keeping with the noble purpose of Padua University, nor could it strengthen the prestige of Italian culture, especially its academic standing, if we were to adopt a smug and grandiloquent attitude towards the multitude who are suffering on the battlefields and in work camps, at a time when everyone is called upon to demonstrate their worth and sense of responsibility. In such an attitude, the desire to show oneself off is much more apparent than the desire to assert an idea.

Having been called upon to teach the philosophy of law which is, like all philosophical subjects, above all an ethical discipline which requires total commitment of whoever professes it, and does not allow for exceptions or compromises, I felt that I would have been betraying the dignity of the position I hold and the trust that the students have placed in me, if I had given my support to a gesture, which in its mystical form, appeared to me to be clearly in conflict with modern culture, which as a university teacher I have the duty to represent and which I support as a scholar of philosophy.

I should add that I believed that I was able to take the decision over whether I attended or not in accordance with my conscience, as it does not come under the performance of my academic duties, and I was not consulted about the ceremony until the decision to have it had been taken.

Norberto Bobbio

Rome, 12 March 1943, Year XXI

RE: Commencement of procedure for dismissal from service in accordance with art. 276 of the Consolidating Act on University Laws.

I am not at all satisfied with the reasons that you have given for your refusal to support an initiative whereby Padua University dedicated a votive lamp for the Memorial Chapel for the Fallen in the Revolution and the Conquest of the Empire.

You argue that at a time like the present 'of great spiritual and moral tension for our citizens' you were under the impression 'that a symbolic gesture, whose symbolism was purely rhetorical and banal, was not in keeping with the noble purpose of Padua University'. You also add that it could not help to strengthen the prestige of Italian culture, 'if we were to adopt a *smug and grandiloquent* attitude towards the multitude who are suffering on the battlefields and in work camps, at a time when everyone is called upon to demonstrate their *worth and sense of responsibility*. In such an attitude, the desire to show oneself off is much more apparent than the desire to assert an idea.'

However, it appears to me that this is precisely the most serious aspect of your attitude: the fact that you could have seen the offering to the Fatherland under arms carried out by the glorious University of Padua to be not a worthy and noble symbolic gesture, but a gesture of rhetorical and banal symbolism, an act lacking in integrity, a show of smug grandiloquence.

This confirms the gravity of your refusal, rather than explaining your reasons, as I find your interpretation of this patriotic act by Padua University to be quite incredible. An act of support is always a purely subjective matter. Therefore, if you had been fully and sincerely affected by the sentiment which should have motivated you to support the ceremony, the ceremony itself would have appeared completely worthy of the nobility and sincerity of that sentiment, and your spirit would not have been able to distort it to the point of seeing it as a rhetorical and banal gesture.

The protest that you have made, all the more serious because you are a member of the party, has placed you in a situation that is incompatible with the Government's general policy directives, and I am therefore notifying you of my absolute intention to commence the procedure for you to be dismissed from service, in accordance with art. 276 of the Consolidating Act on University Laws.

I am granting you a period of ten days from the date of receipt of this letter, for the submission of any rebuttals.

The Minister

I do not remember what happened next. A simple decree requiring my transfer to the University of Cagliari was issued, against which I appealed. A few months went by, and we came to 25 August and the fall of Mussolini. I heard no more of the disciplinary action.

Biggini was one of the seven members of the Fascist Grand Council to vote against Grandi's motion to remove Mussolini from office, because he had been a loyal supporter of Mussolini from the very beginning. The Duce rewarded him by appointing him minister of national education in the new government of the Republic of Salò. He came to Padua, which had been chosen as the location for the ministry, towards the end of 1943. Many things had changed after 8 September. Clandestine activity was much more intense. We had to maintain contacts with the first partisan bands and Patriotic Action Groups [GAP] were being formed even in Padua. When Biggini took over his new post in Padua, he made a declaration of intention similar to that of Gentile in his speeches of the time; namely, that he was there for national reconciliation, in order that Italians did not destroy each other. As a symbolic gesture of reconciliation, the first person he summoned for talks was an oppositionist, Concetto Marchesi, who was appointed rector after 25 July. He then wanted to meet other lecturers, including Carlo Esposito, a well-known expert on constitutional law, and myself. On that occasion, he promised that he would not reintroduce the oath of allegiance to the regime, a promise that he kept. More confidentially, he told me: 'You know that like Mussolini I belong to an old socialist family.' It was a friendly meeting. I got the impression that he realized that everything was falling apart, and that he was attempting to establish a *modus vivendi* with his adversaries. It appears from his biography written by a journalist, Luciano Garibaldi, that he accepted the post of minister without great enthusiasm, out of a sense of loyalty to Mussolini.[18] When I was arrested a few days after this meeting on 6 December, and imprisoned in Verona, my wife went to him, to see if he could get me released. Biggini lifted the phone and called the prefect of Verona, but Valeria got the impression that he was not being taken seriously. Indeed, Biggini was saying on the phone: 'Who is supposed to be the minister of national education, in charge of Bobbio, you or I?'

But let me go back a bit: I got married on 28 April 1943 in Turin. I knew Valeria from when she had been a student at D'Azeglio School. She was part of our circle of friends, along with her sister who had married Roberto Ago, a renowned professor of international law, who was a member of the Court of Justice in The Hague on two occasions. Her father was Professor Cova, who taught gynaecology, and was a native of Vergiate in the province of Varese. He came to Turin from Palermo in 1931, and Valeria always had wonderful memories of Sicily and the years they spent there. Ago and I met the Cova sisters together. In December 1935, when Valeria was seventeen, the four of us went skiing together in Cervinia, which we still used to call Breuil. You would go up on foot from Valtournanche, because, although the road had been built, it was not cleared of snow in the winter. When we got married, I did not know what was going to happen about the case against me for not having taken part in the ceremony at Padua University. As I feared that I would lose my job and salary, I contacted Giulio Einaudi to find out if there was a chance of full-time employment. I had been working with the publishing house since its foundation (1934), and in 1941, they published my critical edition of Tommaso Campanella's *Città del sole* as part of a series of critical editions of Italian classics which was edited by our professor of Romance Philology, Santorre Debenedetti, in secret, because he was barred by the race laws. In 1943, I came up with the idea of a series called the 'Library of Philosophical Culture' which was only started on after the war in 1945, and of another series in collaboration with Antonio Giolitti called the 'Library of Legal Culture', which had a rather troubled existence. 1943 was the year in which my involvement with the publishing house increased with the prospect of the imminent and by then certain fall of the fascist regime.[19]

The fall of fascism on 25 July caught me in the countryside at Rivalta Bormida. I recall that the next day I had to leave early in the morning because I was examining students. I had to take the bus to Alessandria, where I was to take the train to Padua. I knew nothing of what had happened the previous evening. I heard the first confused versions of the news when I reached the town square to take the bus. Then I saw from the train the first jubilant crowds demonstrating at each station. I decided to get out in Milan in order to go to one of the clandestine bases of the Action Party, Adolfo Tino's firm of lawyers, and get precise information on what had happened. I wrote a few notes on that historic day. I found those notes amongst my old papers. As a precaution, I had hidden the identity of the people I met behind pseudonyms.

> I arrive in Milan at ten. In the train, most people's reaction is one of stifled joy. Calm and cautious behaviour. In the corridor, groups of civilians and soldiers comment on the event. The new situation has been greeted favourably by everyone, but their arguments demonstrate the disorientation and political immaturity of the Italian bourgeoisie. However, there is a clear sense of having been freed from an intolerable yoke. On approaching Milan, we see the first crowds demonstrating in the streets. Workers, who have downed tools, stand outside the factories. Groups of women and children wave Italian tricolours in front of the entrances to apartment buildings. Everywhere there is a holiday atmosphere. A child in the middle of a field brandishes a pole with a piece of red cloth attached to it. A railwayman also holds up a

red flag for signalling and laughs in the direction of the travellers leaning out of the train.

In Milan, two armoured cars full of soldiers draw up outside the station, and they get out and line up along the entrance. The trams are not running. I start off for the city centre on foot. There are no processions in the street, just groups of ten or twenty persons, men and women together. They go by on the street, on foot, on bicycles or in vans covered with flags and shouting their support for peace and Badoglio. A worker in his overalls comes out of a warehouse, followed by two or three exultant youngsters. He has a red ribbon on his chest and a printed placard with the words 'Long live Italy, long live Matteotti'. He is carrying a stick, but he does not have a threatening expression. He shouts caustic invectives against the dictator, and everyone laughs. Suddenly a sub-lieutenant in the air force, who looks as though he wants to teach him a lesson, comes up and tells him that that red ribbon on his chest is not the Italian flag. The worker is unperturbed and shouts: 'Long live Italy', and then he adds: 'Long live socialist Italy'. The worker and the sub-lieutenant walk a little distance side by side, but without speaking. Then the worker moves off: neither particularly wants to have an argument.

Graffiti start to appear on the walls and the shop shutters: 'Suitable tips given to anyone who finds a fascist'. On a butcher's shop: 'Mussolini: entrails'. Everywhere: 'Down with the ex-Duce, long live the King'. In Piazza Cavour, soldiers are camped out in front of the offices of *Popolo d'Italia*, the paper founded by Mussolini, and nervous groups of people huddle together.

At Camaino's legal firm, I find the lawyer and the engineer are already with Camaino. I sit down and listen to the news. The Communist Party and the Socialist Party together with the Action Party have decided to produce a joint manifesto asking the masses to demonstrate maximum vigilance at this crucial moment, to stop the country slipping back into reactionary politics. While we are drafting the manifesto (the engineer is doing the writing), the Novara representative and then the Communist representative, A son of A, arrive. They phone us to say that there is also a meeting a Fogazzaro's: we invite those at that meeting to join us. In the meantime, others appear, including Mr Baruffa, a slight little man who describes his speech to the crowd in Piazza del Duomo: he is a socialist. An officer with a ribbon from the Russian campaign took part in the discussion: he is a publisher who is making available the machinery for printing the manifestos. Our group is getting bigger: this time it is the socialists: Asso B, lively eyes, nervous temperament, a man of trust and of action. Every contribution to the debate goes over the question of the two manifestos again, our manifesto and that of A son of A. Although they are very similar, it is difficult to reconcile them. We want to call on the masses to be vigilant, while the others are for continuing the demonstrations, strikes, etc. In the end, the group that had been meeting at Fogazzaro's arrives. Fogazzaro himself is the subject of a certain amount of bowing and scraping from some people, in spite of the atmosphere and the circumstances. Then, among other people, the authoritative leader of democratic Catholics. The argument over the manifestos flares up again. There is disagreement between Fogazzaro and Camaino over the significance of Badoglio's *coup d'état*, and the Catholic proposes that the manifesto be redrafted. Following a noisy and chaotic confusion of voices, it is proposed that the drafting of the manifesto be entrusted to a committee with a representative from all the parties. I leave. When I return, the manifesto is already typewritten. The beginning is by A son of A, the middle section by the Catholic, and the last part by the Action Party. Everyone has signed it.

The lawyer Camaino was Adolfo Tino, a well-known exponent of the Action Party, whose party name was Vesuvio. 'A son of A' was of course Giorgio Amendola, the son of Giovanni. Fogazzaro stood for Tommaso Fulco Gallarati Scotti, a Catholic writer from an aristocratic family, who published a biography of Fogazzaro in 1920. Asso B was an anagram for (Lelio) Basso. Baruffa's real name was Veratti. The 'authoritative leader of the Catholic democrats' was Stefano Iacini. That meeting was also described in Giorgio Amendola's *Lettere a Milano*, where he tells us that he did not take part in the demonstrations in the streets, because he had to contact representatives of the anti-fascist parties:

> I spent many hours at Tino's law firm, where a constitution for a co-ordinating committee for the anti-fascist opposition was decided upon, and the text was approved for an appeal which contained the essential points of the position that we had agreed in our leadership. Parri and Lombardi were there for the Action Party, Basso for the Movement of Proletarian Unity, Veratti for the Italian Socialist Party, Iacini and Gallarati Scotti for the Catholics, and Arpesani for the Liberals. Comrade Grilli, who for some time had established useful links with various anti-fascist groups, also came. Then there was a whole crowd of people who turned that meeting into a truly mass event. The agreement, which we had been patiently seeking to achieve for months and to which each party had been raising objections and concerns, was now reached within a few hours, and all the difficulties were overcome through the momentum. This agreement was even signed at the offices of the lawyer Tino, where a few days earlier, my anti-fascist friend had raised republican objections against an alliance with the Liberals and ideological objections to an alliance with the Communists.
>
> I spoke several times in that meeting and prepared the draft document, which was then approved with few amendments.[20]

That summer, when Badoglio was in power, was full of uncertainties. I spent most of it moving between Turin and holiday resorts in the mountains, at Dejoz in Valtournanche in the company of Federico Chabod and his wife (and dog), and at our family house in Rivalta Bormida. I interrupted the holidays in Val d'Aosta for two days, because I had been invited by Concetto Marchesi to a meeting with a representative of the Principato publishing house (originally based in Messina) to plan a new series of textbooks for the future democratic Italy. I got to Milan, a deserted city, a few days after terrible bombing.

In Turin, I had contacted old friends. I had gone to see Vittorio Foa, who had been released from prison and was staying with his parents. They had been evacuated to Cordova, a little town in the hills below Superga. We spoke of the prospects for the Action Party. Recalling our meeting in his wonderful book *Il cavallo e la torre*, Foa wrote that I thought of the Action Party 'as a tool of democracy that contained many socialist elements'.[21] When the academic year started, I returned to my department at the University of Padua. Valeria and I settled in a flat which had been kindly put at our disposal by a colleague who had been evacuated. After my arrest, my wife came to see me in prison in Verona, but as she was a young married and pregnant woman on her own, we all insisted on her returning to Turin.

I was arrested in Padua on the morning of 6 December 1943. I was initially imprisoned in the barracks of the Republic of Salò Police, and then in the Scalzi Prison in Verona. I was released at the end of February. Two weeks after my release, my first child, Luigi, was born on 16 March 1944 in Turin. The Prefecture of Padua notified the General Police Management at the Ministry of Internal Affairs of my arrest on 13 December 1943, Year XXII of the Fascist Era, in a letter still held in the State Archive:

> RE: Prof. Norberto Bobbio, son of Luigi, born in Turin on 18/10/1909, previously cautioned for political activity.
>
> On the 6th of this month, at the request of the Verona Militia Headquarters, I, the Federal Commissar, proceeded with the arrest of the aforementioned professor, who teaches philosophy of law at Padua University, and transferred him to Verona for investigations of a political nature.
>
> Prof. Bobbio, who has been accused of membership of a secret anti-fascist association called 'Action Committee of the Liberation of Italy', has been held there in a state of arrest.
>
> Chief of the Province[22]

Perhaps Bobbio could have avoided arrest. One of his students in the Arts Faculty, a youth from Verona called Gianfranco De Bosio

who was to become a famous theatre director, had found out that
they were going to arrest the professor. He ran to warn him on the
morning of his arrest: 'Bobbio glared at me, and completely distrusted
this stupid first-year university student, and he let himself be arrested.
Every time we meet, we talk about this episode which perhaps I did
not deal with very well. I should have got the news to him in a more
sober manner. By going there (in the manner I did), I gave him a
shock.'[23] *The youthful De Bosio was in contact with anti-fascist*
groups, and shortly afterwards he joined the Patriotic Action Group
led by Otello Pighin who won the Gold Medal of the Resistance and
was murdered by Carità's gang. De Bosio based a film Il terrorista
on that experience and it is one of the most effective and political
films on the Resistance. However, Bobbio did not underestimate the
information.

I can well remember that De Bosio came to warn me of the danger
at the Regina Hotel, where Valeria and I used to have lunch. One of
the youths in the Action Party, a student of ours who studied under
the Verona lawyer Giuseppe Tommasi, had been arrested along with
Tommasi himself and other members of the group. He had confessed
that Tommasi had arranged to meet me in Padua to establish a direct
contact between the two cities, and he indicated that I was one of
those responsible for the Paduan Committee of Liberation, which
had been set up in October. It was not that I had not taken the
warning seriously. However, I could not escape immediately, as I had
to destroy compromising documents which I had put in the drawer
of my desk at the university, particularly a report that I had been sent
by Antonio Giuriolo, a schoolteacher in Vicenza and hero of the
Resistance, who had already set up a partisan band. I had to warn
other people. I had thought that I would be able to sort these matters
out and leave in the afternoon. However, the new Fascist provincial
secretary, a captain in the Militia from Tuscany who had replaced
the previous one who disappeared after 25 July, was already at the
Regina Hotel by midday. He was very polite: 'My dear professor, we
have to investigate you.' I had not thought that he would come so
early. He made me get into his car, allowed me to go home to collect
some books and then personally drove me to Verona. During the
journey, we entertained each other in political debate. He told me,
amongst other things, that his real enemies were not anti-fascists like
myself, but the party officials guilty of treachery. They took me to a
school that had been converted into barracks close to Porta Vescovo,
and put me in the hands of the person who commanded the firing
squad for Ciano, De Bono and the other party officials condemned to
death at the trial in Verona in January 1944. I remained in the cells

of the new fascist police for about a month. Then they transferred me to cell number 13 of the so-called Scalzi Prison. There were eight of us in the cell. I underwent interrogation, which could on occasions be brutal, but no trial. Towards the middle of February, a commissar came from Rome to conduct a formal interrogation, after one of the two interrogators in the makeshift Provincial Fascist Police had been arrested following internal disagreements. I recently received a copy of the records of the interrogation on 15 February 1944 from one of my fellow accused, which I had completely forgotten about. It shows that I responded to a question on my relationship with Concetto Marchesi by saying: 'I never had discussions of a political nature with the rector of the University of Padua. We all knew that he had always been a communist, but a communist idealist who concerned himself with the doctrine principally for the good of humanity.'

At the beginning of November, Marchesi had opened the academic year with a show of hostility: he invited no one from the Nazi and fascist authorities to attend the ceremony, and he managed to keep away the militiamen who wanted to disrupt the proceedings. He was a great orator, and he gave a speech that contained a memorable portrayal of the university: 'We have gathered in here what must not be destroyed.' By the end of November, he had handed in his resignation and prepared his flight. He disappeared a few days after my arrest, having arranged the distribution around all the university premises during the night of an appeal to join the struggle. The students themselves distributed the appeals. The anger of the fascist can easily be imagined. A party official immediately came to interrogate me. 'Did you know anything?' 'I know nothing,' I replied, but I knew everything. Marchesi had read out his appeal a few days earlier in the house of one of his students. I had been there. Then they told me: 'You will not leave here alive if you don't tell us where Marchesi has ended up.' But they did not follow it up, and after that they left me in peace. I was transferred to regular city jail at the end of the month.[24]

The last two chapters of my book *Italia civile* are devoted to two other people involved in the Paduan episode: Luigi Cosattini who took part in the meeting that set up the Action Party, and Antonio Giuriolo whom I have already referred to in relation to my arrest.

Cosattini, who was four years younger than me and the son of an old socialist deputy (mayor of Udine after the Liberation), was a brilliant scholar of civil law:

> His university career would have developed rapidly towards its natural fruition, if the war had not broken out in the meantime. War, and particularly this war, confronted young people with problems they

could not turn their backs on and, above all, they could not silence the voice of their own consciences. What was the meaning of the war that we were fighting? Why were we fighting? What were we supposed to do when the war was over, whatever its outcome? But unfortunately, by the end of 1942, developments in the war made clear what the outcome would be for us, at least to everyone who was not blinded by fanaticism or duped by propaganda.

. . . [Luigi Cosattini] engaged in audacious and effective liaison work between various clandestine groups, using the opportunity for travel which arose from his teaching posts at the universities of Trieste and Urbino, his family's residence in Udine and his contacts in Padua. Perhaps he was too fearless. He thought that he was protected by the supposedly 'official' nature of his journeys . . . Wanted and pursued by the German police in Udine, he was arrested while returning to his home and taken to prison in Trieste. A few days earlier, he had taken part in a meeting of the Veneto Region Liberation Committee held in Venice.

Although he had been made powerless and weak by the suppression of his freedom, and although he was alone and deserted amongst his enemies, he never lost for a second that inner moral courage which prevented him from making gestures contrary to the demands of his conscience. He could have lied, hidden his essential nature, or at least minimized his responsibilities. He did not choose to do so. Instead he challenged his accusers, telling them the whole truth. He said he was glad to belong to the Action Party and he accused the Germans to their faces of being oppressors and barbarians. After four months, he was deported to Germany on 21 June. The convoy passed through Udine, his native city . . . Luigi managed to notify his family and was able to embrace his father and sister.[25]

Luigi Cosattini was deported to Buchenwald and then to Aschersleben. He then disappeared in the chaos that preceded the fall of the Reich. Having been evacuated from the camp as the allied troops drew close, and required to take part in an absurd forced march while the SS officials disappeared, he had been condemned to death for an attempt to escape. He escaped in the night from a factory where he was detained with other prisoners. From that moment, we know nothing more of him. He was swallowed up by the dregs of an army that was crumbling apart.

A meeting of liberal-socialists in Padua in 1941 was the first occasion on which I met Giuriolo, who was also younger, by three years, and the author of essays on Henry Becque and Antonio Fogazzaro:

We engaged in long discussions at my institute. I would be sitting at my desk and he would be in the armchair next to it. We did not only talk politics, but politics did form part of our conversation. Our projects would appear terribly naive if viewed from the present day. Yet those arguments were sharpening the weapon needed for the struggle to come, the weapon without which there can be no enduring struggle, the weapon without which you tire and once defeated, you capitulate. The weapon of which I speak is a sense of moral outrage against injustice and oppression.

Four or five of us would go to Arzignano. We would take the train to Vicenza, then a branch line to the next station, and a short climb on foot up to the castle. Up there, we could enjoy the freedom of solitude, surrounded by vines on a hill from which you could see a great sweep of countryside around Vicenza. We were away from inquisitive looks. We would usually sit under the pergola, and Toni would start to bring us up bottles with famous names from his cellar, and he would proudly and lovingly explain the meaning, the secrets and the symbolism of those colours and tastes, as though he had invented them himself. Then there was endless debate: we analysed the world and then put it to rights. We were convinced at the time that it was our turn, the turn of our generation and the ideals that we represented, to make history.

My friends, it all comes down to this: he was a man who listened to his own conscience which told him to fight in the name of a civilization which he believed himself to represent, for the solidarity and liberty of humanity. That was his teaching, the noblest teaching that a man can give other men. If we failed to understand that teaching, then Toni really would have died in vain, and today we would be right to ask ourselves why. It is up to us, and only up to us, to make sure that this does not happen, to keep his memory alive so that his beliefs are not lost. We survivors have a duty to bear witness to those who bore witness.[26]

After 8 September, Antonio Giuriolo joined the armed struggle in the mountains of Friuli, and he was a member of the Rosselli Battalion, which was about forty men-strong and took up positions at Subit. He died in action in the Appennine Mountains of Emilia on 12 December 1944.

On leaving prison, Bobbio immediately returned to Turin. He found a city disfigured by bombings. The last heavy aerial bombardment occurred on 8 November 1943. Many buildings, including the Molinette Hospital, Consolata Sanctuary, the Piedmontese Arcade, the Crocetta Church, had been reduced to rubble. The loss of life was immense. Many essential items were impossible to find. 1944 turned out to be a hard year. Police round-ups were a common occurrence and reprisals a daily event. Every morning there were confused rumours about actions carried out by rebels, as the partisans were called. The most eloquent historical document on daily life in the city is a diary kept by a young industrialist called Carlo Chevallard.[27]

On 13 March, Chevallard described 'a pitiful scene' in his notebook:
lorries full of workers arrested after the large-scale strikes proclaimed
in the manufacturing industries. They were picked up from their
workshops on the day they returned to work, and were deported to
concentration camps in Germany without even being able to see their
families. On 31 March, the SS captured members of the Military
Committee of the Piedmontese Committee of National Liberation,
led by General Giuseppe Perotti, the youngest Italian general. Edgardo
Sogno, who was on a mission in Liguria, managed to escape. Their
trial and that of other members of partisan groups then followed and
led to the shooting of eight patriots at the Martinetto firing range.
The thirty-fourth bombing came on 5 June: 'American planes attacked
the city around half past ten. The bombing was particularly violent
and, if not an act of terrorism, then extremely badly executed; apart
from the usual [industrial] area around Lingotto, Borgo San Paolo
was very badly hit. The area around Crocetta was also horribly dev-
astated.' On 20 June, Chevallard noted down the rumour that the
managing director of Fiat, Valletta, had been arrested for collaboration
with the allied forces. The arrest warrant was not issued by the SS
Command in northern Italy until 26 June, but it was immediately
revoked following the intervention of Cardinal Schuster, the arch-
bishop of Milan. On 23 July, the citizens of Turin found the bodies
of six partisans hanging in Corso Vinzaglio and at the bottom of
Corso Giulio Cesare, as a reprisal for the wounding of a fascist offi-
cial in the Republic of Salò. One of the men hanged was Ignazio
Vian who won the Gold Medal and commanded the Boves Group
which later combined with the Mauri Group. On 20 September,
partisans attacked the military prison: 'Yesterday, about twelve
o'clock, a group of about 180 partisans attacked the military prison
in Via Ormea, took all the guards prisoner, and freed the prisoners,
for the most part deserters and men who had failed to report for
military service.' In the winter, the supply of electricity to manufac-
turing was partially suspended, as a result of the exceptionally cold
spell that hit the city, while the problem of bread supplies became
increasingly serious, in spite of rationing. In January, machine-
gunning from the air became increasingly common, and at Orbassano
fighters hit a suburban tram, killing forty-two people.

On 4 March 1945: 'Yesterday, I went for a walk in Vernone, a small
town near Rivalta, where I met several partisans. They made a much
better impression than last year: they are better armed, better equipped
and above all they appear disciplined (military salutes, signs of rank,
and all the same uniforms), which last year was not the case. They

have received a great deal of supplies from the air, something that I have no difficulty in believing as every evening you can hear aircraft passing very low.'

On 18 April 1945: 'As I was going down to the city on bicycle with a friend, we were stopped and they asked us for our documents. I took out my identity card, a partisan looked at it and then asked for another document. I took out my driving licence. 'Anything else? Don't you have bilingual documentation?' he asked me. 'Of course, but I didn't think that you partisans would be interested in a German document.' He laughed, examined my bilingual document with satisfaction and allowed me through. The bilingual document is almighty!'

My wife had moved out to the country with my mother, during my imprisonment. When I returned, Luigi had been born, and we lived with my father-in-law, Professor Cova, in the city centre. I had two other lodgings that I could move around. One was a beautiful flat left by an evacuated colleague. The other, which was more modest, was an empty property that belonged to us. I became a permanent member of the Committee of National Liberation. A Front for Intellectuals had been established at the instigation of the Communist Party, which set up a Schools Committee. I represented the Action Party in both. The Christian Democrats were represented by Giuseppe Grosso, a lecturer in Roman Law, who later became mayor of Turin. They gave the task of organizing the clandestine press to the Front. I knew a small printer who had a workshop in Via Pomba, between Piazza Bodoni and the National Cinema, and I knew that I could trust him. We set up a newspaper with four pages, which we called *L'Ora dell'Azione*. The first issue was distributed in September of 1944. It was mostly written by myself with the assistance of a communist representative from the Schools Committee, Lia Corinaldi. She was courageous and hard-working, and I remember her with affection. It produced my first political article entitled 'Chiarimento' ['Clarification']. I argued that intellectuals had to avoid two errors: political intrigue or in other words political commitment for personal aggrandizement, and political apathy or indifference to politics. Two or three issues of *L'Ora dell'Azione* were published.[28] I remember that there was a problem in finding premises for the committee meetings. We mainly met at the Law Institute and at the Academy of Sciences, whose secretary was an old anti-fascist. It was possible to move about with a certain amount of safety in a big city, in spite of intense police surveillance. When the under-secretary of internal affairs in the Badoglio government, the liberal Aldobrando Medici Tornaquinci, arrived on a mission from the South to contact the Resistance in Turin, I took part in a meeting which was organized in an empty building in Corso Francia with all representatives on the Committee of National Liberation.

Naturally we knew the risks we were running. When you are going around with a bag full of clandestine newspapers, you know very well how things could end up. A distinction has to be made between active resistance, armed resistance and passive resistance. Armed resistance was part of the active resistance. However, there was active resistance that was not armed. It was carried out by those who produced counterfeit documents and membership cards, or who engaged in propaganda activities. They were also running risks, and if they were unfortunate enough to be arrested, they too would end up in the concentration camps. However, there was a grey area, which is now being not only exonerated but also acknowledged as having made an honourable contribution. This grey area was made up of those who sat on the fence and waited to see which way the wind would blow. They were people who did not want to compromise themselves. In reality, none of them wanted the Germans to win, but they stood by as onlookers. They were divided between those who thought Stalin would be coming and those, the majority, who awaited the arrival of the American troops that had already landed in the South. Even when it comes to collaboration, you need to distinguish between voluntary collaborators and coerced collaborators: the collaboration of those who had decided to support the Republic of Salò and the collaboration of those, such as state employees, who were obliged to collaborate. I'm not saying Italians were all on the side of the partisans, but a huge majority of them were certainly not on the side of the Germans. It is also true that some of the people who joined the partisan bands, did so because they felt that it was more dangerous to enrol in the forces of the Italian Social Republic than to go up into the mountains. Many were of the age for conscription. However, it is impossible to put those who fought to free Italy from Nazis and fascists on a par with those who wanted to perpetuate Hitler's domination of the world, as revisionist historians are trying to do.

On the other hand, the historian Renzo De Felice, author of the monumental biography Mussolini, *which is almost 6,000 pages long, has claimed that the 8th September marked the death of the fatherland: he defined it as a 'tragic date for the Italian nation' in a debate with Bobbio published in* L'Unità *and* Panorama *to mark the fiftieth anniversary of the Liberation.*

De Felice: 'The 8th September witnessed a confrontation between two elites, one fascist and one anti-fascist, to which the masses were indifferent and they could not understand why the war for which they were paying the price should continue. Judgement of the partisan movement must always be put in the context of the prevailing mood in that particular moment. Initially the demobbed soldiers on the run from the Germans were helped by the population. Mothers thought of their own sons in the war and did everything they could . . . Everyone helped out in the same spirit of self-sacrifice as long as the partisan band came from their area. However, when the civil war developed into something increasingly violent with attacks and reprisals, the Resistance became very unpopular. The majority did not take part, they waited. The workers, clerks, middle classes and peasants were all waiting. So with various up and downs, you got to the spring of 1945, when it became clear that the Allies were winning, and all that was needed was to put a handkerchief around your neck and become a freedom fighter. Alongside the enthusiasm of the elites who were battling it out, was the general feeling of relief amongst the majority that peace was imminent; it did not matter why.'

Bobbio: 'We might have been a minority, but we changed the direction of events. Today we have to oppose the arguments of those who at the time did not realize the importance for the history of all humanity of fighting against Nazism and fascism actively and not just passively . . . I would challenge De Felice who claims that national identity collapsed after 8 September, by suggesting that 10 June 1940, the day Mussolini took us into the war, was the tragic date in Italian history . . . If anything, 8 September gave Italians and anti-fascists the opportunity to move on, pick themselves up and become active. Although a minority, we were totally convinced that Italy had to lose the war. This is the conviction that divides us: in my opinion, the great majority of Italians were not in favour of entering the war . . . The revision that should be made, I admit, is above all in emphasizing the plurality of behaviour patterns: those fighting for the Resistance, the fascist adversaries and those who remained in the middle. The achievement of more recent historical research is that it has demonstrated this greater complexity. The lack of popular involvement cannot be interpreted as widespread opposition to the partisan movement.'[29]

You often hear it said that fascism was a less savage and more tolerant dictatorship than Nazism. The argument is used in disputes between historians and politicians in order to diminish the historic importance of anti-fascism and the Resistance. I have already said that the regime did allow some liberties, but the race campaign was shameful. But most important of all, you have to go beyond the strict confines of an Italian controversy. You cannot separate the struggle against fascism from the struggle against Nazism. You cannot talk about what was happening in Italy without relating it to what was happening in Europe: the Italian Resistance was just a part of the

European Resistance. There was resistance of varying degrees of intensity in all the countries occupied by the Germans, and the great merit of the Italian Resistance was that it involved Italy in a great European movement. Anyone who forgets this forgets the very nature of Hitler's war of aggression. This is the reason why fascism and anti-fascism must never be put on a par. On the one side, there was a cruel and pitiless war, with all the aggravation of the concentration and extermination camps, and on the other side were the European resisters, regardless of whether or not they were communists. One of the symbols of the European Resistance was General Charles de Gaulle, who was clearly not a communist. Perhaps one should add that the Resistance in Italy, precisely because it was a fascist country, was not only a patriotic war but also a war against fascism, and therefore a civil war. Nevertheless, the Resistance was a way to bring Italy back into the fold of civilized nations. It was at the very roots of our democracy.

The insurrection and liberation of Turin had been planned by the Piedmontese Regional Military Command with a coded order which is still famous: 'Aldo says 26 × 1', which meant that operations were to begin at one o'clock on 26 April. The partisan brigades surrounded the city, and tricolours flew from the roadblocks. Here and there you could hear shooting. The Piedmontese Committee of National Liberation was made up of Franco Antonicelli, chairman, and Paolo Greco for the Italian Liberal Party, Giorgio Amendola and Amedeo Ugolini for the Italian Communist Party, Rodolfo Morandi and Giorgio Montalenti for the Italian Socialist Party, Alessandro Galante Garrone and Mario Andreis for the Action Party, and Andrea Guglieminetti and Eugenio Libois for the Christian Democrats. For two long days, there were dramatic negotiations with the German Command, which was willing to withdraw from the city on condition that two divisions, the 34th Armoured Division and the 5th Alpenjäger, were allowed to keep their arms, but the partisans were demanding unconditional surrender.

Greco writes:

> In the early hours of the morning of the 27th,' writes Greco, 'the Committee of National Liberation was transferred to the Fiorio tanning factory, in whose vicinity there was ongoing firing between the workers barricaded in the factories and the fascist militias who surrounded them. German armoured cars were rushing up and down Corso Francia firing madly. Don Garneri appeared at the Committee of National Liberation carrying the third German request to cross the city with the two divisions, and in the event of a refusal, it threatened 'to turn Turin into another Warsaw.[30]

Following a further refusal by the Committee of National Libera-
tion, the German troops started to withdraw while keeping open
the access to Corso Vittorio Emanuele, in order to be able to leave
Turin towards the north. The Fascist Militias, which had now been
disbanded, joined the Germans, while groups of partisans occupied
buildings in the centre and flushed out the snipers. On 28 April, the
Committee of National Liberation transformed itself into a regional
government and officially took possession of the city. A procession
moved from the Fiorio tanning factory through Piazza Statuto and
along Via Garibaldi to Piazza Castello in the heart of Turin. Ada
Gobetti, the widow of Piero Gobetti, who was appointed assistant
mayor, described the events:

> The procession started with a lorry full of armed partisans, followed
> by our cars and then other lorries of armed men. They were still firing
> from windows and street corners, but the people, unconcerned about
> the danger, filled the streets we passed through, and shouted 'Long live
> Italy! Long live the partisans! Long live the Committee of National
> Liberation!' They threw flowers and lifted their children, holding them
> towards us, so that they could see and would be able to remember.[31]

The Committee of National Liberation made new appointments:
the prefect was Pier Luigi Passoni, a socialist; the mayor was Giovanni
Roveda, a communist, and the head of police was Giorgio Agosti, a
member of the Action Party. Another Action Party member, Augusto
Monti, teacher in the Resistance School, was appointed school
superintendent, but the Allied Command was not to recognize this
appointment.
We should not forget that clandestine activities carried on alongside public ones. In the academic year 1944–5, which was marked by
a particularly cold winter, my colleagues in the Faculty of Law, who
included Paolo Greco the chairman of the Committee of National
Liberation, asked me to run a course at the Law Institute, as the chair
in philosophy of law had been vacant since Solari left in 1942. On
the last day of lessons, Saturday 21 April when the Liberation was
imminent, we undertook to recommence the course in September. I
discovered an unexpected account of this episode in the final pages of
Diario di Leletta, lettera a Barbato (Milan: Angeli, 1993), the diary
of sixteen-year-old Leletta d'Isola, a Catholic and monarchist, which
she had started in 1943 when she espoused the ideals of the liberation
struggle and assisted the communist partisans billeted at her family's
country home in Bagnolo in the province of Cuneo. After a note on
the general strike of 18 April called to demonstrate the will of the

people of Turin that Germans and fascists should leave the city, the diary went on to say:

> A few machine-gun bursts at Valentino, distribution of anti-fascist leaflets, trams running wild in the inexpert hands of Auxiliaries and seamen from '*x-mas*' motor launches.[32] Abbagnano goes on strike, Guzzo gets away with the usual compromise and sits amongst us. Colonel Cabras gets some workers to put up posters similar to the partisan ones (but who bothers to read them any more?).
>
> Bobbio says in the lecture hall: 'Take part in this strike and remember it: it is the prototype for the perfect strike.' Indeed his message spread to all the classes.[33]

Then on Saturday 21 April 1945, a comment which I have to confess I read with surprise and a degree of emotion:

> So Bobbio finished the course on the philosophy of law, having talked about the relationship between power and justice: 'In making the decision we can refer to history, the actual history we are living through, now that power, or rather the abuse of power, is about to be so spectacularly defeated!' (Only those of us who were present can understand how great was Bobbio's courage: at that time fascist power had not yet been defeated. It would have taken just one informant for him to have been liquidated.)[34]

Once the war was over, I returned to teaching in Padua, but in September I kept my promise to the students in Turin. One of these was Umberto Scarpelli, one of the better-known Italian philosophers of law, who died young in 1994. He dedicated his first book, *Marxismo ed esistenzialismo*, to me. In it, he states that after the break and the return to liberty, I started my lesson with a display of continuity by saying: 'Now as we were saying . . .'. In actual fact, I used the expression 'Heri dicebamus' ['Yesterday we were saying . . .']. But the substance was the same.

3

Finding Out About Democracy

In 1945–6 I returned to Padua University. The rector was Egidio Meneghetti, whom we had all given up hope of seeing again after his arrest and the torture he suffered. I was there on 31 July 1945, when he made his speech before the allied authorities at the reopening of the university. He argued for the fundamental tenet of the Action Party's programme: that the principles of liberalism, 'the precondition for all civilized living', are no longer sufficient because 'if you examine your conscience and the facts, you discover that it is difficult for complete freedom to exist where the advancement of the more able is not governed by equal starting positions'.[1] On 12 November 1945, I took part in the inauguration of the academic year, at which Ferruccio Parri spoke: at the time he was the prime minister in the government formed in June by the parties in the Committee of National Liberation. The students who were former partisans crowded around him, and shouted his *nom de guerre* 'Maurizio, Maurizio!' in an unrepeatable atmosphere of enthusiasm and expectation. We were convinced that a new phase in the life of the country was about to begin.

However, the Parri government was forced to resign in November, and on 10 December, De Gasperi formed the first of his three governments with the support of the Socialists and Communists. In the meantime, elections had been called for the Constituent Assembly and for the referendum to choose between the monarchical and republican systems of government. The vote took place on 2 June 1946.

When it came to drawing up lists for the Constituent Assembly, I could not refuse my inclusion as a candidate for the Action Party in the Padua–Vicenza–Verona constituency. I then carried out the only election campaign of my life on behalf of the Action Party. They came to pick me up by car and took me to public meetings. I have to say that I did not do it very willingly. I lacked both the calling and the experience to be a speaker at political rallies. I spoke at rallies in Belluno, Verona, Vicenza, Adria and, of course, Padua. I remember one time when I had just finished speaking, they got me into a car and said: 'No, no, professor, you can't go home. You are expected in another town!' It was a great relief when I had finished my last speech, and I was at last free from a nightmare that had lasted for nearly a month. I went back to Turin to vote. I was living alone in Padua, as Valeria had stayed on in Turin with Luigi and my second son, Andrea, who was a few months old.

In that period, I founded a small newspaper for the electoral campaign, called *La Repubblica*, because the thing which distinguished us from all the other parties was our inflexibility on the question of the republic. I have to say that there were large turnouts for the Action Party events. Indeed, the size of the crowds at the public meetings gave us a false impression. This was especially true of Meneghetti's meetings, where he spoke in a stentorian voice. He proved to be a brilliant street orator. I remember that one of our most applauded orators was a certain Sagramora, who came from I know not where and of whom I have never heard mention since. He held splendid public meetings at which he used all our traditional rhetoric. He would ritually pronounce syllable by syllable the words: 'small and sickly king' to a roar of applause on each occasion. Behind the image of the 'small and sickly king' there was of course the monarchy's responsibilities for fascism, the involvement in the war, and its flight from Rome following the armistice. We campaigned against both the Communists and the Christian Democrats. I would repeat the quip against the Christian Democrats that they were a party which was neither democratic because they were controlled by the Church, nor Christian because they had been compromised by fascism. But the Communists were also our target, in that they were not democratic. I remember a sentence, directed against the Communists, which concluded one of the short articles in *La Repubblica*: 'You write "Long live Stalin" on the walls, while we write "Justice and Freedom"'. But then everything went very badly for the Action Party. In Veneto, the Christian Democrats won an absolute majority, and the Action Party only had a handful of votes. In the preferences I came second, after Meneghetti, but some distance behind. Besides, our party had suffered a catastrophic defeat around the country and did not manage to win in a single regional constituency. The seven Action Party members of parliament were all elected on the national constituency. It was an incredible fiasco. I told myself: 'That's enough, my political career is over.'

In an article written for *GL [Giustizia e Libertà]* during the electoral campaign, 'You can't resuscitate the dead' (March 1946), I was mistaken in predicting that a 'real and lasting' democracy could only be ensured by parties of the left: I thought that the Christian Democrats, being a party of the centre, were destined 'to be crushed between the opposing forces':

> Too weak to dislodge the privileged from their fortresses, it will end up postponing social reform indefinitely, in spite of its good intentions. Equally, as it is too weak to preserve the liberties of all citizens in a situation of discontent on the one hand and renewed enthusiasm for the struggle on the other, it will end up making the country pay for a purely formal liberty by real disorders and disturbances which will eventually lead to a suppression of liberty. By claiming to act as a referee, it will end up as the onlooker, while the other two sides slug it out. A generous but sterile idea. It claims to be the point of equilibrium, but risks sowing discord.[2]

As we all know, the electoral contest was to prove Bobbio wrong. The Christian Democrats won the elections to the Constituent Assembly with 35.2 per cent of the vote. The results of the other lists were: the Italian Socialist Party of Proletarian Unity 20.7 per cent, the Communist Party 18.9 per cent, the National Democratic Union (the liberals) 6.8 per cent, the Front for the Man in the Street [Fronte dell'Uomo Qualunque] 5.3 per cent, the Italian Republican Party 4.4 per cent, the National Coalition of Liberty (formation of monarchist groups) 2.8 per cent, the Action Party 1.5 per cent (with seven seats). All the other lists were under 1 per cent, including Parri's and La Malfa's party, the Republican Democratic Coalition with 0.4 per cent and two seats, and Lussu's party, the Sardinian Action Party with 0.3 per cent and two seats. The failure of the Action Party has been understood by the majority of historians to be the result of the divide between the two souls that coexisted in the party: the socialist one and the democratic one. This led to the split by the Parri–La Malfa faction just before the election. According to Giovanni De Luna, the split created a climate 'of distrust and malaise', a fall in the number of activists, closure of papers and 'a real political and organizational breakdown'.[3] In Paul Ginsborg's opinion, 'Parri, La Malfa and the majority of the moderates abandoned the conference and the party, and Lussu got his Pyrrhic victory'.[4] Pietro Scoppola argues that 'the crisis was primarily the result of Parri's attempt to move the party's centre of gravity towards the middle classes and the bourgeoisie'.[5] *According to Ennio Di Nolfo, 'the very abundance of intellectual talent which marked the Action Party proved to be its weakness, given that it was translated into a profusion of factions which contended for support and majority positions'.*[6]

I reflected a great deal on that defeat in the years that followed. The Action Party fought the election after a split. In February there had been a conference and the party had found itself divided into a moderate faction led by Parri and La Malfa, a liberal-socialist faction led by Calamandrei and Codignola, and a socialist faction led by Emilio Lussu. If it had gone into the elections as a united party, it would have picked up a few more votes, but it would never have managed to compete with the three mass parties, the Christian Democrats, the Communists and the Socialists. We were a party of intellectuals, distant from what were to be called the two subcultures of our nation, the Catholic one and the socialist one. In Italy, it was the Communists who took on the socialist mantle, not us rootless intellectuals. The fact is that the division between whites and reds has always been profoundly rooted in the political life of our country. I remember that as a lad, there were even two opposing bands in a town where we stayed on holiday, one for the socialists and one for the Catholics, and they had to contend for the main square on festival days and in funeral processions. In other words, this was the Peppone and Don Camillo syndrome. Exactly why the socialist subculture was reconstituted around the Communist Party is not something that I believe has yet been explained. In my own town, Rivalta Bormida, where the old mayor before fascism had been a socialist, the new mayor after Liberation was a communist. What had happened? The active resistance to fascism had been carried out in Italy by the Communists, who had become much stronger, partly because of support from the Soviet Union. The young people who had fought against fascism voted for the Communists, not for the Socialists.

The Action Party, which was principally made up of intellectuals with a liberal and democratic background, had little in common with the Communists and Socialists. Without any doubt, it was orientated towards the left, but its roots were in the history of European liberalism. Suffice it to say that it included, albeit in its moderate wing, men like Luigi Salvatorelli, Adolfo Omodeo and Guido de Ruggiero. At various times, the differing inspirations became confused or blended together – now one was stronger, now another, even in the way it was to be interpreted historically and politically. As in reality it was neither communist nor socialist, but split between different identities, the Action Party was floundering right from the beginning. Thus the party that inherited the values of Piero Gobetti and Carlo Rosselli was demolished in the electoral contest. Indeed, it was to be dissolved after the elections. Each activist took his or her own path. The majority, like Franco Venturi, Massimo Mila, Alessandro Galante Garrone, Giorgio Agosti, myself and even the partisan leader Dante Livio Bianco, did not take part in active politics again, but devoted ourselves to our studies and our profession. There was a diaspora and the Action Party philosophy, however you may judge it, disappeared as a political force.

Those who reproach us for incorrect forecasts and for our difficulty in understanding the society of the time, are not wrong. I was one of those who thought that Italy would be poorer but more democratic than it actually became. We were wrong. I believe that the Action Party and the Communist Party itself made an incorrect assessment. It was a colossal mistake. They did not believe that reconstruction could be so rapid and so effective. The intellectuals in the Action Party had no idea of civil society. They did not understand the spontaneous impulse that comes from *homo oeconomicus*. Communists, Socialists and, to some extent, members of the Action Party believed in the planned economy, while in Italy something very surprising happened, whose results are still with us. A network of small enterprises was established at the time and developed rapidly. It was based purely on economic interest. I too had always thought that reconstruction would be slow, and that state intervention would have been needed. I remember that we had the idea that the lira would have to be revalued, but Einaudi said there was no need. One thing should be clear: the reconstruction was done by the right, not the left. The left has always ignored the spontaneous rationale of economic activities. The Action Party specifically supported the mixed economy with the nationalization of large enterprises of public interest.

The left must do some serious soul-searching over what happened at the time, and reassess the role of Alcide De Gasperi and Luigi Einaudi in the reconstruction of the country. Of course there was also the contribution of the left wing of the Christian Democrats, who always had a good understanding of theory. However, the decisive battles were fought by the right wing of the Christian Democrats. Dossetti's left-wing Christian democracy did not really affect the economic policies of reconstruction. In all honesty, it has to be acknowledged that the economic miracle came about in spite of the left's forecasts of catastrophe. The consumer boom left us stunned, and reconstruction occurred behind our backs. Those of us who had been in the Action Party almost did not realize it. This analysis applies to northern Italy, because reconstruction in southern Italy went through a different process, with a centralized role played by the Southern Regional Development Fund [Cassa del Mezzogiorno]. But in any case, it did not happen through the Guido Dorso's 'Southern Revolution'. This was the failure of all the old campaigners for the South, who had theorized about alliances between workers in the North and peasants in the South. This unfortunately was just ideology. The failure of these Southern campaigners has had disastrous consequences. A people who do not attempt to save themselves by their own efforts, but wait for salvation from state assistance, are unavoidably destined to remain behind in the process of economic and social development.

The establishment of democracy, the struggle between parties, the creation of powers from below, and the development of local autonomies were the questions that Italian society faced up to after the war. The return to liberty, the restoration of elections, the rebirth of interest and participation in the fundamental rights of the collectivity and of individuals, represented crucial questions of political theory which could (or should) have been resolved twenty-five years earlier, after another war, when the Socialist Party, but also the Catholic Italian People's Party, had attempted, as Vittorio Foa writes, 'to extend and modernize democracy by politically representing classes who until then had been excluded: the peasants and workers'.[7] The birth of the Republic put back on the agenda the questions that had been raised by the two-year period of factory occupations (il biennio rosso)[8] *and which were suffocated by the defeat of that political and trade-union struggle.*

It was my interest in Carlo Cattaneo that led me to change the direction of my studies to the history of political thought, almost always with some link to current affairs. It was pure accident that I became interested in the Lombard writer, and my marriage had been the pretext. Solari told me to take what I wanted from his library as a wedding present. I had often noticed the seven volumes of Cattaneo's work, published by Le Monnier between 1881 and 1892, and I asked him for them. Thus, during the German occupation, in which it was difficult to get hold of books and the public libraries were either completely closed or hardly ever open, I threw myself into the study of these volumes. However, there was another reason that explains my interest in this writer: he was one of the very few intellectuals of the Risorgimento whom the fascists were not able *to use* (possibly the only one). His concept of the state, defined as a 'grand transaction' is diametrically opposed to the fascist doctrine of the state as the supreme moral arbiter. From a philosophical point of view, Cattaneo also represented for me the antithesis of the spiritualistic philosophies that have prevailed in our country. He was an enlightened reformer, whose ideas could certainly have been considered the ideal philosophical basis for the Action Party's programme. On the other hand, I must point out that, in spite of the lack of success that Cattaneo's thought has had in Italian culture, it had been the subject of studies by liberal and anti-fascist intellectuals under fascism, such as Luigi Einaudi, Mario Fubini, Luigi Salvatorelli and Cesare Spellanzon. For these reasons, I edited a collection of his writings in 1944–5 and wrote a lengthy introduction for it. It was published under the title *Stati Uniti d'Italia* [*United States of Italy*] by a small but creative publishing house in Turin. It was part of a series called 'La Città del Sole' which I had devised and edited.[9] Fortunately for me, the National Library of Turin was not completely closed, which was not the case elsewhere, although in the evening I was forced to stay at home and work, because of the curfew.

It was in this period of transition between an old and a new world that I became interested in existentialist thought, but I never had an opportunity to work on it afterwards. In 1944 the same publisher in Turin brought out my short work *La filosofia del decadentismo*, which was translated into English in 1948 and Spanish in 1949. However the major theme in the years that straddled the Liberation and the Constituent Assembly was democracy. We considered Italy to have never attained a full democracy, so the programme of the Action Party could have been summarized by just two words: 'democratic revolution'. We believed that the country's transition to democracy constituted a revolutionary event. I had an ethical concept of democracy, founded on the recognition of the individual as an entity with rights. In the last course of philosophy of law that I held at Padua before the Liberation, I had written the following conclusion:

> The democratic state is a state in which freedom of coexistence is most fully implemented in line with the ideal model, which means the coexistence of free beings, and is therefore the nearest thing to creating a community of individuals and ultimately the ideal of justice, as far as these are known to contemporary history.

This concept also inspired the articles that I wrote after the Liberation for *GL*, the theoretical journal of the Action Party. These were my first attempts at journalism. Later, I shifted towards a procedural concept of democracy, mainly based on Kelsen, according to which democracy is characterized by the rules that allow a free and peaceable coexistence of individuals in society. At that time, I still saw democracy as the form of government that best allows the independent development of each individual. This was the ideal that motivated my theoretical work on democracy, 'Stato e democrazia', which appeared in three instalments in *Lo Stato Moderno* in the summer of 1945. This magazine was edited by Mario Paggi, who belonged to the moderate wing of the Action Party.

These were my interests when I took part in a group that travelled to England in the autumn of 1945. It was a journey to explore a country considered to be the cradle of democracy, and one that had proved to be stronger than Hitler's V2 bombs. In September there had been a conference of foreign ministers of the five great powers, the United States, the Soviet Union, Great Britain, France and China, which had been given the task of finalizing the peace treaties with the countries allied to Hitler's Germany. Meanwhile, I was leaving our country, which had been almost destroyed and was struggling with the consequences of military defeat and appalling public services. The government, which was made up of the parties of the Committee of National Liberation, was about to confront the choice between monarchy and republic, and a few months later was to take on the task of declaring a new constitution.

The trip was conceived by its organizers, the British Council, as a kind of civic education course designed for people who had passed their formative years under a dictatorship. In order to choose the delegation, which was mainly to be made up of legal experts, as they were more likely to understand democratic institutions, the British Council contacted Professor Pasquale Chiomenti, a lecturer in comparative law at Rome University, who had an Anglo-Saxon educational background and spoke excellent English. I think I was invited to join the group because he was a friend of my brother-in-law Roberto Ago, who was also a member. I recall that the delegation was chosen on the basis of the model that had been used by the Committee of National Liberation. All the parties in the committee were represented. There were two experts in constitutional law: Vezio Crisafulli, who was a communist at the time, and the elderly Gaspare Ambrosini, a Christian democrat. The chairman was Filippo Vassalli, a distinguished liberal, professor of civil law at Rome University and father of Giuliano, a scholar of criminal law. There were fifteen of us altogether. We travelled in October and November, and were in England during the political crisis that affected Parri's government. I remember London as foggy and rather cold. We visited the headquarters of the two large political parties, the Conservatives and Labour, and met their party secretaries. I remember being invited to the House of Commons where Winston Churchill sat, and to the House of Lords.

They also took us to a by-election campaign. I took the opportunity to meet Harold J. Laski, which did not fail to move me. He was a political scientist, a leading member of the Labour Party, and a teacher at the London School of Economics. At Croce's suggestion, Laterza had published his *Liberty in the Modern State* and his *Democracy in Crisis*. I published a summary of our conversation in *GL*: Laski declared that he was an admirer of the Soviet Union and defined Stalin as 'très sage'. Today, such an expression would provoke astonishment or even outrage, but immediately after Hitler's defeat, to which the Soviets had made a decisive contribution at the Battle of Stalingrad, this did not make any particular impression.

I used to write to Valeria almost every day: a considerable pile of letters, which I can no longer find. As we felt it our duty to give an account of our journey, I gave a lecture on my return at the Italo-British Association, which I then repeated in Rome in April 1946. It was entitled 'The political parties in England'. I argued that the lesson of democracy in England, where there had been a tradition, was not yet over, and perhaps was only about to start. What was the lesson to be drawn from the British Constitution? I said it was the need for large democratically organized parties at the service of democracy, which can provide strong government without the dangers of dictatorship. In fact, I saw England as having a stronger government than any other European state, which appeared to be the most significant result of the way the parties were organized:

> The parliament is no longer a sovereign assembly, except in the claims you find in all the textbooks, or made unfailingly by all British politicians, according to whom the parliament can do everything except 'change a man into a woman'. This expression is just a cliché: the reality is quite different, especially since the executive's powers to dictate regulations which are legally binding has been massively increased. If anyone could change a man into woman, it would be the government, and the parliament would give its approval, after a lengthy discussion in which the opposition would put its criticisms across forcefully. Parliament is not a sovereign assembly, but a debating chamber. Mirroring the famous saying that in a constitutional monarchy, a king reigns but does not govern, I would be tempted to say that in the current British parliamentary system, the parliament debates but does not decide. Parliament debates questions, but it does not resolve them itself: it criticizes plans but in the end it approves them. I have already said that in the current British constitutional order, the parliament is not a focal point for the confluence of ideas, but simply a communication line. If there is such a focal point in England today, that is to say, an organism that links the popular political forces and with them determines the government policy directions, then this is no longer the

parliament but the winning party. I therefore do not think I would be going too far in saying that if the British system is offering a constitutional model for our consideration and perhaps for actual implementation on the continent, then this model is much more similar to a new type of multi-party state with the government chosen by the prime minister than it is to parliamentary government in the true sense of the term. In fact, it is closer, in many ways, to presidential government as it exists in the United States of America than it is to unalloyed parliamentary government.[10]

Young Italians educated under fascism did not have much of a democratic culture. The most important book on which we could base our ideas was *La storia del liberalismo europeo* by Guido de Ruggiero, a philosopher and friend of Croce, which was published in 1925 and went through several reprints. We anti-fascists were Anglophiles as a reaction to the Anglophobia of the fascists, which was evident in the slogan 'God damn the English!' that even appeared on badges, and the epithet 'Perfidious Albion'. Carlo Rosselli was an admirer of England and labourism. Guido Calogero, who left his university post in the fifties in order to become the director of the Italian Institute of Culture in London, was another Anglophile. The magazine *Il Ponte*, founded by Calamandrei at the end of the war, was politically influenced by labourism (in a utopian manner). Calamandrei himself went to England in order to collect material for an issue devoted to labourism.

But perhaps the most important example of our interest in English culture is represented by the magazine *Occidente*, which was founded in Milan in 1945. Its creator was a young man called Ernesto De Marchi, who after university went to study in Oxford and made England his ideal home. In fact, he was so fascinated by it that he spoke Italian with an English accent. He was the son of an industrialist and the owner of a beautiful villa on the Lecco branch of Lake Como, where the contributors would sometimes meet. The magazine published many writings by English intellectuals, as its aim was to promote exchanges between the two cultures.

In 1952, Occidente moved to Turin. In 1954, it changed its subtitle from Two-Monthly Review of Political Studies to Anglo-Italian Review of Political Studies. As well as Bobbio, the editorial committee included intellectuals like Riccardo Bauer, Luigi Firpo, Renato Treves and Leo Valiani. The Italian contributors were young academics such as Gastone Cottino, Uberto Scarpelli, Carlo Augusto Viano and Ferruccio Rossi-Landi. The latter also had a passion for England and introduced Gilbert Ryle to Bobbio on a trip by the Italian editorial committee to meet the English editorial committee in Oxford. Ryle, one of the most renowned English philosophers, wrote The Concept of Mind *which Bobbio translated for Einaudi.*[11] *An episode that occurred at the University of Padua on 6 November 1946 could be considered typical of this period.*

The rector, Meneghetti, asked me to make an inaugural speech for the opening ceremony to the academic year, a practice that fascism had done away with, because it was considered an outdated ritual. The then minister of education, Guido Gonella, was there. He was an anti-fascist with a Catholic background in the Veneto tradition, who had sought refuge under fascism in the Vatican and wrote for the 'Acta Diurna' column in the *Osservatore Romano*. The inaugural speech was entitled 'La persona e lo stato' ['The individual and the state'], and took up themes developed in 'Stato e democrazia', which had appeared a year before in *Stato Moderno*, as I have already mentioned. It compared the two opposing negative interpretations of the state, 'as a God and as a machine', both of which, although in opposition to each other, can be found in the work of Hobbes: the mortal God and *homo artificialis*. The fascist concept of the state as the ultimate moral arbiter derives from the former, and the Marxist concept of state power from the second: the two forms of totalitarian state, which contrast with the democratic state:

> We took the traditional definitions of the state as the God-state and the machine-state as our starting point, and described them almost as though they were a nightmare from which we wanted to escape. Gradually, in the course of our studies, we began to make corrections to these two definitions, and the nightmare started to fade. Indeed, our debate brought to light at least two useful concepts, which, although very subtle in their practical application, were indispensable in clarifying our problem: the concept of a *curb* on the powers of the state in relation to the individual citizen, and the concept of *participation* by the citizens in the state within its curbed powers. If then, there is a restraint on the state, it is no longer a mortal God, and its threatening expression becomes a benign one. If, within its curbed powers, the state requests the participation of all its citizens, it is no longer a machine superimposed on the citizen, but it is the citizens who join as equals for the common collective will. Humanity becomes progressively more civilized by freeing itself from its idols.[12]

A month later, I published an article in Calamandrei's *Ponte*, which was entitled 'Open and closed societies', and was devoted to Karl Popper's great work *The Open Society and its Enemies*.[13] I think I was the first in Italy to draw attention to Popper. It was a year after the publication of the English edition, which was to be translated into Italian much later. I do not remember whether I came across it because Giulio Einaudi gave it to me for translation, or because I brought it back from England.

> Unless you want to close your eyes to it, it is very clear that universal suffrage, the guarantee of an individual's rights, the control of public powers and the autonomy of local authorities must express the conviction that the citizen is not a means but an end, and that therefore a society is more advanced and more civilized, the more it increases and encourages a sense of individual responsibility. In other words, democracy as a social, political and legal order represents an open society that aspires to be a society that breaks the monopolistic impulse of each group, and tends to disperse society's obfuscations to reveal the citizen, the individual person in all his or her sacrosanct dignity.[14]

It is claimed that liberal writers like Popper were ignored in Italy, as a result of the dominance of Marxism. The criticism cannot be directed at me. I also wrote a review of Popper's work for *Rivista di Filosofia*.[15] People exaggerate when they talk about Marxist hegemony in Italy after the war. The fact that Popper's book was only translated into Italian twenty years later was due to the weakness of liberalism in Italy at the time. None of the new liberals has given any thought to Luigi Einaudi, a great liberal writer of European standing. I referred to him as the ideal teacher of liberalism in an essay in 1974.[16] His conversations with Croce were published in *Laissez-Faire Economics and Liberalism*,[17] one of the most significant documents reflecting the debate at the time that fascism was drawing to a close. Disappointingly, it was somewhat ignored, even in liberal circles.

On 26 December 1946, Giorgio Almirante, Arturo Michelini, Pino Romualdi and other ex-fascists founded the Italian Social Movement.[18] On 3 January 1947, the prime minister, Alcide De Gasperi, visited the United States, and on his return he dismissed the government. It was the end of the left's involvement in power. A new chapter was also being opened in Bobbio's life. In May 1950, an association was set up in Venice, which took the name European Society of Culture. Bobbio was a founding member, and is now its honorary chairman. It was established in a Europe that had been divided into two opposing blocks, and this division also affected cultural life. The Sovietization of the USSR's satellite states with the signing of the pacts of steel, the Berlin Blockade between the winter of 1948 and the spring of 1949, against which the Americans organized an airlift, the signing of the NATO Treaty in 1949 for the collective defence of western Europe, and the exclusion of communist parties from government in Italy and France in the same year, were all proof of the existence of an

'Iron Curtain', the expression that was coined by Churchill in his speech in 1946 to describe the military and political division of the old continent as a result of the Yalta Conference.

When the European Society of Culture was founded, the Cold War had already started. The idea of Europe appeared to have had its day. World conflict had produced a continent divided into camps, each ready for warfare against the other. Europe was also marked by the outcome of a bloody war that had lasted more than five years: wrecked buildings, bereavements, vast piles of bones and hordes of displaced persons. Perhaps never before could you have seen the evidence of what barbarity can be engendered by the frenzied abuse of power. Paul Hazard's book, *The Crisis of the European Conscience*, which had appeared in 1935, suddenly became extremely topical. We asked ourselves whether there could still exist an ideal European homeland and a shared European consciousness. The European Society of Culture was a response to these concerns by those who saw our continent as having fallen prey to a period of decadence.

The initiator and driving force behind this association was Umberto Campagnolo, whom I met while teaching in Padua. He graduated in philosophy at Padua, and taught there at the Tito Livio High School. When the order came for teachers to enrol in the Fascist Party, he refused and went into exile. He escaped to Geneva, where he attended the school of the distinguished jurist, Hans Kelsen, who was also an exile, as a Jew, from Germany. Campagnolo published a book on international law in France, *Nations et droits*, which was a doctorate thesis supervised by Kelsen. After the war, he returned to Italy and got a job with Olivetti, where he founded the corporate library and laid the basis for the publishing house which was to be called Comunità (but at that time was called Edizioni Ivrea). He set up the European Society of Culture along the lines of the previous experience with the Rencontres Internationales de Genève, which were among the cultural events with greatest resonance immediately after the war. They were organized by a committee chaired by Antony Babel, the rector of the University of Geneva and formerly the professor of economic history. The purpose of these events was to reaffirm the existence of Europe after the catastrophe. The first of these encounters took place in the summer of 1946 on the theme of 'The European spirit', and there was a particularly memorable clash with Jaspers prompted by Lukács's lecture. The events were of a theatrical nature, and indeed they took place in a theatre. The speaker used to stand in the middle of the stage, and behind him would sit other intellectuals who were to take part in the debate. The audience would be in the stalls. I first took part in 1950, when the official speaker

was an Italian, Galvano Della Volpe. Maria José, who lived in Geneva
and was passionately interested in Italian culture, took a very active
part. The acts of the proceedings were published every year.

It was with Babel that Campagnolo planned the establishment of
a venue for cultural events in Italy. The European Society of Culture
was born in May 1950, with Campagnolo as secretary and Babel as
chairman. Its offices were in Venice and its official language was
French. Its magazine, *Comprendre*, is in French. To date, forty-eight
issues have been published, each devoted to one of the major themes
of the contemporary world. After the death of Campagnolo (1976),
I became its editor. Under my editorial control, the last three issues
have dealt with *Le Sens de l'histoire* (1977–8), *Éthique et politique*
(1979–80) and *Violence et dialogue* (1981–3). The choice of Venice
was not accidental: it evoked the city's historic role as a bridge between
the West and the East. In the first issue of *Comprendre* at the time
of the Constituent Assembly, Campagnolo wrote that 'the principal
purpose of the European Society of Culture has to be that of safeguarding the opportunity for debate between persons engaged in
cultural activities, which is being threatened by the intensification of
a political struggle that tends to divide Europe into two camps rigidly
opposed to each other'. In truth, the European Society of Culture was
the sole organization that continued to carry out its annual meetings
with the participation of intellectuals from the East and the West.

Naturally, those from the West were mainly of the left. The French
intelligentsia made a particularly important contribution. I remember
meeting Benda, Sartre and Merleau-Ponty at its meetings, as well
as the entire *gauche* that had been involved in the Resistance and put
the question of *engagement* and commitment at the top of the agenda.
The society was also of great importance to eastern European countries, because it meant keeping contacts alive between intellectuals in
western Europe and Yugoslav, Hungarian, Bohemian, Polish and East
German intellectuals who had managed to maintain a certain independence of thought in countries beyond the Iron Curtain. Meetings
in the interval between assemblies, the Conseils Exécutifs, were sometimes held in the capitals of communist countries. Thanks to these
meetings, I visited Prague, Belgrade, Budapest, Warsaw and Cracow,
and I gave various reports on the question of tolerance (Warsaw), on
Europe (Belgrade) and the question of dialogue and cultural politics
(Budapest).

The society was created to put up moral resistance against the
Cold War, which appeared to be preparing for a Third World War.
We were challenging the politics of politicians with what we called
'ordinary politics' or the 'politics of culture', which were the politics

in which intellectuals engaged above party divisions, whose specific task was to defend the very conditions for the survival of culture threatened by the polarization of the two blocs. We undertook not to argue amongst ourselves over matters of contemporary politics. We recognized that we were united by a common cultural heritage, whether we were in France or Russia, England or Czechoslovakia, Italy or Poland. Cultural Europe did not accept the 'Iron Curtain', which was an exclusively political division. Instead of being divided between East and West, our Europe embraced Pushkin, Dostoyevsky and Kafka, just as much as it did Voltaire, Flaubert and Gide. This Europe had survived a barbarous war that had lasted nearly six years, thanks to its great intellectuals like Julien Benda, who had written *Discours à la nation européenne*, Benedetto Croce, who in 1932 had paid tribute to the 'religion of freedom' in the first chapter of his *History of Europe in the Nineteenth Century*,[19] and Thomas Mann, who almost every day broadcast his 'Warnings to Europe' in which, as a German writer, he denounced the barbarity of the Nazi regime to the world.

On 10 May 1953, Thomas Mann sent the society a letter entitled 'Retour de l'Amérique' in which he wrote:

> Europe's millenary perspective, its experience of suffering, its certainty that everything passes, that everything has its time, and that prudence becomes folly and advantage calamity, its well-developed scepticism, its understanding of what has to be condemned, which is an attitude that runs contrary to the will of the spirit of the world and obstinately clings to that which is unstable, all mean that Europe is more suited to a role as mediator who attempts to avoid an unspeakable catastrophe than to the role of soldier or unilaterally subjected mercenary doomed to be the first victim of this battle between titans.

This was the groundwork on which I based my reflections, which were brought together in *Politica e cultura* (Turin: Einaudi, 1955). My first essay, 'Invito al colloquio' had appeared in *Comprendre* in 1951:

> The task of those engaged in cultural activities is now more than ever to sow the seeds of doubt and not to gather certainties. The history of the false ideologies of improvisers, dilettantes and propagandists with their own agendas is full to the brim with certainties, covered with grandiose myths and produced from harsh dogmas. Culture means moderation, thoughtfulness and circumspection: assessing all the arguments before giving an opinion, checking all the accounts before taking a decision, and never giving an opinion or taking a decision in the style of some oracle on which a final and irrevocable decree is to be made.

The second essay, 'Cultural politics and the politics of culture',[20] was devoted to the ideas that had inspired the European Society of Culture, and attempted to find a response to two extreme positions, two sides of the same coin: politicized culture 'which is subject to the directives, programmes and impositions of politicians' and apolitical culture which is 'detached from the society in which it lives and from the problems that this society discusses'. I proposed that in place of this antithesis there should be:

> a *politics of culture*, which means politics carried out by people involved in cultural activities in as much as they are involved in those activities, and this does not necessarily coincide with the politics carried out by people in their social context.
>
> . . . This differentiates itself from the two extreme positions, but is in no way an intermediate position or an accommodation between the two. It is, as previously stated, a different position which refutes both the others at the same time, because it goes to the root of the problematic relationship between culture and politics. Indeed, before posing the problem of whether or not those engaged in cultural activities should also get involved in politics, this approach poses the question of what kind of politics should be engaged in, in order to create the right conditions for developing the culture of which such people are custodians.

4

Dealings with the Communists

By the end of the war, we were well aware that the Soviet state was a despotic one. On the other hand, we could not forget that the Soviet Union had made a decisive contribution to the allied victory. If it had not been for the desperate and heroic Soviet resistance at Stalingrad, which halted the German advance on Moscow, Hitler might have won the war and Europe would have become a German colony. Part of the European intelligentsia not only acknowledged this Soviet contribution to the final victory, but saw the country, which had become the second world power, as a new society. In 1950 we published at Einaudi an Italian version of *Soviet Communism: A New Civilization*, two large tomes amounting to 1,600 pages, written in 1935 by Beatrice and Sidney Webb, two English intellectuals who, as husband and wife, had been members of the Fabian Society and had held positions within the Labour Party. They travelled all over the Soviet Union in the thirties, and became convinced that a *new civilization* had been born. The translation of this book and its title are today a bit disconcerting: it is evidence of the muddled thinking that existed even amongst non-communists. As I have already said, Laski, whom I met in London, did not disguise his admiration for what we now call 'real' communism,[1] which is opposed to the real capitalism of the United States. Of course, not all intellectuals on the left had allowed themselves to be fooled. André Gide's disappointment on his return from a trip to the Soviet Union is well known. Less familiar is the experience of Bertrand Russell, a man of the left, self-declared socialist and fervent pacifist. In his autobiography, he told the story of how he had visited the Soviet Union full of hope and had been admitted to the Kremlin for a meeting with Lenin, but came out depressed and alarmed, having had the impression that he had just been talking to a fanatic: 'Lenin, with whom I had an hour's conversation, rather disappointed me. I do not think that I should have guessed him to be a great man, but in the course of our conversation I was chiefly conscious of his intellectual limitations, and his rather narrow Marxian orthodoxy, as well as a distinct vein of impish cruelty.'[2]

To members of the Action Party, it was obvious that the Soviet state was a dictatorship. Perhaps we had not yet seen all of its 'demonic features', but the great question with which we challenged the communists was that of liberty. Mila tells how he responded to Pajetta who was trying to indoctrinate him by saying: 'But doesn't freedom come into all this?'

In his last writings before his death, Carlo Rosselli, who inspired the more uncompromising wing of the Action Party, proposed the unification of all the anti-fascist forces, including the communists, but his judgement of their doctrine and way of doing things was severe: 'They pervert the political struggle in that they reduce it purely to tactics or a means to an end.' That perversion was the result of the 'over-centralized, hierarchical and almost military [nature] of their party'.[3]

The last battle that the former members of the Action Party fought together with the communists was against the so-called *legge truffa* ['swindle law'], as the opposition parties called the electoral law approved by Parliament at the beginning of 1953, by which a large advantage in terms of seats was to be given to a coalition that exceeded 50 per cent of the votes. The law was the subject of bitter debate, during which the left resorted to filibustering. The campaign for the June elections was hard fought with fractious propaganda. The former members of the Action Party set up a small party called the Party of Popular Unity, which was led by Piero Calamandrei and Ferruccio Parri. My painful political disagreement with Franco Antonicelli goes back to this time, as he decided to join the list of dissident liberal candidates: the National Democratic Alliance, established by Epicarmo Corbino, a former Treasury minister. Our list won 0.6 per cent of the vote for the Chamber of Deputies and 0.7 per cent for the Senate, while Corbino's list managed just 0.5 per cent. Neither party won a seat, but they proved to be crucial in depriving the centre coalition of the votes required for benefiting from the bonus for achieving a majority. The coalition of parties made up of the Christian Democrats, the Italian Social Democratic Party, the Italian Liberal Party, the Italian Republican Party, the South Tyrol People's Party [Südtiroler Volkspartei] and the Sardinian Action Party, stopped just short at

49.8 per cent. If they had achieved 50.01 per cent, the majority bonus would have come into play and the history of our country would have been different. Would it have been better or worse? In the current climate of historical revisionism, which on occasions is quite belligerent, it is asked whether the fight against the *legge truffa* was not perhaps a mistake which delayed the modernization of Italian political life. It is a legitimate question, but it ignores the historical situation in which the election campaign was fought. We must not forget that we were in the middle of the Cold War, and a victory by the centrists would have almost certainly not meant a switch to a democracy based on alternating governments, but to the permanent exclusion of the left from participation in government.

My position in relation to the Communists, at the time (the early fifties) could best be summed up by the title of an article I wrote a few years ago for the magazine *Nuvole*: 'Neither for them nor against them'.[4] Although I have never been a communist and have never thought of becoming one, I realized however that communism was the agent behind enormous transformations, an actual revolution in the original sense of the term. At the same time, I had reached the conclusion that we members of the Action Party had to differentiate ourselves from the communist positions, albeit acknowledging the battles that had been fought together, because we had not forgotten what were the general premises for the modern state. I, therefore, looked on the Communists (particularly the Italian ones, as I have already said) not as adversaries but as people with whom we had to enter into a dialogue.

This was the conviction on which I based the articles that were published in *Politica e cultura*. Besides, I believe that it is in my character not to exaggerate disputes or exasperate differences, but rather to seek out where people whose ideas differ from my own are right. I have always sought to have a civil debate with everyone: both Catholics and communists. As far as I am concerned, I have endeavoured to use a method of reasoning that weighs up the pros and cons, without closing off all space for another's position, and that does not make it impossible for him to respond with his own arguments. This approach has meant that not only have I maintained friendly relations with communists who are my personal friends but also with the party and its leadership. The debate that gave rise to the articles in *Politica e cultura* commenced with a very civil exchange mainly with Ranuccio Bandinelli and Galvano Della Volpe. I realize that my emphasis on this personal circumstance may appear bizarre to someone who is not familiar with that period in Italian life. Today, it is difficult to understand the crusading spirit that pervaded both the opposing parties, and how little readiness there was to listen to the arguments of the other side. The articles compiled in *Politica e cultura* represent an attempt to breach the wall that divided us. They showed that dialogue was possible, even in the darkest hours of the Cold War.

Moreover my relations with Palmiro Togliatti[5] were very courteous. I could see that he belonged to a particular tradition of political intellectuals who shaped the history of the Italian Communist Party. After the war, Italian society did not at all develop in the direction that the Communist Party had expected. The reconstruction of our country and its accelerated development quickly brought about an economic recovery that was not achieved by the 'masses' dear to the Communists, but was the fruit of the unfettered resourcefulness of small and large enterprises, as I have already stated. For the members of the Action Party, the event that dramatically displayed the communist leader's strategic abilities was the famous debate on article 7 of the Constitutional Charter, which assimilated the Lateran Pacts. Piero Calamandrei said that after all the compromises our constitution would be reduced to a middle-aged man with an old lover who tears out his black hairs and a young lover who tears out his white hairs, so that he ends up completely bald. However, my relations with Togliatti at the time of the controversy between Galvano Della Volpe and myself were based on the mutual respect that I think should be the distinguishing feature of disputes between intellectuals. I recall that Togliatti came to Turin in 1961 for a conference organized by the Resistance Association. At one of the events organized to celebrate the centenary of Italian Unification, it fell to me, as the association chairman, to introduce him in the crowded hall of the Gallery of Modern Art. Franco Antonicelli invited him to lunch at his home. The three of us were there at the table, and no other guests. I can remember nothing of the conversation, which I do not think was particularly interesting.

Besides, although there were disagreements between the Communists and myself, they never turned into open warfare. We never stopped co-operating on this or that initiative. For several years, I was involved with the National Popular Book Centre, and I also became its chairman. The purpose of the centre was to promote the reading of literary texts amongst working people. Its office was at the Trade Union Offices. We used to tour with book presentations, which were followed by debates, and some of these were held at Communist Party branches. I particularly remember the presentation of *Letters from Members of the Italian Resistance Facing the Death Sentence* in 1952, and *Letters from Members of the European Resistance Facing the Death Sentence* in 1954, both published by Einaudi and edited by Piero Malvezzi and Giovanni Pirelli.[6] Some record of my work has remained in *Letture per Tutti*, the small magazine published by the centre,[7] and the pages of *L'Unità* which published a couple of the articles I wrote in my capacity as chairman of the National Popular Book Centre.

In 1955, Bobbio was one of the members of the first Italian cultural delegation to visit Mao's China, which had maintained no official diplomatic links with Italy. Six years had passed since 1 October 1949 when Mao Zedong had proclaimed the birth of the Chinese People's Republic, but Western countries still recognized the nationalist government of Chiang Kai-shek, who had taken refuge in Taiwan. Jean-Paul Sartre had published La Chine que j'ai vue. *Cultural visits were a way in which People's China could maintain relations with Europe, during the period in which it presented itself to the world as a new power, after its intervention had proved decisive in the Korean War. For the majority of Westerners, the country that emerged from the Long March was still something mysterious, but it had shown (at the Mao–Khrushchev Summit in 1954) that it was not willing to be a satellite power of the Soviet Union.*

The month-long trip started on 24 September. The delegation was led by Piero Calamandrei, who was a deputy in the Constituent Assembly. A communist, Antonello Trombadori, was the secretary. The delegation was made up of literary figures like Carlo Cassola, Franco Fortini, Franco Antonicelli and Carlo Bernari, as well as the film critic Umberto Barbaro, the psychoanalyst Cesare Musatti, the painter Ernesto Treccani, the architect Franco Berlanda and the scientist Rodolfo Margaria. Nearly all the delegates wrote accounts of the trip in the form of either books or articles. Il Ponte *edited by Calamandrei, brought out an issue of over 700 pages, including an article by Bobbio on the Chinese constitution. Antonicelli, a keen photographer, brought out a book illustrated with his pictures. Bernari and Cassola wrote books. However, the best account was produced by Franco Fortini: it was called* Asia Maggiore *and was published by Einaudi the following year. It also contained an extraordinary portrayal of Bobbio:*

Delle Carte. He must be between forty and fifty years old. His entire person exudes not so much intellectual force as a kind of deep-rooted education and a loyalty to parents and grandparents. The energy behind his convictions has, in his case, the sole weakness of expressing itself for precisely what it is: namely energy. You feel that he is well aware of the virtues of order, tenacity, sober thinking and intellectual honesty. Such would perhaps have been accompanied by a kind of didactic intensity, if it were not offset every now and then by a smile which is both embarrassed and ironic. It is ironic, every time his speech indulges in a superfluous adjective or a tone that is just slightly more passionate than usual. It is embarrassment or even timidity when it suggests a hint of worldliness or nonchalance. It is clear that as a boy he must have been diligent and clever, and must have despised all forms of sentimental frailty. He does not relax when he sleeps. His morality is always controlled and extremely urbane. You have to admire and respect him, but you feel that his preferences and his judgements of things and people arise from his horror of ambiguity and uncertainty. His preferred moral approach is unquestionably the following: 'Now let me see . . .'. He is profoundly conservative by effort of will rather than by conviction, so that he has overcome decadence and reached the age of reason and precision in which there is a return to the virtues of his grandparents and his great-grandparents: conciseness, clarity and decorum. In order to achieve this, and in order never to lose the opportunity of becoming part of the society of the competent in this chaotic and revolutionary world, he needs a citadel to resist the tendency to disorder, and that citadel is not a critical spirit based on freethinking but rather a critical spirit based on science (I believe that even as a child he liked to divide the world between the competent and the amateurish). So if there is someone in our group who does not succumb to laughter and tears, but only to the intellect, it is Bobbio, or rather Delle Carte, as I want to call him for his similarity to Descartes. He reacts to the antics of his university colleagues as he must have reacted to the outbursts of his school friends: outward indulgence but mainly disapproval. Thus his frequent condemnation of the casual attitude and inconsequence of Latin peoples, his inflated complex about northern Europeans, and his unshakeable belief that the development of the peoples who surround us, that is the Chinese, could never be guided by that rational perception of the world which sprang up in Europe after the Reformation. This is undoubtedly true, for there cannot be industrialization without a scientific approach, and there cannot be the latter without the West, without Europe. But in the case of Delle Carte, this wholly correct, indeed obvious, truth cannot be separated from a belief in the unarguable superiority of Western civilization, so that when you talk with him, you are constantly obliged to emphasize the substantial shared human identity between us Westerners and the Oriental Chinese, to negate the existence of the 'mysteriousness of China', which is a Western invention, and to point out the traditional features of this civilization which should perhaps be saved in a future fusion of cultures. The gentleman Delle Carte has misgivings about the future; the future is black. These misgivings could be foreboding, but they are not cowardly foreboding. They are the projection forward of a pessimistic view of the past and of history. Only twice did I see Delle Carte display enthusiasm: the first time at the parade on 1 October, and the second time on hearing Bizet's 'Habanera'. His enthusiasm was short-lived, and immediately regretted. The devil shows his cloven hoof, and then conceals himself again.[8]

It was an unforgettable journey, which had a profound affect on me. While the trip to England meant the discovery of democracy, the one to China was an encounter with communism as it actually is. I have never visited the Soviet Union except for a very brief stay there on our way to China. I never even had the desire to go to the Soviet Union, in spite of the invitations from the Italy–USSR Association. The European Society of Culture had organized some of its annual executive meetings in Moscow, but I never went. I knew very well that the 'intellectuals' that they would have had us meet would really have been party officials. On our trip to China, we left Zürich on a Soviet plane and we stopped in Prague, Minsk and Moscow. In Moscow, they took us to an old hotel in Red Square, where they took all the delegations, but my knowledge of Russia was limited to what I could see along the way from the airport to the city centre, and a short walk around Red Square. The stops in Novosibirsk and Irkutsk were more interesting, particularly Irkutsk, which was a completely new city. It struck me as a stunning example of modernization within a peasant society. The impression we had when we landed in Ulan Bator, the capital of Mongolia, was very different. We got off the plane in an enormous open space, and it felt as though we had been placed in a world a thousand years back in time. Then there was the long haul to Peking over the Gobi Desert. At the airport, Piero Calamandrei and his wife, Ada, who accompanied him, were hoping to embrace their son Franco, who at the time was the correspondent for *L'Unità* in Peking, and to see their granddaughter, but they were disappointed as Franco had had to leave for Tibet. We were put up in a hotel full of foreign delegations, who had been invited for the anniversary of the Chinese Revolution. Jean-Paul Sartre and Simone de Beauvoir were also there.

It was a fascinating but exhausting journey. Every day we were engaged in a busy programme of visits and meetings: museums, schools, imperial palaces, council housing, factories, shipyards and farming communities. They took us to see the building where prostitutes were re-educated, and cultural centres where they could show us how popular chess was in China. The evening generally involved going to the theatre where the plot was always the same: the courageous and warm-hearted soldier in Mao's army ultimately defeats the perfidious soldier in Chiang Kai-shek's army. On occasions we went to the circus, a form of entertainment for which the Chinese are famous around the world. We travelled north to industrialized Manchuria, and south down to Canton. Of course, we went up onto the Great Wall. We went by train from Shanghai to Canton on a beautiful sleeper-van that had belonged to the colonial railways, and the journey took two days. I had never been on the same train for two days, and it was an experience I was never to repeat. I remember very clearly the incredible cleanliness: not a piece of paper or peel on the carriage floor or under the station canopies. You got the impression that even the less well off had a tremendous sense of decorum: to this day I am not sure whether this was imposed or simply their culture. We were all disposed to admire a people who expressed a civilization that was thousands of years old through their extremely well-mannered behaviour: courteous, not loud, serene and smiling. The impressive popular demonstration in Tienanmen Square for the national holiday on 1 October was the most extraordinary spectacle I have witnessed in my whole life. After a brief military parade came an enormous procession of dancers, acrobats and jugglers. Garlands of flowers and female singers filled the square with colours and graceful movements. From the steps, we had a good view of Mao Zedong who was high up on the stand with all his General Staff. I can honestly say that they looked at him with admiration. The Long March is one of the most incredible and inspiring episodes of modern history.

We were none of us naive. Indeed, many of us had started the journey with the precise intention of not being deceived by the propaganda. When we met Chinese intellectuals and visited universities, we tried to bring the conversation around to questions of freedom and democracy, with the result that our discussions trailed off into an atmosphere of chilly embarrassment, which Fortini described brilliantly in *Asia Maggiore*. We would ask for news of people whom we knew were being persecuted, such as the writer Hu Feng. His writings were banned, and they explained unconvincingly that this measure did not concern his views, but his participation in a plot. We never got much more than embarrassed smiles in response to political questions. We knew that the visits had been organized down to the last detail, and that when they took us to a farm or a house of correction, these had not been chosen at random. We knew we were travelling through scenery made up of spurious images. We realized that there was a rigid system of police controls. I had a personal experience of this when at Peking airport they seized a book I had by Kao Kang, a Communist Party leader who had fallen out of favour. It was an English-language version published by the Chinese state which I had brought with me from Italy. I was immediately subjected to an interrogation. They wanted to know where I had purchased the book. It was useless to explain that I had brought it with me, and the book was confiscated. In spite of this, we all got the impression of a people who had woken up after a long sleep, leaping from the Middle Ages straight to modern times. Of course, they showed us the old women with deformed feet as part of the propaganda, but it was also true that this oppressive custom had been abolished and that there would be no more old women with deformed feet in the future. Equally, it was true that enormous housing estates had been built for working people in a few years. The people who filled the gardens, museums and theatres seemed content, and it was difficult to deny that the Chinese had achieved a better standard of living. Above all, you had the impression that there was something profoundly new in the way people related to each other, an account of which is given in *Asia Maggiore*. This aspect could have led to a more perfect society or, as actually happened, to despotism. At the time, even those who did not consider themselves to be communists, felt that the transformation could have led to an excellent republic rather than an abominable one. Naturally the communists amongst us, like Barbaro and Trombadori, saw the new Chinese society as a great leap forward by the Revolution, which had imposed the historical acceleration required by a country that had remained very backward. They put their faith in this benevolent interpretation, and closed their eyes to irregularities that they sensed were there, but did not want to follow through. The others, non-communists like myself, felt ambivalent. We admired the big changes, but were worried about the limitations on freedom. We left the country with the sensation of having just had an unrepeatable experience: the chance to see from the inside how communism undertook the enormous endeavour of transforming a backward society, albeit with all its many flaws. Canton and Hong Kong were divided by no man's land. They accompanied us for a bit, and then left us on our own to reach the barrier that marked the border. When we arrived in Hong Kong, we were confronted with an incredible reversal of the situation: from the new world of the Revolution to the triumph of capitalism. Then Antonicelli and I, along with some of the others, asked to return to Italy through India, stopping at Bombay. We were travelling around the world for another month.

In Asia Maggiore, *Franco Fortini wrote that the intellectual generation to which he and Bobbio belonged had spent their adolescence dreaming of Europe, not China. They had been fascinated by Paris, London, Madrid and Germany, but not the rest of the world. 'To speak of China was like speaking of the moon.' He confessed: 'In this, I am not modern. L'Inde and* la Chine *are remote, almost unreal places, just as they were a century ago, which rhyme with* amours enfantines.' *The trip in 1995 was a sudden encounter with an unknown reality, not only because of its structural elements – the economy, the politics and the material conditions of the population – but also because of its culture, its patterns of behaviour and methods of expression (apart from Kao Kang's book which was confiscated, Bobbio also brought Claude Roy's essay 'Clefs pour la Chine', which was published in 1953). The encounter with communism involved the anniversary of the Revolution, visits to factories, the discovery of Chinese traditional theatre, the Peking opera and the Stalinist interpretation of Western culture in a populist manner, but also the difficulties in discussing the most pressing problems. Towards the end of* Asia Maggiore *in a section entitled 'Dialogue with teachers of Marxism', Fortini recounts what happened to Bobbio:*

Bobbio told me that in the evening he was to have a conversation with two professors of philosophy, and he invited me to come along. At nine in the evening, we entered a badly lit room in our Shanghai hotel where there were two people waiting for us, who introduced themselves solemnly. They were the two Chinese closest to the Hollywood stereotype of generic-perfidious-intractable-enigmatic Chinese person that I have ever met. They were both tall, cold and self-possessed with inscrutable expressions.

Although embarrassed by their stiff appearance, Bobbio started to speak. After the first few questions, we realized that it would be ridiculous to count on the kind of professional camaraderie which in Italy exists between so-called cultured persons and, in any case, academics. The two gentlemen were not lecturers in philosophy at all, but party officials particularly well versed in Marxism–Leninism–*Stalinism*, and were responsible for providing political and historical courses at Shanghai University. Hence our embarrassment, and theirs. Long silences. We had thought we were going to meet lecturers who were in a position to give us information about the teaching of philosophy in Chinese universities. What we got was very general information from these two men who must have been as uneasy as we were, but attempted with extreme courtesy not to make it apparent. Their job in Shanghai was to teach historical and dialectical materialism (our first objections immediately came to our lips). They were organizing courses for both students and faculty in political economy and the histories of the Soviet and Chinese Communist Parties.

'But', asked Bobbio, 'isn't there a Faculty of Philosophy where Western philosophy is taught?' They replied that there was in Peking, and again apologized for not having more information. 'Which writers do they study?' 'The great figures in the history of philosophy.' 'Are there any translations of Hegel in Chinese?' 'Yes, Hume, Kant, Hegel and Fichte, for example, have been translated into Chinese, as well, of course, as the classical Marxist texts. However, the majority of the philosophy students read the texts in their original languages or in their Russian translations.' 'Are there any courses on logic?' 'Exams in logic are obligatory in the faculties of law, history and journalism.'

'What is the current position of Fung Yu-lan?' 'He is professor of philosophy in Peking, and has publicly explained his support for Marxist materialism.'

The replies were all of this kind, expressed in a few words without a trace of friendliness, without giving any opportunity to develop a conversation. No one knew how to bring the interview to an end. It was clear that the two men were either suspicious about our questions or frozen by embarrassment. But the most unpleasant thing was their furtive smiles of agreement which every now and then flashed across their lips, when, for example, we asked how many philosophy students there were in Peking or about Fung Yu-lan, the historian of philosophy.

We tried with difficulty to formulate a few more questions. 'What are the main questions currently discussed by your philosophical scholars?' 'The influence of Dewey's thought on two of our greatest philosophers, one of whom is on the side of the Kuomintang and the other lives in China. The problem of the critical assessment of our classical literature. The validity of our traditional empirical medicine. Pedagogy.'

There was nothing to be done. It was like drawing blood from a stone. There was no point in trying to understand. For the first time, we found ourselves up against a brick wall. The two gentlemen had come because they had had to come, but they refused to get involved in a conversation. The mood was frosty when we took our leave. The interview lasted less than half an hour. Bobbio was concerned and irritated, and I could not blame him. For the first time, we had had to deal with two party officials who were convinced that it was a waste of time to attempt to persuade Westerners. This was typical of Shanghai, and of the harsh struggle taking place in a troubled, corrupt and hostile city. This time it was not us who did not want to understand. They were the ones who observed us with irony from behind the lenses of their glasses, because they knew the high cost of their battle and they had lost the taste for conversation.[9]

Our return was spoilt by an unpleasant and ridiculous controversy. *Il Ponte* published an issue devoted to China (*La Cina oggi*, April 1956, 727 pages and 100 illustrations), which contained a photograph showing Calamandrei writing a message on a blackboard in a factory to express greetings to the Chinese workers. This photograph annoyed someone we all knew and admired: Nicola Chiaromonte, who was close to Ignazio Silone at the time. He wrote an article in *Tempo Presente*, the magazine which he edited, accusing Italian intellectuals of flattering tyranny and claiming that *Il Ponte*'s special issue amounted to the glorification of Mao's regime. On the photograph at the factory, he wrote:

It shows Professor Calamandrei from the side, while he writes 'Greetings from the Italian workers to the Chinese workers' on a blackboard erected at the entrance to a steelworks. The gesture is a sham, the words are a sham, the situation is a sham, and the man in that situation is a sham. These are things which you do because you are obliged and are unnatural. They are not done by those who breathe the more 'enlivening air of freedom'.[10]

The latter expression belonged to the journalist Robert Guilain, who had visited Mao's China twice, once in 1949 and again in 1955. His reports from his second trip (eighteen articles published in *Le Monde*) denounced the lack of freedom which they were suffering in China, and the air of oppression he had to breathe. Chiaromonte's criticism was cutting, and Calamandrei was mortified by it. He responded with an article entitled 'Il tempo della malafede' ['Time of bad faith'] in *Il Ponte*, one of his last writings (in issue 8–9 of 1956). It was partly ironic, but it was the irony that arises from hurt feelings. He replied that it was not a matter of making a theoretical choice between the Chinese Republic and a Western democracy, but of understanding 'whether the Chinese regime represented real progress for that people towards justice and also towards freedom, in comparison with the governments that had come before'. I can go along wholeheartedly with this position. I recently commented on that journey, and recalled that at the time the choice between the old liberal civilization and the new communist civilization was not so easy as it is now. I concluded:

> Now the choice appears much simpler. There is no longer any need to pose the question, either with trepidation or hope according to your point of view: 'And what if the experiment works?' Well, the experiment has not worked. The difference is in the meaning that you wish to give to this catastrophic result: whether it was the inevitable result of the plan to exterminate the middle class, as Ernst Nolte has recently repeated, or the failure of a grand design to change history, which millions of people believed and placed their hope in. A great victory over an immense crime, or a utopia turned on its head?[11] Of these two possible conclusions, the latter is without doubt the most tragic.[12]

The day after Nikita Khrushchev's speech to the XX Congress of the Communist Party of the Soviet Union (14–25 February 1956) on the misdeeds of Stalinism, Alberto Carocci and Alberto Moravia launched an inquest in their magazine Nuovi Argomenti, *inviting left-wing intellectuals to reply to the 'nine questions about Stalinism'. Bobbio also received this invitation. Initially, he did not want to take part, because each question appeared too daunting for reply without first reflecting at some length. After some pressure from Carocci, he agreed to take part in the second group of contributions, but his statement did not in reality respond to any of the questions posed: 'It is a matter of assessing', he wrote to Carocci, 'whether what happened in Russia has not undermined theoretical Marxism itself (by which we mean the Marxist philosophy of history) or at least obliged Marxism to treat 2000 years of political thought with greater caution.' He was interested in the ancient antithesis between 'tyranny and liberty, which has remained the central theme of political thought from Plato to the present day'.*

My response to the nine questions written in the summer of 1956 and entitled 'Further comments on Stalinism', was published in *Nuovi Argomenti*, and started with a quotation from Engels's *Antidühring* on the effects of the French Revolution:

'When the French Revolution achieved this society in accordance with reason and this state in accordance with reason, the new institutions proved to be absolutely irrational, however rational they might have appeared when compared with the previous state of affairs. The state according to reason had gone entirely up in smoke. . . . In short, when compared with the pompous predictions of the Enlightenment, the social and political institutions that were established with the triumph of reason proved to be caricatures and bitter disappointments.'

I would imagine that many communists would have recalled these words after having read Khrushchev's report. Ultimately, that report is the most thorough recantation of revolutionary delusions: the state based on justice 'had gone entirely up in smoke'. If compared with the 'pompous predictions' of Marxist theoreticians, the social and political institutions established by the triumph of dialectical materialism had proved to be 'caricatures and bitter disappointments'. By disproving the predictions of theoreticians, the events that followed the French Revolution had, according to Engels, undermined the Enlightenment's theory of state and power. Have the events that followed Stalin's death disproved the predictions made by Marxist theoreticians and undermined the Marxist doctrine of state and power?[13]

In reality, I had no idea what was going to happen in the world of 'real' socialism. What interested me was Marxism's claim to be the only real science of society. To me this claim appeared to be invalidated by three defects: socialist utopianism, by which the new society declared itself to be perfect and sheltered from the storms and upheavals of history; historical determinism, by which the forward march of humanity was circumscribed by the grand design of an ideal and classless society; and the supremacy of economic relations over political institutions, to the extent that the latter are determined by the former. I do not believe that there is much point in going into the first two weaknesses in the doctrine, which have been widely discussed by theoretical Marxism. The question that is still relevant today concerns the relationship between economics and politics, because it poses the theoretical question of forms of government. I argued that Marxism 'clearly demonstrated a complete disregard for the theory of governmental forms' that had been the cornerstone of traditional political doctrines. According to Marxists, forms of government were incapable of modifying the structure of society and the so-called social base, as they belonged to the superstructure. I used to quote Lenin to illustrate my criticism: 'Forms of government were extraordinarily varied. But in spite of this difference, the state at the time of slavery was a slave-state, whether it was monarchical or republican, and if republican, whether it was aristocratic or democratic.' These general reflections on the political philosophy of Marxism were taken up many years later, and provoked a wide-ranging debate inside and outside Italy, as I will explain later.

> We see political theory as the theory of power, of the maximum power that man can exert over other men. There are two classical themes of political theory or supreme power: how to seize it and how to exercise it. Theoretical Marxism examined the first of these two themes, but not the second. In short, Marxian political theory lacks a doctrine on the exercise of power, while it has developed an enormous theoretical corpus on the seizure of power. Machiavelli taught the prince of old how to seize power and how to maintain the state, while Lenin has taught the modern prince, the proletarian vanguard party, only how to seize power.
>
> . . .
>
> The most important branch of the theory of the exercise of power is the one concerned with the abuse of power. While liberal doctrine makes the abuse of power the core of its thinking, communist political doctrine generally ignores it. Anyone who is familiar with Marxist and non-Marxist texts on political doctrine cannot have failed to notice one of the most significant differences between liberal and communist doctrine is the emphasis that the former puts on the abuse of power as a phenomenon demonstrated by lengthy and objective observation of history, compared with the indifference of the latter.[14]

I saw Khrushchev's report to the XX Congress as a return to traditional political doctrine and the reaffirmation of liberal principles and concerns, in that he condemned the abuse of power and returned to the distinction between power restricted by the law and power that goes beyond such restrictions. It seemed to me to be an explicit disavowal of the justification that Marxists used to deny the abuse of power: power cannot be abused because it is in itself just (a charismatic theory of power), or state power cannot be abusive because it is unlimited, having no restriction other than force (a sceptical theory of power). Both arguments have been used at different times by communist political doctrine. Indeed, communists have responded to critics who accused them of condoning tyrannical government in two different ways: (1) as it is governed by the Communist Party, which *correctly* interprets the needs of the majority by means of the Marxist social science, the Soviet state has no need of restrictions (the charismatic theory); (2) all states are dictatorships, so why should the Soviet state not be one too? (the sceptical theory).

As always, I was particularly interested in procedural questions, and the end of my response to the 'Nine Questions on Stalinism', I considered at length the principle of authority as a criterion of truth. What was Khrushchev's report if not the correction of a political doctrine on the basis of the principle of authority? The aberrations of Marxism–Leninism during the Stalinist period witnessed the triumph of the principle of authority through the personality cult, but those aberrations, including the personality cult itself, have been corrected by those whom the system had authorized to take action. Therefore I asked myself: do they not have, in their turn, any restriction on what they do to rectify the doctrine? And if there were any restrictions, had Khrushchev exceeded them? In order to better explain my response to this problem, I investigated a fundamental problem in political philosophy. We know that all political systems are governed by two types of norms: fundamental ones, which concern the principle to which the system aspires, and the formal ones, which concern *how* the system functions. When the fundamental principles are altered, we are usually confronted with a change in the political regime, but when the formal principles are altered, there is usually a change in the form of government. Well, it seemed to me that the upheaval that Khrushchev brought about affected not only the form but also the substance of the Soviet system, and constituted the beginning of profound change that questioned not only the formal organization, by bringing to an end the principle of authority as a criterion of truth and recognizing the opposite principle empirical inquiry, but also 'some fundamental principles'. Today we know that there was still a very long way to go. Not only did they fail to continue along that way, but the ideological, political and economic system which was created by the October Revolution also continued to degenerate until it fell apart.

Marxists gave my essay a very hostile reception. I was particularly struck by two reviews, both of which were negative: Valentino Gerratana's 'Bobbio e lo stalinismo', published in *Contemporaneo* (III, no. 4, October 1956), and Franco Fortini's 'Il lusso della monotonia', which appeared in *Ragionamenti* (II, no. 7, October–November, 1956).

Gerratana acknowledged that my article did have the merit of pointing out a theoretical question which Marxists would have to examine more closely, but he reproached me for having ignored a passage in which Lenin dealt with the question of dictatorship: 'The irrefutable evidence of history demonstrates that, in the history of revolutionary movements, personal dictatorship has often been the expression, the vehicle and the agent of the dictatorship of the revolutionary classes.'

Fortini was harsher, and condemned me for allowing myself the luxury, typical of conservatives, of extolling the monotony of history and perceiving it as immutable rather than changing. He accused my analysis of being based on 'such obvious examples of polemical and ideological distortions as to sacrifice the very scientific cool-headedness and objectivity that [Bobbio] accuses the communists of lacking'. In other words, I was supposed to have attempted to show that Marxism and Stalinism were the same thing. I confess that I felt rather upset, as I had only wanted to show that the crisis of Stalinism reflected a flaw in Marxism. I did not bother to respond either publicly or privately. The misunderstanding was too great for it to be worthwhile. I did not return to the argument for another twenty years, when I reconsidered the relationship between Marxism and the state in the first chapter of *Which Socialism?*[15] Besides, I was distancing myself from the political struggle at the time, and returning to my studies.

Former members of the Action Party were divided over how to view communism. Augusto Monti continued to write for *L'Unità*, while remaining faithful to the Action Party. On the other hand, Franco Venturi, who had been the cultural attaché under the Italian ambassador in Moscow, Manlio Brosio, was asking us to abandon any expectations we might have had of the Soviet Union.

On 17 October 1964, Amendola wrote an article in *Rinascita* entitled 'The figures do not add up',[16] which argued that Italy could not be governed without the communists, and he based this assertion on the economic and institutional crisis the country was going through (an attempted coup attributed to General De Lorenzo appeared to involve the president of the Republic, Segni, to some extent). His essential argument was: 'If you do not include us in your calculations, the figures will not add up.' I do not know exactly why I decided to write to him and express my opinion. However, the occasion was the sudden removal of Khrushchev from power, which I took as my starting point to express my amazement that after so many years, the change from one head of government to the next in the Soviet Union did not occur on the basis of a fundamental law, as even occurs in the case of absolute monarchies, but by means of a *coup d'état*. Amendola replied to me on 5 November, saying that he intended to publish my letter in *Rinascita*. It appeared in the issue of 7 November, followed by his long reply. In my letter, I had written that Italy was now ready for a large working-class party, but concluded: 'We need your strength, but you cannot do without our principles.' In his reply, Amendola distanced himself from 'real socialism', proposing an independent way forward for the working-class movement in Western countries, which could only be achieved through the unity of working-class parties, because this is the only way to make an impact 'that would guarantee in practice the necessary link between socialism and freedom'. The last sentence in my letter on their strength and our principles was clearly provocative. Amendola commented on it by claiming that there would be room in this one great party of the working class for communists, socialists and persons like myself 'who represented the continuation of the struggle for liberalism started by Piero Gobetti'. I responded with what was now a public rather than a private letter and it appeared along with another article by Amendola, entitled 'The possibility of reunification'.[17] I said that I was fully in agreement with the idea of reunification, and pointed out that in the context of our constitution there was only room for one socialist and democratic party. Social-democratic policies, I continued, would always be better than no policies at all. I concluded again with an intentional provocation: 'The historian who will be writing the history of this twenty-year period in fifty years time . . . will not be looking for documents on the profound changes in Italian society in the archives of our largest working-class party.' In his next reply, Amendola argued that the united party of the working class would have to be a new party that would undertake a path that would be neither communist nor social-democratic, but finally represented a 'third way'.

I had occasion to recall this conclusion some years later when, picking up on the political debate within the left, I started a dialogue with the communists on the theme 'The third way does not exist'.[18] This was proof yet again of the slowness with which ideas develop in our country in relation to the speed of the transformations that occur in society. At the time, I wrote that the third way does not exist, because, given that the Leninist option has been blocked off and was therefore unrepeatable, as by then even the communists were suggesting, it would have been a serious mistake for them to turn their backs scornfully on what had already been achieved, albeit partially, by the European social-democracies. Instead of contriving new solutions out of understandable loyalty to their sense of self, they should have made an effort to develop those that had already been commenced. I insisted on arguing that the only way to pursue a left-wing policy without abandoning the rules of democracy was to take action on chosen objectives that produced better results than those already attained, rather than going off in search of a third way whose whereabouts nobody seemed to know. You cannot avoid the real difficulties that the social-democracies have not managed to resolve by fantasizing about a third way. You need to strengthen the organization of the working-class movement in order to continue the democratic path to socialism, which is everywhere the same. A wide-ranging debate developed around this question, in which intellectuals and politicians from communists to republicans took part (thus providing a range of views to the left and the right of the Socialist Party). In an article written at Christmas 1978, I took up an amusing parable invented by my friend Luciano Cafagna, in order to conclude the debate and take the heat out of it. He told the story of a capricious princess who wanted to have a 'leoncorn' for the royal menagerie at all costs. In vain her old father attempted to explain that there was a lion, a ferocious and frightening animal, and a horse, an attractive and mild animal, but an animal which has a lion's head and a horse's tail has never existed. The obstinate princess attempted to mate them, but the only result was that the horse was torn to pieces by the lion.

Curiously, the image of 'leoncorn' (or unicorn)[19] reappeared a few years later in Giorgio Napolitano's introductory lecture to the conference organized by the Gramsci Institute in Piedmont in March 1982, on the changes taking place in the Communist Party.[20] At the end of his speech, 'The Italian Communist Party as seen by the Italian Communist Party', on the party's peculiarities which made it different to traditional social-democratic parties in spite of the changes that were taking place, Napolitano wondered whether the party should be compared, as in Togliatti's famous metaphor, with a giraffe, which is a real animal, albeit a strange one, or with the mythical unicorn, the animal that represented purity in the Middle Ages. He left the question unanswered, but gave the impression that he preferred the first simile to the second. It was then my turn in the following lecture, 'The Italian Communist Party as seen from outside', to challenge one by one the various 'peculiarities' that Napolitano had argued for, and to conclude that the Italian Communist Party had become increasingly similar to a European social-democratic party and had increasingly detached itself from the communist parties strictly following the Soviet line, as in eastern Europe.

Amongst my communist friends such as Napolitano, Aldo Tortorella and Pietro Ingrao, I would also like to recall Gian Carlo Pajetta whom I had known since my high-school days. When he wrote *Il ragazzo rosso va alla guerra* (Milan: Mondadori, 1986), I was amongst those launching his book at the Press Centre. As is well known, he was an energetic man with a fiercely polemical nature, but also kind and witty. When Enrico Belinguer died on 11 June 1984, I was invited to take part in the commemoration in Turin at Piazza San Carlo which was crowded with people. On that occasion, talking of the praise that you give to adversaries in the face of death, I compared it to the homage that vice renders to virtue. A month later, President Sandro Pertini appointed Carlo Bo and myself senators for life. Amongst the telegrams of congratulations, I received one from Pajetta which said: 'This is the homage that virtue pays to virtue.'

A few years later, when he was interviewed by Nello Ajello for La Repubblica *when the crack in the edifice of communism had widened to the point of bringing it crashing down, Bobbio saw the fall of the Berlin Wall and the end of the USSR not as a defeat for the left, but as a chance for regeneration: 'The left has not disappeared with the wall. It is only the bad left that has disappeared. In pursuit of the ideal of egalitarianism, it had acted in a repressive and despotic manner. Now that that left is no more, another can come into existence. Indeed there has already been a left in Italy that has had nothing to do with the Soviet left.'*

'Is the era of left-wing despotism now just a bad memory?' asked Ajello. 'One can only hope so,' replied Bobbio. 'Hegel defined despotism as that form of government in which only one person, "the ruler", is free, and beneath him there is a multitude of servants. In a democracy on the other hand, everyone is equally free. Equally: that adverb is fundamental. This equality must, in my opinion, also acknowledge the social rights, starting with the essential ones (education, work and health), which also make it possible to exercise one's libertarian rights better. Social rights and the commitment to satisfy and defend them: that is the basic principle which distinguishes the left from the right.'[21]

5

My Teaching Experience

If I look back over the years, as old men are wont to do, I have no doubt about what was my principle activity: university teaching. Once my political passions had died down after 18 April 1948, I went back to a peaceful life, just as many others did, having become involved in politics for ethical reasons. Following my teaching experience in Camerino, Siena and Padua, I started teaching at Turin University in the academic year 1948–9 as Solari's successor in the chair of philosophy of law, and I remained at that university until I retired in 1984, as emeritus professor. For the majority of my life, therefore, I have had two very difficult duties to carry out: teaching and writing. I must confess that I have always been afflicted by the doubt that I was not up to these two formidable tasks.

The bookshelves that cover the walls of Bobbio's study, contain a series of black folders bound with a rather cheap cardboard, without inscriptions on the covers or spines other than an occasional faded piece of paper glued to the cardboard. These are the course lectures for the early Paduan courses, cyclostyled by some diligent students, as they did in those days. They start with Lessons on the Philosophy of Law *for the 1940–1 academic year which were collected by two students, P. Antonelli and G. Chiesura.*[1] *The latter is the writer and poet Giorgio Chiesura, who gave himself up to the Germans after 8 September, thus choosing the Calvary of the concentration camp in preference to fighting the Germans. He devoted his novel in verse,* La zona immobile, *to this process of mortification: 'I am here because I am tired of deceits.' In 1993, he published* Sicilia 1943, *the diary (July–September 1943) he kept during the days when the regime collapsed up to his decision to obey the proclamation and become a prisoner: 'War is a separate world, that is to say, one of those situations in which you live through experiences, emotions and sensations that could not possibly be repeated or continued in normal life.'*[2] *After forty years of silence, he wanted to see Bobbio again, and he and his wife had lunch with his old professor.*

The course lectures also include Lessons on the Philosophy of Law *for the 1941–2 academic year, put together by his student Giulio Pasetti Bombarella, now professor of civil law at the University of Rome, and* The Origins of Modern Natural Law and its Development in the XVII Century *for the 1945–6 academic year, put together by his students G. Milner and R. Toso. In his course for the 1942–3 academic year, Bobbio said:*

> Every man has the possibility of differentiating himself from others in accordance with his own intrinsic law, which is his own freedom, and therefore of being valued in a manner that corresponds to this differentiation . . . But that which constitutes a man's own particular nature and gives him the chance to differentiate himself from other beings and other men is his *liberty*. Therefore justice is not simply equality, an abstract principle, but equality with reference to liberty, a concrete principle. This means it is not purely and simply equality, but *equality in freedom*, or rather and more specifically, the equal opportunity to use one's own freedom. By establishing freedom as the basis for assessing justice in this manner, the question of justice shifts: it passes from being a concept of justice as abstract equality to a concept of justice as equality in freedom, that is equality in the free expression of one's own personality. By using this principle, justice does not mean that I am the same as you, but that I am equal to you in the opportunity to express my own personality. Thus abstract equality becomes a concrete reality through liberty.[3]

His loyalty to teaching was stronger than the fascist censor. It can be easily imagined what effect these lectures would have had on many students. One of these was a German, Heinz Riedt, who had managed to avoid military service through sickness, and had won a scholarship to an Italian university. In the lecture halls of the old faculty building, he came into contact with anti-fascist groups and after 8 September he took part in the Resistance as a member of a Patriotic Action Group. Following the war, he returned to Germany and was the translator of the German edition of Primo Levi's If this is a man. *Levi called him an 'anomalous German' in his later work* The Drowned and the Saved. *Riedt said that 'Coming from Germany I felt as though I was in a free country', and recalled his experience at*

Padua University and Bobbio's lectures.[4] *The conclusion to Bobbio's course on the philosophy of law was as follows:*

> The nature of the democratic state is this: that the individual and the state are no longer at daggers drawn, but identify with the same general will, which is the will of everyone that dictates to everyone individually. In the struggle between liberalism and socialism which broke out in the last century and continues to this day, democracy represented the salvation of the liberal state which did not want to transform itself into its opposite, the socialist state, and also the salvation of the socialist state which did not want to descend into anarchy. It has been invoked on different occasions as a corrective for either of these. As such, it has even represented an area of agreement between the opposing tendencies. Today it undoubtedly represents where we are going in our present situation.
>
> Of course, I am not saying that democracy is possible today, especially in Europe. I am merely saying that democracy, as the term that unites the two opposing and integrated requirements of justice, is the direction in which our civilization is moving. Whether it is achieved earlier or later depends on the greater or lesser development of our civic conscience.[5]

On my return to Turin, I taught at Palazzo Campana (the building which had been the Fascist Provincial Headquarters), in a small classroom on the first floor. Initially, I did not have many students. Later I was moved downstairs to the so-called main hall, because it was larger than the others, although equally unadorned. You could enter directly through a small door that opened onto the main road, without having to go through entrance and corridors. The hall was very noisy because the trams passed outside. I gave my lectures in Palazzo Campana for another twenty years, until the faculty was moved in 1968 to its new premises in Palazzo Nuovo. However, my best-known courses took place in the old building where I was surrounded by its rather grey walls with bad acoustics. Palazzo Campana, which is alongside the Egyptian Museum and faces onto Piazza Carlo Alberto, is where the student protests literally exploded twenty years after I entered it, with the first occupation of a university building in Italian history which occurred towards the end of 1967. Meanwhile, two more children had been born: Andrea, who has already been mentioned, on 24 February 1946, and Marco on 5 September 1951. In 1953, we bought a 'second home', a four-roomed flat in the first 'skyscraper' built in Cervinia, where the boys learned to ski under the guidance of their mother, whom they soon surpassed, and we used to spend summer holidays there, as Valeria and I continue to do to this day.[6]

Our faculty had a reputation for being very strict. The first exams were considered particularly hard: foundations of private law with Mario Allara, who was rector for a long time, including the period of protests and occupation, and history of Roman law with Giuseppe Grosso, the mayor of Turin and the chairman of the province, an incorruptible member of a political class that has now disappeared. Foundations of Roman law with Silvio Romano was also considered a difficult test. Students had to pass these three exams, and many failed to do so. This caused a veritable exodus to minor universities. One of the lecturers who enhanced the faculty's standing was Paolo Greco, a renowned scholar of commercial law, who was de facto the chairman of the Committee of National Liberation during the German occupation, and Francesco Antolisei, who established a school of criminal law: his textbook was for many years the standard text for public prosecutors and magistrates.

I therefore found myself teaching in a conscientious faculty, which had a good reputation and was not to be trifled with. Philosophy of law was a first-year subject, devoted to general concepts of law which every student has to know before dealing with more specialized legal disciplines. I always tried to repeat the same course as little as possible. This involved the hard work of preparing a course on one particular subject every year. I prepared many of them, and in the end volumes of lectures were published by Giappichelli, partly on the basis of my notes and partly thanks to the notes written down by the students. Two of these volumes are still in use, as can be seen from the royalties that I continue to receive from the publisher. They cover two courses that were given towards the end of the fifties, later revised and continuously reprinted: *The Theory of Legal Principle* and *The Theory of Legal Systems*, and these courses were interconnected.[7] Latterly Giappichelli has changed them from course textbooks into a book in a single volume, *The General Theory of Law*, partly because it had already been published in this form in Spanish.[8] Each year, I alternated between theoretical and historical courses, the former essentially devoted to the clarification of questions of an introductory nature, the latter devoted to outlining the thought of the great figures and currents in the philosophy of law. Of the courses on individual thinkers, the most famous were the ones on Kant (1957) and Locke (1963), whose reflections could be considered the basis for the liberal theory of the state.[9] Of the courses on currents of thought in the philosophy of law, I devoted one course to *Legal Positivism* (1961),[10] which has been reprinted several times.

At the beginning of the fifties, I concerned myself with the nature of the science of law, an old problem which was more speculative than real. It has often interested jurists, who have never renounced the idea that a jurist's work was scientific, especially during the century of positivism triumphant. It was a question of finding out the position of the 'science' of law, or rather the law as a science, within the increasingly complex groupings of sciences. I had been fascinated by the problem since beginning my studies. One of my first articles was entitled 'Science and technique of the law' (1934).[11]

Immediately after the war, I had become familiar with neo-positivism through my work with the Centre for Methodological Studies, and with Anglo-Saxon analytical philosophy which had created the so-called 'linguistic turn'. According to the latter, to put it very briefly, 'linguistic analysis' has the therapeutic virtue of freeing philosophy from many artificial problems. The Centre for Methodological Studies had been founded in Turin by Ludovico Geymonat. It included academics from different backgrounds: philosophers like Nicola Abbagnano, jurists like Bruno Leoni, economists like Ferdinando Di Fenizio and scientists like Eugenio Frola, Piero Buzano, Prospero Nuvoli, Enrico Persico and Cesare Codegone, whose ambition was to overcome the traditional barriers that divided scientific culture from humanist culture.

In March 1949, I was invited by friends at the centre to give a lecture on the science of law, to which I gave the title 'Science of law and linguistic analysis'. I argued that logical positivism had developed a theory of science based more on the concept of rigorous methodology than the truth of its content, which finally made it possible for jurists to consider their work, which is quintessentially the task of making legislative language precise, as a science. Although the argument was original, it was anything but well founded. All the same, the lecture was published in the prestigious *Rivista Trimestrale di Diritto e Procedure Civile*. The article was a success and provoked a certain amount of debate. In the same year, I gave a course on this theme and published a coursebook entitled *Theory of the Science of Law*.[12] I returned to the subject again with a lecture at a conference organized by the Centre for Methodological Studies in 1952, which I entitled 'The precision of the science of law'. In the second half of the fifties, I abandoned this line of inquiry, which I had not studied in enough depth, but my article is considered the beginning of the so-called Turin School of the science of law, which has produced some distinguished figures who were much more capable of developing the discipline than I had been – the most important of these was Uberto Scarpelli.

The logic of normative propositions was a branch of the philosophy of law that was entirely new, and I devoted articles and lectures to it for about ten years. Later it was called deontic logic. If I say: all men are mortal, Socrates is a man, Socrates is mortal, then I am in the field of assertive logic, which goes all the way back to Aristotle. Deontic logic, which includes legal logic, is a logic that asserts not what something is, but what it should be. For example: 'Murder *ought* to be punished, Jack has committed murder, Jack *ought* to be punished.' Deontic logic deals with the modal categories of *should be* and *can be*, which means saying 'one ought not to do' is like saying 'one can do', just as saying 'one ought to not do' is like saying 'one cannot do'. I do not want to go any further with these linguistic games, which have always engrossed me, but which I have not worked on for some time.

I believe that in 1954 I was the first to become interested in deontic logic in Italy, although I only got as far as the rudiments, and it was up to others to take the credit for transforming it from this trickle of knowledge into a university discipline and a philosophical school. My curiosity about this subject started with two books that appeared in 1951, and both had the words 'legal logic' in their titles: *Introducción a la lógica jurídica* by the Mexican Eduardo García Máynez, and *Jüristische Logik* by Ulrich Klug. The real founder of deontic logic was Georg Henrik von Wright, a pupil of Wittgenstein, of whose works I recall *Deontic Logic* and *An Essay on Modal Logic*. In 1954, I wrote an article on this argument, which constituted a kind of introduction to deontic logic.

The most renowned scholar of this discipline in Italy is Amedeo Conte, who says that he became fascinated by it following my lecture at the Collegio Ghisleri in Pavia. Conte at the time was a student at the Faculty of Law, and not even twenty years old. He recently showed me incontrovertible written evidence: the *Ghisleri College Yearbooks for 1952, 1953 and 1954*, edited by the Student Association, which give accounts of the lectures held over the three-year period. These include: 'Prof. Norberto Bobbio, for the University of Turin: "Law and logic"'. I myself found the full text amongst my papers: twenty-two sheets of paper in a tiny handwriting, entitled: ' "Law and logic", a lecture held in Pavia on 29 April 1954'.

In the preamble, I emphasized the importance of defining the words we use, and quoted a line of Montaigne: 'La plus part des occasions des troubles du monde sont grammairiennes.'[13] I also quoted Balzac's novel *Les Employés*: 'A côté du besoin de définir, se trouve le danger de s'embrouiller.'[14] I wrote to Conte about this discovery, and he used the letter as the preface to his second volume containing his studies on the philosophy of normative language.[15]

You claim that the nineteen-year-old who was introduced to me by the college rector, Prof. Aurelio Bernardi, discovered his own vocation while listening to my lecture. I have no reason to dispute your words, even though I am always a little doubtful about the search for exemplary moments long after the event by those who are narrating their own life and who, without realizing, idealize it, as you do in your letter of the 2nd of last January, in which you refer to that meeting as 'epoch-making', an exaggeration (which was intentional, and not without a certain irony). It was epoch-making, moreover, not only for you, but also for me, given that that lecture was a public trial of the article I was to write in the following summer on the work of García Máynez, which was published at the end of 1954 in *Rivista Internazionale di Filosofia del Diritto*. And while we're at it, why not epoch-making for the future of deontic logic in Italy?[16]

I was his professor and he my disciple who was destined to outshine me in this specific subject. The reader might be interested to know how Conte defines deontic logic: '*Metaphysics* investigates *tò òn* (being, the *Sein*) in its constitutive ontology; *deontics* investigates *tò déon* (ought, the *Sollen*) in its constitutive deontology. The definition of the concept of *déon* (ought, *sollen*, *devoir être*, or *dover essere*) and the definition of the relationship between *déon* and *òn* (between ought and is, *sollen* and *sein*, *devoir être* and *être*, or *dover essere* and *essere*) are the two principal tasks of a critical analysis of deontic reason.'[17] His premise is amusing:

> A piece of graffiti appeared one day on the wall of the New York subway: 'God is the answer'. The next day, another one appeared below it: 'What was the question?'
>   This anecdote illustrates the spirit in which the research contained in *Filosofia del linguaggio normativo* was carried out. What was the question? My research intends to determine not just the *reply* to individual questions on deontics (*Deontik*, *déontique*, *deontica*) perceived as a philosophical science, but also the *question* itself. In this sense, they represent junctures in the critical analysis of deontic reason, of a *Kritik der deontischen Vernunft*.[18]

What was even more amusing was that Conte and his disciples formed a football team, which created a strip with *déon* written across the middle. The strip had two versions: blue with red lettering, and white with blue lettering. Both were presented to me as a symbolic gesture to the supposed founding father.

As I inherited the chair from Gioele Solari, you might wonder whether the transfer from teacher to disciple was characterized by continuity or a rift. I can say that the continuity was mainly sentimental. Solari was principally a historian of philosophy. His course, which was partly published after his death, was in reality a course on the history of the philosophy of law, from the Greeks to modern times. His main works, *The Concept of the Individual in Private Law* (1911) and *Historicism and Private Law* (1915),[19] were both of a historical nature: the first is an account of the Enlightenment in law, and the second a study into the historicism of law, particularly the historical school of law founded by the great German jurist von Savigny. He wrote many studies of individual thinkers: Grotius, Spinoza, Locke, Kant, Hegel and Rosmini, which were collected together in *Historical Studies on the Philosophy of Law* (1949),[20] which contained a wonderful and affectionate introduction by Luigi Einaudi.

The general theory of law, which I concentrated on, went in a completely different direction, not to mention of course my interest in deontic logic. The book, which was successfully used for my application for promotion back in 1938, was entitled *Analogy in Legal Logic*,[21] was itself a study into legal logic, as its title implies. It concerned the practice of overcoming gaps in the law with norms taken from similar cases. Part of the book was historical, but the part dealing with the theoretical basis for reasoning by analogy was the most important and ambitious. Solari's courses would have been perfectly suited to a faculty of philosophy. Besides, the Faculty of Law in Turin had at that time a long humanistic tradition, as can be seen from the eminent academics that taught there: Francesco Ruffini, Luigi Einaudi, Achille Loria and Pasquale Jannaccone. When I took over from Solari (in 1948), I initiated the teaching of the general theory of law in a manner that I considered more relevant to an increasingly vocational faculty of law. I liked to point out the profound difference between the philosophers' philosophy of law and the jurists' philosophy of law. The essence of Solari's teaching, which I attempted to put across as much as I could in my teaching too, was what he called the civic function of the philosophy of law, which turns problems of a political nature into philosophical questions, and ultimately into questions of conscience.

At that time, the academic world was much more exclusive and cloistered than it is today: lecturers with tenure were an elite, no more than about fifteen in our faculty, so that many of us were allocated other tasks in order to cover all the teaching required by the faculty. For example, I taught politics as well as the philosophy of law for many years, starting in 1962. Things changed in the seventies, with the sudden and inordinate increase in the number of students, following the easing of entrance requirements in response to pressure from new social groups who had taken their studies beyond school-leaving age. Necessarily this led to an increase in departments, a proliferation of teaching posts, an expansion in particular of specialist subjects and the subsequent formation of a substantial category of associate lecturers. However, the most noticeable difference between the state of universities then and now is in the separation between students and teaching staff: on the whole, students used to be passive listeners. There was no tradition of personal contacts between students and teachers, as is typical of American and British universities. Indeed, at the beginning of the student protests, there was a legitimate demand for a change in the relationship between students and professors. The only reference point for students in the faculty was the janitor. For information about exams, interviews, theses or anything else, students had to go through the janitor, a position that today is no longer even remembered.

My lessons were rather crowded, only because it was a subject that nearly all students studied in their first year. I was one of the few who held seminars. 'Holding a seminar' meant putting together a select group of students who would meet once a week to discuss a specific theme or a text. For many years after I had definitively left the department, I would happen to meet some former student, who used to attend one of these seminars and in the meantime had become a judge in the lower court, a lawyer, or even a university lecturer, like Gustavo Zagrebelsky, who is now a judge in the constitutional court, and they would greet me with 'Professor, do you remember the seminar on "punishment"'?

The twenty years that passed between the commencement of my teaching in Turin and the 'turmoil' of 1968 were rather monotonous. They were years in which nothing much happened in my public life worthy of narrating. I conducted the normal life of a university professor: lectures and exams, and every now and then some article in an academic magazine and some book bringing together the more interesting articles. Apart from the course books already mentioned, during this period I also published *Studies into the General Theory of Law* (1955), *Natural Law and Scientific Law* (1965), a collection of my writings on the fierce debate between the exponents of natural law and the exponents of positive law, of which I was one, and another better-known collection of essays, *Studies for a General Theory of the Law* (1970). I also produced a collection of essays on Pareto, Mosca and elitism in Italy, which I entitled *Essays on Political Science in Italy* (1969).[22] These were the years in which my fame unexpectedly grew to the point of my being invited to give the introductory lecture on Hegel and natural law to the VI Congress of the Hegel Society held in Prague in 1966, and on 'Legal science in relation to *is* and *ought*' for the International Conference of the Philosophy of Law held in Gardone in 1967.

Two thinkers had a particularly strong influence on the development of my studies: the jurist Hans Kelsen and the philosopher Thomas Hobbes. When I won the Balzan Prize in 1994, I said that it was reading Kelsen that inspired me to perceive democracy as a system of rules that makes it possible to establish and develop free and peaceful coexistence. I first wrote about Kelsen in 1954.[23] I only met the Austrian jurist on one occasion. It was in 1957 when I was giving a lecture, 'Quelques arguments contre le droit naturel', at a conference organized by the Institut International de Philosophie Politique in Paris. I have written encyclopedia entries, articles and reviews on him, as well as a book of essays, which was published in 1992 and contains ten articles written between 1954 and 1986.[24]

Kelsen occupies a fundamental place not only in my studies on the theory of law, but also in those on political theory. It is to Kelsen that I owe the procedural perception of democracy, which goes back to Schumpeter's idea of democracy as competition between elites in amassing electoral support in free elections. 'The democratic method', he wrote, 'is the institutional instrument for taking political decisions, on the basis of which individuals obtain the power to decide through a competition aimed at the popular vote.'[25] Kelsen, the founder of the Vienna School and father of the Austrian constitution, took up this idea of Schumpeter, and divided forms of government into two basic models: democracy, founded on power from below, and autocracy, in which power derives from above (a distinction that reflects the similar Kantian one between autonomy and heteronomy). It follows from this that the selection of the political class takes place through election in democracies and through appointment in autocracies. This means perceiving democracy as a method, or rather a system of rules for taking collective decisions with the greatest consensus of the agents involved in those decisions. Contrary to the critics who deny the procedural concept of democracy, I have pointed out many times, albeit with little success, that, although this is certainly a minimal definition of democracy, it is in no way value-free. It is a definition that sets the minimal formal requirements that a democratic system must possess, but this does not preclude reference to some important values. The perception of democracy as an instrument that regulates competition between elites to control consensus implies reference to values such as the equality of citizens in relation to their right to vote, freedom of choice in relation to the vote, and, consequently, the peaceful resolution of social conflicts. I would also like to mention that the first and very important Italian translation of Kelsen's work was by my friend Renato Treves, who met the great Austrian jurist in Cologne while we were on our trip to Germany in 1932, and that Kelsen's most comprehensive work, *General Theory of Law and the State*, which appeared in America in 1946, was translated for the publisher Comunità by Sergio Cotta, who was my assistant at the time.[26]

Thomas Hobbes is the philosopher with the greatest number of entries in the *Bibliography* of my writing (and the second author overall, after Piero Gobetti, with forty-two entries). I first began to study him in 1939, when I reviewed Carl Schmitt's essay on the *Leviathan*. Then in 1948, I edited UTET's edition of *De cive*, in the series 'Political Classics' edited by Luigi Firpo.[27] I spoke of my passion for this English philosopher at my eightieth-birthday celebrations at Turin University.

> I admit it: Hobbes was one of my authors. I have studied him off and on throughout my life. But I do not claim any credit other than for realizing the central importance of Hobbes's thought at a time when he was still little known in Italy. But that was understandable: under fascism he was viewed with suspicion. We did not realize that, instead of representing the totalitarian state, the Leviathan represents the modern state, the great modern territorial state that rises from the ashes of medieval society. It is a political body that manifested itself in various forms of government, and of course, these included autocratic government. Principally the Leviathan maintains a monopoly over legitimate force, which is legitimate in that it is based on the citizens' consent. I had realized the importance of Hobbes during a study that I had previously made of Samuel von Pufendorf's legal system, and Pufendorf was, in his own way, a Hobbesian.[28] I was particularly struck by the novelty of Hobbes's method. Hobbes's arguments were no longer based on the principle of authority, whether historical or revealed, but solely on reason, on rational arguments. It is correct to say that Hobbes's influence on the development of my ideas was more to do with method. However, I believe that even the substance of his ideas has contributed to the formation of my political thought. I will give three instances: individualism, contractualism and the idea of peace through the constitution of a common authority. I could also add a certain pessimism over human nature and history. When I started to examine Hobbes, I could not have imagined that his thought would increase in importance so suddenly and with such far-reaching consequences in Italy, and outside Italy too. Commentaries on Hobbes are now so numerous that one book says it all. It is called *Which Hobbes?* That is precisely what it asks: which Hobbes? I would give a simple and perhaps even banal answer: Hobbes interpreted with a modicum of common sense and historical awareness, which in my opinion are sadly lacking in scholars who have searched for originality at all costs. They recently published an existentialist and Heideggerian interpretation of Hobbes. That is like mixing up the prince of light with the prince of darkness.[29]

Hobbes was linked to my curious relationship with Carl Schmitt. I had met him in Berlin in 1937. That year, I spent part of my holiday in Germany in order to finish a study of Max Scheler, the final part of phenomenological studies, which was published as 'La personalità di Max Scheler' in *Rivista di Filosofia* the following year. During this period in Germany, I met Schmitt, who was then about fifty. As I said to Antonio Gnoli, in an interview in *La Repubblica*,[30] I am still amazed that someone like Carl Schmitt would receive an unknown youngster with such friendliness. He invited me to supper and we continued our conversation in the garden. He gave me some of his works, including a youthful essay of 1912, 'Gesetz und Urteil' ['Law and judgment'] and a rare pamphlet, *Politische Theologie*, of 1924, with a brief dedication: 'Mit besten Grüssen' ('With my warmest greetings'), signed C. S. and dated '10.X.37'. The following year, he sent me his new book on Hobbes, *Der Leviathan in der Staatslehre des Thomas Hobbes*, which I reviewed in *Rivista di Filosofia*. Ten years later, he and I were to have a lively exchange of letters.

It was the famous German jurist and philosopher who made contact in 1948 to ask for a copy of De cive, *which he reviewed in* Universitas *in March 1949. This request initiated correspondence which continued until 1953, with a surprising epilogue in 1980 (five years before Schmitt's death).*

The Schmitt–Bobbio letters have been published and carefully annotated by Piet Tommissen in Diritto e Cultura *at the request of A. Carrino (V, no. 1, January–June 1995). It consists of nine letters in German by Schmitt and eleven in Italian by Bobbio. After the first two letters in 1948, there were eleven in 1949, one in 1950, three in 1951, one in 1953, and two in 1980.[31] The first two letters reflect the climate of uncertainty in which European intellectuals attempted to piece together their relationships after the war.*

Plettenberg (Westphalia)
(British Zone) 15/XII 48

Most distinguished Prof. Bobbio,

I hope you won't mind if an old admirer and student of Hobbes contacts you directly to ask you if it would be possible to have a copy of your edition of *De cive*?

I would be very pleased to see your edition. I lost my large and beautiful collection of books, but to my particular joy, I saved your edition of Campanella's *Città del sole*. If the dispatch of books to Germany involves particular problems, could I ask you to send a copy to Mr Armin Mohler, Registr. 36, Basel, Switzerland?

Hobbes's name appeared again in my brief personal essay, *Ex captivitate salus*, in 1946. I could send you a copy, if you would be so good as to provide your address. In the *Bulletin of the Faculty of Law* at Coimbra of 1948 (vol. XXIV, no. 1), you'll find my essay: 'Historiographia in nuce' (on Tocqueville). In the same issue, I found a reference by Prof. Mereo (of Coimbra) to a book by Passerin d'Entrèves on Filmer. If it is not an indiscrete question, could I ask you how Mr Passerin d'Entrèves is, and where he is at the moment?

Please treat my questions with friendly indulgence. But: 'on se lasse de tout excepté de penser'. With all my sincere esteem.

Turin, 26 December 1948
Via Sacchi 66

Dear Professor Schmitt,

Just think that since the end of the war, your letter is the first time that I have heard from the Germany of learning, with which, as you know, I had close personal links as well as cultural ones. I therefore greeted this letter as a much appreciated sign that intellectual life has not been extinguished, even when faced with enormous difficulties, and I hope that this represents the beginning of new relations to which, for my part, I am happy to make my small contribution.

I have asked the publisher to send a copy of my edition of *De cive* to the address you gave me. So that it isn't a disappointment, I should add that it is an Italian translation of the famous text, with my commentary and introduction of a general nature, which is more of a presentation to educated people than an example of personal scientific research. In any case, I hope you will find it acceptable.

I don't know d'Entrèves writings on Filmer. I doubt that it exists. I keep a close eye on my friend's work, and I have never heard mention of such a work. Perhaps it is a magazine article. For further information, you could write yourself to D'Entrèves, who has been professor of Italian studies at Oxford University since the end of the war. His address is 13 Charlbury Road, Oxford.

Now I have a favour to ask of you. I am the general editor of *Rivista di Filosofia*, which regularly gives out news about philosophy in Italy and abroad. Unfortunately, however, we know nothing or almost nothing about Germany. To date, we have an exchange with only one journal, *Die Wandlung*, which is not a specifically philosophical publication. We would be very interested in setting up exchanges with other journals more closely related to the subject. Do they still publish the distinguished long-running philosophical periodicals, such as *Logos*, *Kantstudien*, etc.? Are they publishing new ones? Who are the publishers and who the editors? Could you send me or have sent to me some information about this? The information that you could give me, or the contacts with which you could provide me, would be extremely useful.

This year, I have started teaching at the University of Turin, my native city, after eight years at Padua. I am now married with two children. After many wanderings, I have returned to my old home in Turin at Via Sacchi 66. I would be very pleased to hear your personal news and about your studies.

I apologise for writing in Italian, but after many years without practice, I fear that I no longer know how to write in readable German.

Please accept my warmest greetings with fond memories.

In the following letter, the German philosopher makes a brief reference to his adversities before the courts. When Nazism fell, he was deprived of his chair at Berlin University, because he had been a member of the Prussian Council of State and chairman of the Association of National-Socialist Jurists. He was arrested and tried, and after two years of prison, he was acquitted.

Plettenberg (Westphalia)
30 January 1949

Dear Professor Bobbio
Most distinguished colleague!

Your letter of 26 December reached me in the middle of January. I was extremely happy to receive it and sincerely thank you. I was particularly interested to hear news of what had happened to you. I too have returned home, after many 'wanderings'. I lived through the taking of Berlin by the Russians, I was three times in the jaws of the Leviathan, and I found refuge in a small township, at my parents' home, and with my wife and seventeen-year-old daughter. Perhaps you will be interested in the account of the prison camp which I have enclosed, *Salus ex captivitate*[*sic*], which includes a passage on Hobbes. Your *De cive* has not yet arrived . . .

There followed information about German philosophical periodicals, in response to Bobbio's request. Three days later, on 2 February 1949, Schmitt sent another letter to announce that he had received De cive: *'I am very happy', he wrote, 'about this precious gift, and I am keen to inform you of its arrival and manifest my heartfelt thanks. I have already read a bit, and am fully satisfied with this edition.' Bobbio replied on 20 February.*

Dear Professor Schmitt,

I have received your letters of 30 January and 2 February, and with the former, your *Ex captivitate salus*, which I read with great interest and an intense feeling of involvement, not only because of the passage on Hobbes (I share your opinion and admiration), but also because of your evaluation of the history of legal thought and because of the profound autobiographical 'pathos'. But is silence really the only way forward, when surrounded by so much ruin? Or is your silence just a necessary pause in which to gather your thoughts so that you can return to the world with a more peaceful conscience and face the work you have already completed and the work still to be done with a renewed and stronger sense of purpose?

Thank you for your kind words about my Hobbes. I would be happy if you took the opportunity to write about it in a German periodical. I would have liked to continue to work on this open-minded destroyer of myths, if I hadn't been distracted by all the other work I have at the moment. However, it is certainly an argument to which I will return sooner or later, partly because Hobbes has, for me, a paradigmatic value, and reading his works has been profusely suggestive and enlightening . . .

In the following letters, they wrote further about books, periodicals, editions of Hobbes and a mistake in Schmitt's review of Bobbio's De cive. *On 3 July 1949, inspired by an article he had read, the German philosopher asked Bobbio for his judgement on the term 'state', in German 'Staat'. Bobbio replied on the 23rd of that month.*

A year later, on 10 December 1950, Bobbio sent Schmitt a letter in which he commented on the autobiographical passages in Ex captivitate salus, *the short book on Schmitt's imprisonment (which was to be published by Adelphi in 1987). When read today, the letter suggests something of a value judgement on the crisis that European civilization was experiencing:*

As far as the autobiographical pages of your book are concerned, I fully understand the sense of bitterness and almost dismay that emanates from them. I understand and admire the noble manner in which you have expressed this, thus making your meaning the more intense and moving. But I do not feel that I can entirely agree with it. The European catastrophe, in which both the victors and the defeated are victims, is not only the end of a certain period in history, but also the beginning of another. Do we have to take note only of that which is ending in our era, and not that which is beginning? And isn't that which is beginning, albeit in a tragic and terrifying situation, worthy of being viewed with some hope, I would say almost with respect? Are not the revolts of the poorest classes against the voracious holders of wealth (in our country we know something about this) and the rebellions of colonial peoples against centuries of massacres (initiated by Donoso's compatriots and blessed by theologians like him)[32] a struggle for justice and the law?

I mean that we are defeated if we want to uphold a civilization that is finished, and we continue to lament the passing of a paradise that has been irredeemably lost. We are defeated only to the extent that we believe that the struggle for justice in the world is over, that there is nothing that can be done except resign ourselves to our future, that the world is an immense turmoil from which we can only free ourselves by looking towards the next world.

I am not a Marxist, and still less a communist. My admiration for the Enlightenment writers has taught me to fend off the temptation towards fanaticism. But behind Marx, I see peoples with a 'thirst for justice', while behind theologians like Donoso, I only see the powerful with a thirst for more and more power.

Dear Professor Schmitt, please accept these words of mine (which you will find vague and naive) as the expression of a desire to continue our dialogue, a desire that I have long held as a result of my reading your books, my admiration for you as a scholar and a jurist, and my memory of that distant conversation fifteen years ago in Berlin at your home in Dahlem (am I right?) and which we continued out on the lawn. The much appreciated gift of your books provided an immediate opportunity to meet that desire. Today, we feel the need for dialogue more than ever, *lest we are too late again*!

In 1951, Schmitt suggested a conference to Bobbio to commemorate the third centenary of the publication of the Leviathan. *Later, he sent him his article on Hobbes which was published in* Die Tat. *Bobbio used it as a cue to clarify his own views on Hobbes, and to distinguish between theoretical analysis and practical action (in two letters, the first on 4 February and the second on 24 April).*

After thirty years of silence, and having retired from his university post, Bobbio wrote again to Carl Schmitt in 1980, and received an answer almost by return of post. It was occasioned by an article in the weekly magazine L'Espresso *which devoted an article to Schmitt ('Alti e bassi di una carriera', in issue no. 45 of 1979). Bobbio's letter and Schmitt's reply have the feeling of a final leave-taking:*

66, Via Sacchi, 10128 Turin
4 January 1980

Dear Prof. Schmitt,

I have never forgotten when I visited you in Berlin in the summer of 1937. I was twenty-eight years old, and I was not only young but also unknown. I have often had occasion to recall that meeting now that your name has begun to reappear increasingly often in academic publications and recently in a mass circulation current-affairs magazine such as *L'Espresso*. I have never failed to express my surprise that a professor who at the time was at the height of his fame, as you were at that time, should so amiably receive a youngster who had only just embarked on his studies . . . Not only did you receive me and listen to my bad German (I have now almost entirely forgotten it, except for reading), but you invited me to stay for supper with you and your family, and we also spent some time in a small garden and played with your children . . .

I have had several occasions to think of you over the last few years, and for some time, I have been meaning to write to you. But I have been putting it off, partly out of laziness and partly because I was waiting for an opportune moment. The article about you in *L'Espresso* and the correspondence with Miglio that followed gave me that opportunity. I remember that you dedicated your essay *Ex captivitate salus* to me with the words: 'Doceo sed frustra' ['I teach but to no purpose']. Now, you could not repeat *frustra*, if we go by what they write about you at the moment in Italy. One of my students, Pier Paolo Portinaro, is studying your thought, particularly *Verfassungslehre*, which is your least-known work in Italy.[33]

I finished teaching on 1 November, having reached seventy years in October. The youngster of that time is no longer so young! I would like to wish you the customary Happy New Year. But with all that is happening in the world (even in our poor country), I daren't pronounce this word 'happy', even under my breath.

I wish you good health, of course, and hope your work goes well. Please accept my warmest greetings with fond memories.

D 597 Plettenberg – Pasel 11C
10 February 1980

Dear Prof. Norberto Bobbio
Dear and esteemed colleague

On 23 January, I received your friendly and meaningful letter of 4 January. I read it with profound emotion and sincere appreciation for your loyal and repeated memory of the Berlin years. Our common experiences and the events we have lived through, typical of a risky science, have laid the basis for a particular form of friendship. By profession, we are both jurists and not revolutionaries, and I only regret not having had the pleasure of coming to see you in person and repeating by word of mouth the admiration that I have publicly declared for your *De cive*.

I was particularly touched that you mentioned my short book *Ex captivitate*. This interest in me displayed by a travelling companion is something of unparalleled value to me. I have taken the liberty of enclosing the Spanish edition of my memoirs, as a sign of my appreciation. In the German edition, there was of course no *Prólogo a la edición Española*. The remorse shown at the end of Hobbes's autobiographical poem will say more to you, my dear and esteemed colleague, than to any other reader, because you are a great Hobbesian scholar and go-between.

With best wishes for your retirement, I wish you good health and hope your work goes well. My regards with fond memories.

The events of 1968 destroyed the quiet life into which Professor Bobbio had withdrawn. The epicentre of the earthquake was Turin itself. On 27 November 1967, the students' movement decided to occupy Palazzo Campana, and remained in occupation for a month, until the police cleared them out between Christmas and New Year. Curiously, the ruling class failed to understand the importance of an event that sparked off protests which were to spread to all the universities like a contagion, expressing a generation's rebellion and political grievances in an unrepeatable cultural upheaval: La Stampa *devoted only a brief article to it, four columns at the bottom of the page for local news.*

We academics were also completely taken by surprise. Personally I thought that the centre-left government was by then well established, and that our institutions were entering a period of greater democracy and more rapid modernization. Contrary to what is argued by neo-liberals, the country was decidedly under the influence of the United States in relation to the world of social sciences, and certainly not of Marxism. A work that reflects this attitude was Gino Martinoli's *The University as a Business Enterprise*,[34] which appeared in 1967, and starting from the premise that Italian universities were very unproductive, as Aldo Visalberghi wrote in the introduction. It proposed to apply the theory of corporate organization to the temples of learning. What happened was that the students revolted precisely because they did not want universities reduced to corporations. I was conscious of the fact that the protests were aimed at real failings, particularly in the relationship between teachers and students, but not to the point of justifying a state of collective folly: self-managed courses, in which students would decide what to study, and would simply bring *papers* to exams, which had been written by them not individually but as a group, on current affairs such as the Vietnam War, the Chinese Revolution or the Prague Uprising. I was against group exams and group marks, because, as I said at the time, an exam is an act of individual responsibility. But this was not what they wanted to hear. Above all, I was against the aggressive language that often accompanied the protesters' demands, permeated their documents and filled the pages of *Lotta Continua* (and on occasions the aggression was not only verbal). That newspaper was delivered to my home every day, and I believe that I am one of the few who has the complete collection of its issues.

Unfortunately, we university teachers were unprepared for confronting the rebellion: the protests came crashing in on us without the least expectation. As I have said, I expected an increasingly rapid normalization of our democracy. We witnessed its crisis precisely at the time when we thought the country was moving towards becoming a conventional democracy. In the evolution towards a stable democracy, something happened that no one had imagined: the explosion of revolutionary hysteria fraught with terrible dangers (as was to be proved later with the outbreak of terrorism). For intellectuals of my generation and experience, it was not only surprising but outrageous to question the democracy that had resulted from the Resistance. We should not forget that the rector Allara, had been appointed by the Committee of National Liberation. This explains why some of us believed that the protesters had adopted a fascist approach, although I personally was not of that opinion. 'You are rejecting the democracy that brought you up free' was the reproach that the protesters of 1968 had to face. Perhaps the most talked-about and symbolic case was Franco Venturi, who had been one of the leading figures in the Piedmontese Resistance and editor of the newspaper *Giustizia e Libertà*, from 1945 to 1946. He rejected all the protests as a fascist provocation. He was one of Italy's greatest historians, and yet he was reduced to giving lectures to a handful of students who remained loyal to him. In reality, the protesters were not rejecting the Resistance, but accusing us of having betrayed its revolutionary ideals. More precisely, they were accusing the communists of this, and reproaching them for having lost their revolutionary momentum. Mao's China had replaced Brezhnev's Soviet Union as the ideal country.

I cannot avoid mentioning that, in my case, the conflict between professor and student was paralleled by a family conflict, which in some ways made it more dramatic, but in other ways less so. Luigi, my eldest son, was one of the leaders of the student movement. He had become the secretary of Interfacoltà, the student representative body, which the left took control of for the first time in 1967. The left-wing slate, UGI, which included communists and socialists, had defeated the 'Coalition', a grouping of Catholic students. He was the one who signed the edicts to the rector, the deans, the Board of Governors and the Senate. I can remember an unruly confrontation in the main hall between the Senate and the various groupings in the student movement with their leaders, including Luigi. The rector, Allara, was huddled on the cathedra where he usually gave his lectures: he was pale, subdued and incapable of understanding what was going on. I also remember a dramatic phone call, while I was attending an Einaudi editorial committee meeting, the well-known 'Wednesdays' at Einaudi: 'Listen Bobbio, you must do something, because the room where we were holding the Board of Governors' meeting has been occupied by the students, and your son is among them. They are preventing us from getting on with our work.' Of course, I told him that there was absolutely nothing I could do. I did not have any 'political' influence over my son, and even if I had had, I would not have used it. The only time that I asked him to moderate his attitude in order to avoid embarrassment to me, was at the inauguration of the 1968–9 academic year, at which, in accordance with tradition, the Interfacoltà secretary was supposed to give a speech. The previous year, we had witnessed an awkward scene, because Allara had driven off the student representative before he had managed to finish his speech. I have to say that Luigi did not want to upset me, and the event passed off without incident.

There are a few slight traces of Bobbio's involvement in the controversies of 1968 in his bibliography: four articles published in Resistenza *between January and June of 1968, in which he comments on the shortcomings of Italian universities.*[35] *He had direct experience of a confrontation with the student movement when he accepted the appointment to the Organizing Committee, along with Marcello Boldrini of the Catholic University and Beniamino Andreatta of Bologna University, which was set up to oversee and direct the College of Social Sciences in Trento, as it switched in 1968 from a provincial college to a state-run university faculty: it was to be one of the major flashpoints in the Italian student revolts.*[36]

Over the nearly thirty years that divide us from the upheaval of 1968, there have been many reminiscences and many explanations of that cultural and political fault-line which stands out as a unique event in the second half of this century. The final episode of the unrest affecting society and behaviour that started in the late fifties and early sixties is reflected in the events of 1968: it marked the end of a long process, but the protest movement did leave its own enduring imprint of new and radical features. However, in the long term, trends were to go in the opposite direction to the social and political projects that the protests fed on, as Paul Ginsborg has written: 'The essential values that they put forward – anti-capitalism, collectivism and egalitarianism – were to be defeated.'[37]

In the two years of my Trento appointment, the student movement was constantly in a state of upheaval. The protests were aggravated in Trento, a city famous for its Counter-Reformation Council, both because it had no university tradition and because the college that had been founded a few years before was devoted exclusively to teaching sociology, a discipline that was very attractive at the time on account of its novelty and the (vain) hopes it instilled in the young. Add to that the fact that entrance was possible from technical colleges and business schools, which, before the reform liberalizing university entrance, only qualified entrance to the faculties of economics and business. The young came in from all over Italy, and when they arrived in swarms, particularly at exam time, they were living in complete freedom, away from their families. The student protest found very fertile ground for its expansion.

Within a few years, thousands had registered as students. Although those who actually resided in the city, thanks to friendly halls of residence, were only a small part of those registered, they still constituted a quite large group for the city. Moreover, they had few forms of entertainment and spent all their time together, very frequently, given the mood of that time, in political assemblies. It was often up to us to meet them when, in their tempestuous meetings, they presented us with their demands with fervid and harsh words that did not stop short of insults. Fortunately there were verbal clashes, sometimes not without comic aspects. I remember one day in which Andreatta, the youngest of us three, jumped to his feet quite suddenly at the lecture stand in order to take better control of the situation, and laughter broke out, which reduced the tension.

As a member of the Organizing Committee, I was part of the Faculty Committee, made up of about thirty full-time lecturers from other universities. When Boldrini died the following year, I had to take over as dean. Our meetings were endless, and often lasted the entire day. Every now and then, we would be interrupted by the more unruly elements who would stream into the room where we were holding our meetings without so much as a by your leave. There was always some reason or other for protesting. We tend to forget now that the most extreme group used to called itself the 'Katangans': the name itself was not exactly reassuring.[38]

Fortunately, we teachers were a very close-knit group. Our sense of common purpose was partly the result of the impression we had of being in a fortress under siege. My colleagues, who were mostly much younger than I, had more of a taste for change. I got on very well with them, and I have fond memories of those meetings, in spite of the fact that they were tiring, just as I have fond memories of the periods I spent in the city. I was also part of the Board of Governors, chaired with an iron fist, but also much wisdom, by Bruno Kessler, who had been one of the principal campaigners for setting up the institution. The administrative manager was the patient Doctor Tarcisio Andreolli, who never lost his temper. Kessler died young a few years ago, after having become a Christian democrat senator. Indeed, our last meeting was in the Senate many years later.

The committee's task was to set up a normal Faculty Committee made up of at least three permanent lecturers. The first we appointed

1. Bobbio (third from left) next to his brother Antonio, with his cousins Norberto and Luigi Caviglia at Rivalta Bormidia in the old family house (summer of 1916).

2. Fifth year D'Azeglio School, 1923–4 academic year. Bobbio is the third from the left in the second row. First at the top on the left is Ugo Borgogno, and the penultimate in the same row is Giorgio Agosti.

3. On the terrace of the house in Rivalta with Leone Ginzburg, who is standing second from left. Bobbio is the fifth from the left in the same row (taken towards the end of the twenties).

4. Bobbio with his cousins, Norberto and Bicetta, dressed up in old house-clothes at Rivalta.

5. Professor Zini's guests at Zoagli in the summer of 1933. Franco Antonicelli is in the foreground and Bobbio is directly behind him.

6. Drawing by Renato Gottuso that records one of the early clandestine meetings of the Liberal-Socialist Movement in Umberto Morra's villa near Cortona (Meteliano), in 1939. From the left: Bobbio, Luporini, Capitini, Morra. Foreground: Calogero and the back of Gottuso's head.

7. The wedding of Bobbio and Valeria Cova in the San Carlo Church in Turin on 28 April 1943.

8. Bobbio with his first child, Luigi, who was born on 16 March 1944.

9. With Guido Calogero at the Rencontres Internationales de Genève
(September 1953)

10. A photo of the trip to England (November – December 1945). Second to the right of Bobbio is Roberto Ago and second to the left is Professor Mario Sarfatti, an exile in England and the group's leader.

11. Trip to China. Tomb of the hero We-Fe in Hangchow (October 1955).

12. The First Congress of the National Popular Book Centre in Turin on 30 October 1950. Augusto Monti is on Bobbio's left, and Diego Novelli can be seen between them.

13. On the Peace March with Fausto Amodei on 24 September 1961.

14. At the Italian section of the Bertrand Russell Peace Foundation with Joyce Lussu (Rome, 2 October 1965).

15. With Ada Gobetti and Franco Antonicelli for the visit by President Saragat (seen from the back) to the Gobetti Centre (Turin, March 1966).

16. At home with Valeria in May 1986.

17. The students' banner greeting Bobbio to the Law Faculty in Valparaiso (Chile), where he had been invited to give a lecture on democracy on 29 April 1986, when Chile was still under Pinochet's regime.

18. Vittorio Foa's eightieth birthday, with Natalia Ginzburg (Barolo, 4 October 1990).

19. The entire family at Valeria's and Norberto's golden wedding anniversary (Pino Torinese, 28 April 1993). At the back, from left: Marco (senior), Nicoletta, Luigi (whose hand is on Emanuele's shoulder), Marco (junior) and Simone. In the second row: Patrizia, Federico, Valeria, Norberto, Tommaso and Cia. At the front, Andrea.

was Francesco Alberoni, who came from the Catholic University of Milan and had passed that year one of the first selection processes for lecturers in sociology. He also became the director of the College of Social Sciences and suddenly found himself in contact with a mass of students that was not easy to control. He managed to tame the beast by taking control and then on occasions letting it run wild with a free rein, as it were.

The student movement was a libertarian movement. However, one of the liberties that it demanded loudest, indeed with such a deafening roar that it nearly always got what it wanted, was the freedom from the hard grind of study and the strictures of exams. The most detested lecturer was the extremely mild-mannered Mario Volpato who taught mathematics, a subject for which you could not study and pass exams by yet another research group on Vietnam or Black Power. You had to study it, and many could not manage it. Exasperated by the continuous attacks against him and not being responsible for the difficult nature of the subject he taught, he retired and left us.

The student leaders we mainly had to deal with were Mauro Rostagno and Marco Boato. The period of Curcio was over, and I do not remember ever having met him. Both Rostagno and Boato were good speakers, who were listened to by their comrades but also by us. Many years later, Boato became a senator, and we met again in the Senate, our ancient disagreements long forgotten. As is well known, Rostagno tragically died in Sicily fighting against the Mafia, and as usually happens in Italy, to date nothing has been found out about the cause and the authors of that crime.

Every year, the number of students grew exponentially, quite out of proportion to the capacity of the university and of the city itself. The citizens of that peaceful, quiet, well-mannered city found it difficult to put up with them. 'Sociologist' became an insult in local parlance. Kessler, who was the key person responsible for the institution, took the decision, or rather was forced to take the decision, to introduce a fixed number of student places at the end of the 1969–70 academic year. The Board of Governors approved the decision, and it was up to me to announce this reform to an extremely crowded and hostile assembly. I was embarrassed to do it, because I knew just how unpopular this move would be. I had to make a virtue of necessity. Meanwhile, we had managed to obtain other lecturers for the permanent staff from further selection procedures, and so the 1970–1 academic year started with a properly constituted Faculty Committee. Consequently our committee was dissolved at the end of the year. The adventure in Trento was over. I still have a polite letter, which Kessler sent me on 2 February 1971, thanking me and informing me that student numbers had settled down at around 3,200 and that lessons were proceeding in an entirely normal manner.

I had been to Trento many years before in April 1943 on my honeymoon no less, and in search of a rare manuscript of Tommaso Campanella's *Città del sole*. I have also returned at other times in recent years, once to attend a conference on the far from inflammatory subject of the theory of normative systems, organized by Professor Giuliano di Bernardo. By then the memory of those tumultuous years seemed very distant.

I am convinced that the hostility towards all forms of traditional power, the radical transformation of relations between the sexes, and the subjective value of political commitment all arose from a profound trauma which had affected the left in Italy. The crisis of 1968, at least in Italy, was the result of a split that ran right through the sixties. The crisis in the Italian Communist Party following 1956 and the Socialist Party's participation in the government coalition opened up a vacuum which was taken up by a new party, the PSIUP [the Italian Socialist Party of Proletarian Unity]. This party was created in 1964 when the left wing of the Socialist Party finally split off from the main party led by Nenni. It included people like Vittorio Foa and Lelio Basso. In Turin, there was Gianni Alasia who had experienced a harsh workerist experience. PSIUP in Turin had been a breeding ground for many of the young participants in 1968: they had no time for social-democrats who had allied themselves with the Christian Democrats, and equally no time for the Marxist–Leninist orthodoxy of the Communists. A second split had been caused as a reaction to the Chinese Cultural Revolution. Mao's star was rising, and it was the time when China was discovered, while the USSR, following the end of the Khrushchev era and the beginning of the Brezhnev one, represented the end of any hope of renewal. One of the protest groups, *Servire il popolo* ['To serve the people'], considered Mao's China to be the ideal model. The Chinese Revolution was the myth to which the majority of the protesters looked. I remember my discussions with Laura De Rossi, Luigi's first wife and an enthusiastic supporter of the Cultural Revolution and the Red Guards. She held up to me as an example to be copied the re-education of old teachers from the period of colonial bourgeoisie who were forced to clean lavatories. It seemed to me at the time, and still does today, that this was one of the many forms of revolt by children against their parents. When I was young, the students used to sing 'Giovinezza'.[39] That too had been a generational rebellion: the sons, who chose impetuous fascism, against their liberal and socialist fathers, who wished to return to their peacetime occupations after the disruption of war.

Giulio Einaudi gave a lively and critical account of my attitude to the events of 1968 at my eighty-seventh birthday celebrations, which coincided with the publication of my last book, *Old Age and Other Essays*.[40] Einaudi reminded us that I had intended a final chapter for *Ideological Profile of Twentieth-Century Italy*, which I wrote in 1968 and published in 1969, and that chapter which was never written was to be entitled 'A useless freedom'.[41] 'What was the prevailing mood', asked Einaudi, 'which induced you to think that liberty, so painfully achieved in Italy, could be useless? You, who had devoted such passion to teaching, could not endure the acritical extremisms that culminated in the student movement.' He reminded me of a letter I sent him in September 1968 in response to the enthusiasm he and some of his colleagues had expressed in relation to the student movement.

> Culture is intellectual balance, critical reflection, discernment, and horror of all simplifications, Manichaeism and partiality.
>   Above all, I did not believe that I would have to repeat this to you and to my friends at the publishing house, because we have learnt together to appreciate the value of intellectual freedom, not without difficulties and sufferings.

I was shocked and seriously worried by the verbal aggression of the protesters. But at the time, I was far from thinking that the extremist fringes would shift from verbal aggression, of which I had experienced so much at Trento, to physical violence. In January 1971, when I was taking part in a counter-inauguration of the judicial year in Brescia, organized by the periodical produced by left-wing magistrates, *Quale Giustizia*, I expressed my conviction that the violence of these revolutionary groups was purely verbal, and only right-wing subversives were responsible for terrorist acts. The Piazza Fontana Massacre, which I never doubted to be the act of extreme right-wing groups, helped and protected by the secret services, had occurred a little over a year before (in December 1969). I gave a speech at the Eliseo Theatre in Rome on 14 November 1971, on behalf of the University Teachers' Defence Committee for Giuseppe Pinelli and Pietro Valpreda. In that speech, I complained that some magistrates had done everything they could to make the official version of the massacre in Milan sound credible.[42] A few years later, in 'La democrazia e il potere invisibile', an article on this subject to which I have returned many times, I expressed my firm belief that Italian democracy was being undermined by dark forces, particularly within the secret services, in view of the Piazza Fontana Massacre and the conclusions of the first trial (but more reasons were to come later):

I will limit myself to restating the suspicion we were left with after the trial's conclusion, that state secrecy was used to protect the secrets of the anti-state. I would like to refer back to the Piazza Fontana Massacre, even at the risk of appearing still wrapped up in a remote event (not so much remote as removed from view), which may be returning to haunt us. I am doing so, because the decline of our democratic system started then, that is to say, at the moment in which an *arcanum*, in its proper sense of a concealed and mysterious fact, suddenly and unexpectedly became part of our collective life, throwing it into confusion. It has since been followed by other events that were no less serious and are still incomprehensible.[43]

I have not changed my opinion. Many court proceedings were devoted to finding the guilty parties over many years, until the ruling of the Court of Appeal in Catanzaro, on which I made the following comment in a Resistance publication:

> The Catanzaro ruling has provoked surprise and indignation around the country. If you reflect on the various stages through which these lengthy proceedings have passed over many, many years, you get a feeling of vertigo. I am not so much talking about the various stages in the legal process as different theories that have been put forward at those stages. There are four theories: (1) those responsible for the massacre were anarchists; (2) those guilty for the massacre were fascists (with the complicity of the secret services); (3) those guilty were both anarchists and fascists; (4) neither the fascists nor the anarchists are guilty. Everyone has been acquitted. It would seem a farce, a macabre farce, if it were not for the reality of those who died and have had no justice.[44]

The Piazza Fontana Massacre was followed by other outrages, and this repetition of criminal acts was given a name that encapsulated them all: the 'strategy of tension'. I was not totally convinced that this term was appropriate, and I have often discussed it with my friend Franco Ferraresi, who has long been investigating this question and is the author of the most informed book on the history of right-wing massacres in Italy,[45] and in a lengthy correspondence with Falco Accame, an academic who has been looking at the strategy.[46] I argued that there was only sense in talking about a strategy if there was a well-ordered series of actions aimed at a single purpose, carried out by an organized group. But is there a clearly defined purpose for terrorists? Not knowing exactly what their objective is, we attempt to establish it by using a word which is both vague and misleading: 'tension'. However, the use of such an obscure word is the very proof of how little we know as we vainly blunder around. In the meantime, the anxiety of our powerlessness increases.

I returned to the argument in the preface I wrote to the sentence of remittal for the Bologna Station Massacre written by two courageous investigating magistrates, Vito Zincani and Sergio Castaldo. I denounced the incredible, perverse and systematic attempts by the secret services to mislead the inquiries, and argued that they 'belonged to the state and not the anti-state, and their task was not to assist subversion but to offer all the means, which only a secret organization can have at its disposal, in order to fight against it'. I continued:

> Obstructing the course of justice can take many forms, all of which appear to have been used, including the most perfidious: . . . failure to pass on information, providing information too late by artfully delaying it, misinformation, slanted information, even intentionally false or falsified information, or, to use the jargon, 'leaving a false trail' . . . The most outrageous and morally despicable cases are where there has been a conscious attempt, with a precise political purpose, to shift the investigations from one subversive group to another in order to protect the guilty and throw the blame onto innocent persons who are disliked for political reasons. It should be remembered that, to date, all these attempts to lead the investigations astray have gone in one particular direction: there is proof that in some cases there have been attempts to ascribe atrocities carried out by the right to groups on the left, while the opposite has never occurred.[47]

When the last terrorist bombs exploded during the night of 20 July 1993 (now that the Soviet system has fallen, there should not be any reason for right-wing terrorism to continue), I commented the very evening after the event that we were going through one of the most tragic moments in the history of our Republic: 'Italy has always been a tragic country, in spite of the fact that the masks by which we are known to foreigners are the comic masks of the cheerful servant and his master who has been duped. A tragic country, even if the majority of Italians do not know it or pretend not to know it. Or perhaps I should say that they do not want to know it.'[48]

A few years before, another terrible incident shook the conscience of Italians when on 23 December 1984, there was a terrific explosion on the Naples to Milan express. At the time, I asked myself what was the purpose of these acts of terrorism, and I could not find a convincing reply:

> So far the massacres have had no effect other than to disseminate panic, provoke indignation and cause grief whose private consequences are infinitely greater than the public and political ones. Would the course of events in our country have been different if these massacres

had not taken place? Would we have had more stable governments, less controversial policies, or different levels of inflation or employment? Wouldn't then an earthquake have been equally destabilizing? Do not innocent victims also die in a shipwreck?[49]

The murder of my friend Carlo Casalegno, the assistant editor on *La Stampa*, painfully opened my eyes to left-wing terrorism, if, that is, my eyes were not already open. I immediately wrote about it in our newspaper, recalling our long friendship and 'our shared passion for democracy'. On the first anniversary of his death, I again repeated the question, to which I can find no answer, on the meaning and consequences of a terrorist action, and pointed out the disproportion between the enormity of the event and its result. I asked myself:

> What result? What is the result, other than the actual reality of death, which does not go beyond itself? An exemplary punishment? But a punishment implies some guilt, and always implies proportion between the crime and the punishment . . . What other message can these executioners be giving, if not the message of hate, death and, if justice is proportionality, the weighing up of right and wrong and balance between crime and punishment, than absolute injustice?[50]

The purpose is certainly to create terror, but 'if I investigate my mental reactions to this event, I have to say that terror is not the dominant feeling, but if anything, it is horror, a very much deeper, more indescribable and almost unfathomable emotion'. I attempted to explain the difference: 'I have terror of a thunderstorm, because a lightning bolt might hit me on the way. On the other hand, I have horror of the sight of blood, of a child slowly killing a defenceless cat, or of the spectacle of dead bodies abandoned on a battlefield.'[51]

A few months earlier, after some jurors deserted the trial in Turin against the Red Brigades as a response to the murder of the elderly and gentlemanly president of the Turin Order of Lawyers by that terrorist organization, Eugenio Montale agreed with the jurors' decision. This declaration provoked a debate on 'Intellectuals and fear', to which I contributed with an article in which I asserted the need to be pessimistic:

> I am quite happy to leave the pleasure of being optimistic to fanatics, by which I mean those who long for catastrophe, and to the fatuous, by which I mean those who think that everything comes right in the end. Today pessimism is a civic duty, if you will allow me to use that impolitic term. It is a civic duty, because only radical and rational pessimism can induce some slight reaction in those who, on one side

or the other, have shown themselves to be unaware that when reason slumbers, monsters are created.[52]

In 1972, I was appointed to the chair of political philosophy at the newly created Faculty of Political Sciences. I found myself teaching in a new environment, whose teaching resources had been stretched by the twin liberalization of university entrance and of study plans. Even the physical environment had changed, as, in the meantime, the arts faculties had been transferred from Palazzo Campana to Palazzo Nuovo, a rectangular building of steel and glass which was soon to display all its architectural inadequacy under the burden of the mass university. Thus, following the disturbances of 1968, a second period in my teaching career started in 1972 and lasted until 1979.

The invitation to transfer to Political Sciences was partly due to the fact that I had been teaching political science since 1962. The subject had a great tradition in Italy, thanks to Gaetano Mosca, author at the turn of the century of a work now considered a classic: *Elementi di scienza della politica*. The final edition, which was published in 1923 with an introduction by Croce, was reviewed by Einaudi. It was a text before its time, and indeed, in the thirties, it was translated into English and published in the United States, which was unusual for an Italian book of political essays. The success of political science faded in our country under fascism. I believe that the first two chairs in this subject were mine in Turin and Giovanni Sartori's in Florence, which he obtained as the first person to pass the university lecturer selection process in the discipline. My courses dealt with the principal argument in political science: political parties. I used the text of one of the major European constitutionalists, Maurice Duverger, who had been translated into Italian by the publisher Edizioni di Comunità. Of my students, I remember with particular emotion Paolo Farneti, who died tragically on the mid-August public holiday of 1980, in a car accident.[53]

When the Faculty of Political Sciences was established in Turin in 1969, the chair of political philosophy was given to Alessandro Passerin d'Entrèves, who came from Jurisprudence. Born in 1902, he retired in 1972. He asked me to take his place: 'We must establish a tradition. You cannot refuse me.' Even though I never wanted administrative academic posts, indeed I detested them, I had to be dean for three years after d'Entrèves's departure, as I was the oldest lecturer. The course that was most successful and most widely known, was published as a textbook,[54] in which I studied how the categorization of forms of government had changed over the centuries, starting with the famous classical tripartition between monarchy, aristocracy and democracy, and finishing in the nineteenth century with Marx. I also taught a course on the concept of revolution, using book 5 of Aristotle's *Politics*, which deals with 'constitutional changes', as my starting point. Michelangelo Bovero, who was then my assistant and is now my successor, collected notes from the best students, and these produced two large volumes, which I have never had the patience to revise and prepare for publication. My career in university teaching ended in 1979, at the age of seventy, after a period of over forty years.

The last lesson was on 16 May, a Wednesday. There was a large bunch of flowers on the lectern with a note: 'From the students of your last course'. Bobbio quoted Max Weber: 'University teaching is neither for demagogues nor prophets.' When interviewed by La Stampa, *the professor declared: 'The last lesson was a natural and predictable event. In life, we are only taken unawares by extraordinary events.'*[55]

6

Political Battles

In December 1957, a conference was held for the defence of democratic freedoms at the workplace. This was in the middle of the 'tough years at Fiat' as the communist trade unionists Emilio Pugno and Sergio Garavini called them in their embittered book. The fifties were the decade of the country's great economic reconstruction, but also of the trade union's historic defeat: 'All the elements of paternalism and discrimination were successfully put into effect at that time: attacks on the right to strike, compulsion through threats to jobs, political discrimination, and the encouragement of company-run trade unions with no-strike agreements. The mechanisms of the "Cold War" were used to the full, and at their heart was the threat of "American orders"'.[1] Fiat became an isolated reality within Italian industry, labour relations based on discrimination between 'constructive' and 'destructive' elements: 'the CISL benefited from the situation by adopting American methods of company bargaining and adopting a loyal and co-operative attitude in its dealings with the company. On the other hand, the CGIL[2] lost ground both because of the continuing redundancies carried out on a strictly political basis, and because of changes within the working class which were becoming increasingly evident.'[3] In 1955, FIOM[4] published a white paper entitled *Documents Concerning the Attack on the Rights of Liberty of Fiat Workers*. In 1958, the magazine *Nuovi Argomenti* published an *Inquiry into Fiat*.[5] The Turin conference for the defence of democratic liberties in factories was organized to break the isolation in which the class-based trade union found itself: 'Workers knew that nothing could stop their inclusion in the first mass redundancies, if Fiat took a dislike to them for political or trade-union reasons.'[6] The aim of the conference was typical of left-wing initiatives at the time: that of creating a dialogue between factory workers and intellectuals. This was because the city was divided, as Diego Novelli, a journalist for *L'Unità* at the time and the communist mayor in 1975, pointed out: 'In those days, Turin lived two parallel lives: the life of workers, the trade union and the comrades, and the other life, that of the bourgeoisie, which seemed impervious to the hardships of the proletariat.'[7]

I took part in the 1957 conference and gave a speech against political discrimination in the factories, which was published by *Risorgimento*, a publication produced by the Catholic Resistance, edited by Enrico Martini Mauri, the former commander of the Autonomous Brigade of the Langhe.

> This conference on civil liberties in the factories must create the opportunity to discuss one of the most serious problems of contemporary constitutional law: the problem of defending libertarian rights not only in relation to public authorities, but also in relation to powers that continue to be called private. A constitution that has solved the former problem but not the second, cannot be considered a democratic constitution. In reality, the constitutions of the current democratic states were born from a centuries-long struggle against the state, that is against those, who having conquered the highest power over men, were the only ones in a position to abuse it. They are the result of a slow and gradual conquest of individual liberties, and therefore increasingly wide spheres of action in which citizens are able to determine their own behaviour without reference to norms other than those dictated by their own conscience. Briefly, they represent the citizen's guarantee against the abuse of power by the state. The fundamental meaning of a democratic constitution is the assertion that power over citizens, whatever it is and by whatever group or person it is exercised, must have legally established limits, and nothing is more inimical to the implementation of stable and peaceful coexistence amongst citizens, which is the purpose of the state, than power that is unlimited in its nature and arbitrary in its implementation.
>
> Now, the affirmation of civil liberties would be a dead letter and the prime objective of constitutional guarantees would be void, if the citizen's liberties that have been upheld against the organs of the state, were not applied and upheld against private powers. One of the distinguishing features of modern capitalist society is the concentration of enormous powers in the hands of private institutions. We realize that these powers are so great as to suspend, hamper or indeed render worthless some fundamental liberties, which until now only appeared threatened by organs of state power. Our constitution recognizes and protects religious freedom. Suppose a large enterprise makes recruitment

of its employees conditional upon their profession of a certain religion. In this case, citizens would be free to profess their own religion as far as the state is concerned, but not as far as the enterprise is concerned. I ask myself: in this situation does religious freedom exist or not? Our constitution recognizes and protects freedom of thought. Suppose a large enterprise makes recruitment of its employees conditional upon their support for a certain political tendency? In this case too, citizens would be free to hold their own political opinion in relation to the state, but would no longer be able to do so in relation to the private enterprise. I ask myself: in such a situation does political freedom exist or not? You might object that the private body, whatever it does, does not impose a certain belief or political opinion, it merely considers one or the other to be a condition for obtaining work. I would reply that you could argue that even the most tyrannical state does not impose a belief or an opinion, but merely restricts itself to setting certain conditions for being considered citizens with full rights, that is to say, it gives the freedom of choice to accept a certain belief or opinion which it imposes, or to end up in prison.

A democratic constitution is one that not only affirms civil liberties, but also creates bodies and laws to ensure that those liberties are effective and safeguarded against everyone. When the dikes built against abuses of power rupture or threaten to rupture, it is capable of making immediate repairs and raising new defences. Our constitution makes provisions for dealing with this danger. But for this danger to be confronted, three things are necessary: the awareness that the danger exists, an equally clear investigation into the remedial action, and the agreed will to live together in a democratic society.[8]

The problem which I was posing then was a real problem, which was to lead to the demands for liberty in the factories and the condemnation of all forms of political discrimination within factories. It was to be dealt with by the Workers' Statute, brought before Parliament by the minister Giacomo Brodolini and passed on 20 June 1969.

In that period, I was no longer concerned with politics, as I devoted my time exclusively to my studies and teaching. I became involved with that conference because I had always maintained a dialogue with the left. The magazine for which I used to write, *Nuovi Argomenti*, edited by Alberto Carocci and Alberto Moravia, was also interested in the conference. However, it was an isolated incident. It is true that, at the time, we lived in a divided world, and an intellectual devoted to his studies and teaching had very few opportunities to encounter the realities of industrial work, not out of any lack of interest or from personal choice, but simply because these two worlds, the intellectual one and the working-class one, had very few channels of communication. Moreover, I would not say that things have changed very much.

My return to political activity came about many years later, when the Italian Socialist Party and the Italian Social-Democratic Party decided to merge into a single party. As I was a democratic socialist, I believed that it was my duty to make a personal contribution to a development that appeared to open a completely new phase in political life.

In 1966, the XXXVII Congress of the Italian Socialist Party and the XV Congress of the Italian Social-Democratic Party both came to the decision to merge. A few days later, on 30 October, the new party, which took the name of United Socialist Party (PSU), was founded at the Sports Centre in Rome which was packed with a large crowd. 'Perhaps the largest assembly in the name of Italian socialism ever', wrote the newspapers. There was talk of 30,000 people squeezed into the large arena for socialism's constituent assembly.[9] Bobbio was among them.

This was the high point for the centre-left. In February, Aldo Moro's third government was appointed, with Nenni as the deputy prime minister. Gianni Agnelli had been asked to replace Vittorio Valletta as chairman of Fiat. In May, the Chamber of Deputies had passed a law specifying the situations in which dismissals and redundancies could take place. When Il Mondo was closed in the spring, Bobbio wrote to Mario Pannunzio in order to express his regret at the newspaper's passing, even though he had never actually written for it. Pannunzio replied at length:

Rome, 12.3.66

Dear Bobbio,

Thank you for your friendly letter. I would like to be able to reply to your questions, but I fear that I am not up to it. Perhaps *Il Mondo* has gone on for too long. Newspapers like this one, which set themselves the task not only of observing events, but also of commenting on them, making appeals and taking initiatives, have an irredeemably difficult life. You only have to look around: any enterprise in Italy that gives the slightest sign of a moral or political commitment always encounters a strange hostility, which is inured to conflict, tenacious and invincible. In order to confront it, you need continuous drive, patient ardour, genuine agreement amongst a large number of people animated by the same goals. But far from it! The democratic left is divided, quarrelsome and distrustful. The centre-left has demonstrated a high degree of immaturity and a lack of preparation. We are now experiencing a climate of lethargy and dissipation of our energies. The young, who until recently were many and full of energy, now devote themselves to private professions and read material lacking in political commitment. A newspaper is a kind of observatory, and seventeen years at *Il Mondo* has made me aware of incredible changes. For example, I remember the times of De Gasperi: conformism was dominant, but there were dozens of fervent and resolute 'protestants' who would not give up. Where are they now? Many of them have disappeared, and I would say that the most lively ones are no longer around.

But I'm not a pessimist. You are quite right: we need to reorganize the democratic left. We should all give it a bit of thought, and consider what is to be done. As far as I am concerned, I'm certain that something will come out of it. Just recently, with regret being expressed by so many friends over the demise of *Il Mondo*, I have felt that certain beliefs never go away, and it is our duty, as you say, 'to stimulate ideas and prepare'. I don't believe that I am the only one who feels this way.

Thank you again, my dear Bobbio. Excuse the long letter. Kind regards,

Mario Pannunzio[10]

The assembly proceedings were opened by Sandro Pertini. A message was received from Giuseppe Saragat, the president of the Republic. Pietro Nenni was elected president of the United Socialist Party, while Francesco De Martino, ex-PSI, and Mario Tanassi, ex-PSDI,[11] were appointed joint party secretaries. In the Charter of Unification, an attempt was made at a compromise between the Marxist tradition and the social-democratic one, in order not to leave too much political space to the left for the Communist Party and the Italian Socialist Party of Proletarian Unity. The new party espoused 'the doctrinal experiences, commencing from the fundamental Marxist one, and the political experiences that have matured over three-quarters of a century of class struggles, always hard-fought and often bloody'. They wanted to create 'a society freed from the contradictions and pressures arising from the division into classes produced by the capitalist system'. The following day, newspapers published a picture of Nenni smiling behind his thick glasses and standing between Tanassi and De Martino who were shaking hands. Unification was to last only two years. Bobbio's old friend, Vittorio Foa, who at the time found himself on the other side, wrote: 'The affirmation of an independent socialist position was not enough, they had to define its content beyond the alliance with the Christian Democrats. I often thought that the Socialists, once they had split from the Communists, should have developed their own "opposition". The united party's electoral defeat demonstrated that the independent socialist position was still only an intention.'[12]

I was not a member of the Socialist Party, but I was invited to the Constituent Assembly because I had signed an appeal for unification put forward by Aldo Garosci. I explained my reasons for joining the United Socialist Party in a statement written on behalf of a group of intellectuals who had been members of the Action Party. I did not get an opportunity to read the statement at the assembly but it was published in *Avanti!*. That was the only time I joined a party after the defeat of the Action Party, thus displaying an uncharacteristic trust and optimism. This time too, harsh realities were very quickly to prove them to be quite unwarranted.

Intellectuals have the natural tendency to form individual factions. This tendency can be easily explained, and has been studied and analysed exhaustively. I do not know how 'intellectual' can be defined, or if there is only one definition, but in general by intellectual we mean a person who embodies or should embody the critical spirit that is not appeased or should not be appeased by any fully worked-out or established doctrine: the intellectual disseminates doubts, and is impatient of all disciplines and unyieldingly spreads dissent.

In recent years, intellectuals have played this part to perfection, and they could not have done otherwise. In relation to political parties, they have been more on the outside than on the inside. They joined and they left. They were more at ease in small groups, which were parties in name but not in fact, and which they created and dissolved at will. They were a little to the right of the left and little to the left of the right, in the restless search for a position which did not correspond to that of the established power groups, like a roulette ball, if you'll excuse the slightly irreverent metaphor, which continues to jump around the roulette wheel in order to escape the demeaning and banal destiny of ending up on either red or black.

I am not saying that some of these groups did not fight memorable battles, and have not therefore made real and positive contributions to ordinary politics, albeit through their unconventional activities. Too often, however, they have remained on the margins, waiting and even more often displaying suspiciousness, a tendency towards recriminations and the attitude of someone who, unable to save the motherland, has decided at least to save his soul. It seemed that the only choice was between short-lived power at the price of one's own independence or the freedom of an ultimately dismal impotence.

Today, the creation of a great socialist and democratic party, through a reunification open to the whole range of the democratic left, promises to take up a broad enough space within our political spectrum to allow us to move around with freedom, without doctrinal prejudices, without sectarian strictures, in a single direction while starting from different points of view and perhaps safeguarding one's own vocation for being in the minority.

We need to distinguish between this vocation for being in the minority and a rigid, obstinate and sterile schismatic attitude.

Groups, small groups, tiny sects of initiated persons, and confraternities of flagellants or more often flagellators, all conform to the historical and moral necessity of the moment of torment, uncertainty and things falling apart. Today, they no longer have any reason to exist, as at the moment we are commencing the opposite process of converging towards common goals. This is all the more the case now we are convinced that the attraction of other parts of the political spectrum towards democratic socialism is inevitable and certain to increase in the current situation of Italy's democratic development.

I would also like to add that if the area of democratic socialism was not destined to increase, it would be a bad sign not only for socialism, but for democracy as well. For years, we have been in this strange situation of preaching commitment, and then immediately afterwards asking ourselves: 'commitment for whom?' Today, we believe that we can reply, without fear of contradicting ourselves and without too much self-deception, that the commitment to build a modern socialist and democratic party in our country is a commitment that is worth making, even though we have no guarantee that this experiment will turn out in accordance with our desires and our hopes. Indeed we might think that this experiment is going to be very difficult, but this is, if anything, a reason for not drawing back and not giving up hope before we take the first step. And that first step is to join the new party.

After twenty years of democratic life, albeit difficult and confused, and far from the ideal, democracy has definitely put down roots in our country. In order to distinguish between a regime that is accepted from one that is only obeyed, political scientists invoke the principle of legitimacy. Well the legitimacy of democracy in Italy today is taken for granted by most Italians. Democracy has always been hard-won in Italian history, and not just in 1945. The working-class movement has always made an indispensable contribution to its realization, one that was decisive in 1945.

. . .

At a time when we are building a democratic socialist party for our future, it is extremely important to become aware that the democracy we hold dear is the shared foundation of the house that we are building and in which we would hope to live for many years. This democracy is firmly linked to the history of socialism, at least in our country. It is equally important that those to our left acquire the same awareness.

In relation to socialism lacking in democracy, recent history is littered with terrible lessons, which it hands out with the pedantic severity of an inflexible teacher. So terrible that there is not a pupil, however obstinate, lazy or presumptuous, that has not been able to learn from them. I am sure that this lesson has even been learnt by those who cannot admit it or cannot admit it yet. Our old friend Hegel, that master of realism, would have said: 'the prattling falls quiet when faced with the well-founded counter-arguments of history'.

Today, we must hope that the 'well-founded counter-arguments of history' have convincingly taught us never to separate our enthusiasm for socialism from democratic practice. Togliatti used to say of the communists: 'We come from afar.' Well, we can say that we come from even farther away. But we must say it without self-importance. We have committed too many errors to set ourselves up as the authority. Both we and the communists cannot afford to turn our backs on each other: we are too closely packed together in the same boat which is by no means out of the storm. On the other hand, we will have proved ourselves good learners if we have taken on board this lesson on humility. Besides, my friends and I have one strength, which is that of not having any ambitions to follow, and still less any interests to defend. We look on political activity as a civic duty, one that is often disagreeable. Once we used to say that it was a duty to the nation, but now that our nation is the whole world, our duty is towards the great nation of all human beings held together by our common destiny of life and death.

In this nation, our place is on the side of the underprivileged, the oppressed, the victims and those who fight and die for freedom. By joining the united party, we are giving a voice to our original convictions, we are expressing the need for consistency, we are professing our faith and we are taking on a task. We are also articulating our hope that unification goes beyond the expediency from which it arises, and opens a path towards the democratic development of our country that is new, less arduous, safer and more direct.[13]

I returned to these arguments in an article published in January 1967 in *Resistenza*, a magazine founded by former members of the Action Party in Turin. The article was entitled 'After Unification'. Reading it now, you feel that it could be held up as an example or even a caricature of the difference between practice and theory. According to theory, or the interpretation that I gave of unification, unification came at the opportune moment for a push towards greater democracy in our political system. I even spoke of a necessary 'rationalization' of our system. I wrote:

In the current situation and for the foreseeable future, there is no room for either challenging the system at a global level or transforming it from inside, which has been the traditional aim of social-democratic parties ... From this point of view, socialist unification corresponds to a shift in the historical situation and can be considered part of a process of natural readjustment. Following the disarray into which Stalinism has fallen, there has been an increasing awareness of not only the instrumental but also the essential importance of formal democracy, that is to say that the rules of the game play an integral role as well as having procedural importance, and there needs to be prior agreement that they will be respected by everyone.

I concluded that:

> The fundamental problem for the left, in Italy and in other countries too, is to find the right point for grafting together the consolidation of democracy and the development of socialism. It is not an easy problem to resolve and probably it is a problem that only allows for stopgap solutions. However, it is a problem that must engage the efforts of all those who perceive the gradual unification of the Italian left as a process of rationalization which this time will involve the whole system and not just part of it.[14]

In theory the argument appeared flawless, but in practice events were soon to prove it wrong. My support for unification was based on association with the centre-left. I believed that the centre-left was the right choice for the future of the country, and I felt that the socialist wing of the coalition had to be strengthened by ending the arguments that divided the left.

The politician I most trusted was an old friend I have already mentioned, Antonio Giolitti. He was a communist deputy in the Constituent Assembly and the Chamber of Deputies, who left the Communist Party in 1957, transferring to the ranks of the socialist left. He was appointed Minister for Budgeting and Planning in the period 1963–4. I was under the false impression that the centre-left was capable of carrying out the wide-ranging reforms that our democracy needed. Unfortunately, the socialists had lost a lot of their strength in the 1964 split that created the Italian Socialist Party of Proletarian Unity.[15] I am convinced that this breakaway, which weakened the left in the coalition, was a serious mistake. I have always strongly believed that in order to strengthen Italian democracy, you needed to widen its base. This necessity, essential for the country, was made especially clear to me after the defeat of the Popular Front in 1948 and the battle over the *legge truffa* in 1953. Indeed, I viewed the centre-left as the realization of the old dream of a political alliance between democratic Catholics and democratic socialists: hadn't we always said that if Don Sturzo and Turati had come to an agreement, fascism would never have happened?

Our generation was obsessed with the danger of the right. We had arrived at the conclusion that fascism was, as Gobetti put it, the 'combination of all Italy's traditional sicknesses'. However, we also had to deal with the problem posed by the Communist Party and its difficulty in renouncing Stalinism once and for all. The awareness of this structural instability in Italian democracy convinced us that we had to achieve a political alliance between the democratic centre and the democratic left. We developed the idea that Italian democracy was fragile because its democratic components were divided. It was a question of putting in the past what Giovanni Sartori called 'polarized pluralism', so that those who considered themselves steadfastly and loyally democratic could come together and support Nenni's separation from the Italian Communist Party. Why couldn't the alliance that failed to materialize between Sturzo and Turati be achieved between Moro and Nenni? At that point, it became absurd to have a division between two socialist parties which both considered themselves democratic, and had both come to the conclusion that any form of alliance with the Communist Party was by then out of the question, even though they did so at different times. Reunification formally endorsed this process, which tended to stabilize our democracy.

Unfortunately, the birth of the new party proved to be based on a mistaken forecast. In the 1968 general elections, the unified party achieved an overall result that was lower than the one that the Socialist Party and the Social-Democratic Party would have obtained if they had submitted separate lists.[16] I believed that we had to be patient and learn to wait. But the politicians' fear of losing votes led to disagreements that ended up in the dissolution of the new party.[17] The fifth legislature from 1963 to 1968 was the last one to survive the full five-year term. After that came the short legislatures, which showed that democracy had been weakened rather than strengthened.

For the second time, following the failure of the Action Party, my direct involvement in political activity had turned out to be a resounding failure. The disappointment confirmed my belief that there is a profound difference between someone who chooses politics as a full-time activity and someone who is involved in something completely different and occasionally enters the political arena. I have kept the letter from Pietro Nenni, in which he asked me to be a candidate in the United Socialist Party's lists for the 1968 elections.

Rome, 15 December 1967

Dear Professor,

I have been talking to our mutual friends Garosci and Paonni of my sincere desire (and more importantly the party's interest) that you commit yourselves to taking part in the coming election campaign.

Paonni tells me of your instinctive aversion to public life. In that case, your candidacy for the Senate in the Central Turin constituency would ensure the party has your personal participation in the election campaign, while there would be little chance of election, although a senatorial constituency can switch unexpectedly, according to the personality of the candidate.

Dear Professor, please give it some thought, and if you say yes, you can count on it giving us all great pleasure.

Best regards and best wishes for the coming festivities, yours Nenni

I politely refused. I knew very well that I had no aptitude for political life. I also knew that entering politics would mean giving up my studies and my teaching, a sacrifice that would have been all the more serious at a time when university life was showing the early-warning signs of the coming upheavals of 1968. I explained this in my reply to Nenni dated 18 December:

Apart from my instinctive and uncontrollable reluctance to take an active part in politics, I currently find myself in a situation where it would be absolutely impossible from a moral point of view to accept this candidature.

As you know, protests have exploded in the universities more or less everywhere in Italy, but more seriously and acutely in Turin, and these are undermining the structure of our university which in any case was pretty antiquated. Our best students, those who are leading these protests, are demanding, and are right to demand, higher moral standards in the life of the university. In particular, they want greater commitment from the lecturers in the fulfilment of their academic duties. I am entirely on their side and against the majority of my colleagues. If this struggle has been radicalized during the year into forms of revolutionary extremism that are a worry to everyone who is concerned about the future of university education, this is due to the fact that too many lecturers are deaf to any demand that distracts them from their activities outside the university.

Just recently, we heard speeches in Parliament by university lecturers who upheld their right to be members of parliament and university lecturers at the same time. These speeches have once again outraged our more conscientious students, whom I meet on a daily basis. Italian universities can only be saved by lecturers who fulfil their duties conscientiously and with the required dedication. We have to realize that the majority of students are completely left to themselves once they go to university. The four or five years that they spend at university are for most of them an enormous waste of energy (I am mainly speaking of arts subjects). Only those who live through the reality of our universities are aware that we have reached breaking point.

For years I have been preaching in the desert. I have now taken the opportunity presented by these protests to contact student-workers and have given them a genuine and sincere undertaking to work together with them in order to put my teaching work on a new foundation. I believe that this is the only way to give justice to those who are defending a just cause, even though they do not always do so through legitimate means. I have prepared with them and for them a common

programme of multiple seminars which will require my constant attention. I cannot afford to fail when faced with students who have put me
to the test and colleagues who regard me with suspicion. Above all, I
cannot afford just now to take part in a political contest that would
distract me from work that I have freely undertaken and which would
appear to contradict my repeated attacks on the laxity of academic
practice.

Please understand these concerns of mine in the sense in which they
are intended, namely that I do not want to deny the university my
feeble but unshakeable energies, which would be wasted in an election
campaign to which I am not suited.

I was certain that my vocation was that of a scholar, and my place
in society was that of a teacher. I repeated this nearly ten years later
for the 1976 election, in a telegram to Francesco De Martino, then
general secretary of the Italian Socialist Party, and in a letter to the
Socialists' provincial office in Turin. I know myself well enough to
know that I am not suited to politics. On the whole, I have had very
few contacts with politicians. If anything, I have been in contact with
intellectuals in various parties. Lelio Basso was one of the few party
leaders with whom I met frequently and whom I considered a friend,
but, whilst maintaining our friendship, we were constantly in disagreement over which political policies should be implemented. We
met at the beginning of the thirties on a trip organized by Barbara
Allason on Easter Monday to her holiday home in Pecetto Torinese.
The purpose of the cheerful gathering of friends was to introduce
Basso and his wife, both very young at the time.

I doubt that I knew at the time that that young lawyer had written for
Rivoluzione Liberale, and was already well known as a political writer.
After that meeting, I heard him being referred to, during the years
of anti-fascist underground, in connection with the formation of a
clandestine group that had split from the Italian Socialist Party with
the intention of undergoing a profound renewal. This split created the
Movement of Proletarian Unity which recruited many friends whom
we would have liked to have had as comrades in the Action Party.
Lelio Basso was one of the founders of the movement and his name
was prominent amongst the most authoritative leaders of the groups
that opposed fascism. As my memory of events linked to the Liberation is still very sharp, and my memory of the following years in
which I returned to teaching and my studies is equally vague, I cannot
remember how we met up again.

Basso always considered himself a Marxist, but as is well known,
his Marxism was based on an interpretation of Rosa Luxemburg, who
rejected Bernstein's revisionism at the beginning of the century, and

later rejected Lenin's authoritarianism. At the beginning of the sixties, we had conversations and an exchange of letters about the possibility of publishing a collection of Luxemburg's writings that he had suggested to Einaudi and that he himself had translated on different occasions. In fact, his books on Luxemburg were published elsewhere, for reasons that I can no longer remember. I do, however, remember that I invited him to give a lecture on Rosa Luxemburg to inaugurate the academic year at the Piero Gobetti Research Institute, which comes in February, the month in which Gobetti died. He also maintained friendly relations with the centre, but relations between Basso and Gobetti himself could be the subject of a long and interesting study.

Basso was an accomplished orator whom I always admired and even slightly envied. He did not indulge in the usual rhetoric of politicians who are also lawyers. He was clear, concise, incisive and persuasive. He would have been a brilliant university lecturer. In fact, I was so convinced that I invited him twice to give seminars for students at the Institute of Political Science when, in the early sixties (with 1968 just round the corner), I realized that students wanted to hear other points of view, and that we needed to break the isolation of universities and bring them closer to society and the political struggle unfolding within it. Basso was the right man. His powerful political calling never distracted him from his studies, which enlivened his essays and speeches that were published in various Italian and foreign magazines. One of these, *Problemi del Socialismo*, quickly proved itself to be a weighty political magazine. Precisely because of his qualities as man of culture completely lacking in amateurishness, he was one of the few Italian politicians whose writings were widely published in foreign magazines, and was also known outside Italy for the work he did for the Peoples' Tribunal.[18]

However, I am also unsuited to politics, because I suffer from the academic's typical professional deficiency, that of being an eternal doubter. If you carry out research, especially in the field of human sciences, you can, once you have examined all the pros and cons, end your study with a question mark. My friends often reproach me for often ending my books with expressions of doubt. As can be seen, there are profound existential reasons that have contributed to keeping me from public office: a politician has to be a man of action, which I am not by any stretch of the imagination. If I have to choose between an active life and a contemplative one, I will always choose the latter, as I said at the launch of *Maestri e compagni*:

All [my friends and comrades] had a lively interest in politics, as I have said, but they were not politicians in the real sense of the word. Only occasionally did they become involved in actual political activity. Were they unpolitical? Yes, in a way.

> They were unpolitical in the narrow sense of the word, if by politics, you mean action within one's own citadel, one's own little citadel beyond which there are other citadels, each with its own walls, its own drawbridge and its own guards armed and ready to attack the enemy. With its own walls, and what's worse, with its own gods.[19]

The failure of the centre-left government convinced me that democracy in Italy had always had and was always going to have a difficult time, because it is squeezed between an extreme right and an extreme left, which hampers gradual steps forward. This was the thread running through the first draft of my *Profilo ideologico del Novecento*. In the sixties, questions about democracy were again settled in relation to the contribution that Marxism could provide, now that it had been revitalized by the explosion of youth movements: the question was whether the creation of a socialist democracy could in some way make use of the Marxist theory of the state. My response was that it was definitely not possible, as I explained in an article published in a book to celebrate Pietro Nenni's eightieth birthday by *Quaderni di Mondoperaio*, the Socialist Party's magazine edited by Federico Coen.[20] This gave rise to a debate that involved intellectuals across the whole of the left – socialists, communists, social-democrats and extra-parliamentarians – on the question: 'Is there a Marxist theory of the state?' This debate gave rise to my book *Which Socialism?*,[21] which I have defined as 'my second extramural outpouring', that is to my second book relating to beyond the walls of the academic citadel, after *Politica e cultura*. The part I played in the debate amongst socialists led to my personal involvement in the political battle that took the Italian Socialist Party out of the hands of Francesco De Martino and into those of Bettino Craxi.

Craxi was elected general secretary in 1976. The previous year had seen communist successes in the local elections. At the XL Congress (Rome, 2–7 March 1976), the socialists kept Francesco De Martino as general secretary. Strategy was based on the assumption that the parties of the left could achieve 51 per cent of the vote. But the factions led by Craxi and Mancini did not hide their preference for an alternative strategy, based on a belief that the balance of forces between the Communists and Socialists could shift back in their favour. In April, the Christian Democrats, with the support of the fascist party, the Italian Social Movement, defeated the bill on abortion. May brought the fall of Moro's government, which was made up solely of the Christian Democrats with the external support of the Socialists. At the elections called early on 20 June 1976, the left achieved 46.79 per cent of the vote: the best result since the war, but the Italian Socialist Party had to face up to 'a disappointing election result'.[22] *The bombshell came at a meeting of the Central Committee held at the Midas Hotel (Rome, 13–15 July), and it put the leader of the autonomist faction, Bettino Craxi, at the top of the party. He was supported by a coalition which included the faction led by Lombardi and Mancini, as well as the one led by Manca with positions close to De Martini. As far as* Il Manifesto *was concerned, 'Craxi the Amerikan had won'.*

In this climate, Mondoperaio *organized a conference on 'The socialist question after 20 June' (Rome, 20–1 July), in which Bobbio read the introductory paper: 'The socialist question and the communist question', which caused something of a stir. In August,* L'Espresso *published part of it under the curious title 'The Eaglet, the Partridge and the Sphinx'. In September, the text of his speech was published in* Mondoperaio. *In the first part, Bobbio examined the historical position of the Socialist Party:*

> There is just one, very clear starting point for our reflections. In thirty years, that is from 1946 to 1976, the Socialist Party has seen its votes halved from 20% in the elections to the Constituent Assembly to 10% in the 1972 and 1976 elections. At the same time, the Communist Party has moved in the opposite direction and has nearly doubled its number of voters from 19% in 1946 to 34.5%, and this is why you cannot talk about the socialist question without mentioning the communist question.
>
> The eaglet did not manage to fly simply because, in all probability, it was not an eaglet, but a partridge which made a short hop and then had to rest. Leaving aside metaphor, let us consider Duverger's well-known categories for party size, according to which parties can be divided into large ones with a majority calling, medium-sized ones and small ones. The Socialist Party, which has been trimmed from both the left and the right as its current 10% showing demonstrates, is a medium-sized party, that is, a classic coalition party, whether with the right, the left or the centre, whether in government or opposition.

In the second part, 'the most authoritative intellectual associated with socialism', as Paolo Mieli defined him in L'Espresso, *identified the fundamental difference between communists and socialists:*

> I have never believed that there was room for so many different socialisms. There are just two great historical currents of socialism, the revolutionary one and the reformist one. Nor do I believe that revolutionary socialism and reformist socialism are incompatible in the absolute sense. There are historical periods, cultural traditions,

social and political conditions, and class structures that favour democratic socialism over revolutionary socialism. I am not saying that
we did not precede them in the obstacle race towards the full democratization of post-war socialism, but they have undoubtedly caught
up with us. Naturally, the Socialists know very well that their political
space would be greater if they were not so overshadowed by their
brothers competing against them. How do you maintain the distance
when the others come close to you and you stay still? Or rather when
the others come close, and you call on them and tell them that you
can do nothing without them? In other words, there is a communist
question that the Socialist Party has to deal with, given that the party's
strength is directly proportional to the differentiation that it can
maintain in relation to the Communist Party. The problem of a critical
distinction (not a purely tactical or strategic one) between the Communist Party and non-communism (which is very different to the
anti-communism shared by the Christian Democrats and the Social
Democrats) is a fundamental problem for the Socialist Party. You have
to admit that the solution to this problem is becoming increasingly
difficult in the current situation.
. . .
I believe that the difference between communists and socialists has
to be found at a deeper level. I believe that it has to be traced back
to a difference, which is probably insurmountable, concerning our
visions of humanity, its history and its future. In order to sum up this
difference in a few words, I would speak of a secular concept as opposed
to a totalizing concept of history, where by 'secular concept' we mean
that while history is the product of human beings, in order for it to be
humanized, it cannot be perceived as the product of human beings
who believe themselves, like gods, to be in possession of an absolute
truth that has to be imposed even on the recalcitrant. It means that there
is no longer any room for princes: not for the old prince to whom
Machiavelli entrusted the task of liberating Italy from 'barbarian rule',
and not for the new prince to whom Gramsci entrusted the task of
transforming society. The elements of this concept are a sense of history's enormous complexity and thus the denial of all purely consolatory
utopias, the conviction that once the principle of freedom, by which
I mean individual freedom and the freedom of social groups, has
entered into history following I know not how much blood and tears,
any attempt to suffocate it is a step backwards. This secular concept is
based on the idea of conflict driving history, a sense of the multiplicity
of opinions, whose only remedy is tolerance, the use of persuasion in
the place of violence, the conviction that there are no final solutions,
and that you have to take one step at a time, not ever believing that
you can start again right from the beginning, even though you do have
to be ready to turn back. History should be portrayed as an immense
forest in which no path has been previously marked out and indeed
you cannot even be sure that there is a way out.[23]

The paper had a certain resonance. La Stampa *spoke of a 'merciless and harsh ideological diagnosis, which we believe was more agreeable to intellectuals than it was to socialist politicians'.*[24] Paese Sera *acknowledged that Bobbio had 'the capacity and the strength to speak his mind without deferring to anyone'.*[25] *According to* Corriere della Sera, *'it is to him that those attempting to refound the Socialist Party are turning in search of ideas to secure the future of their party'.*[26] *Bobbio's home received messages from members throughout Italy.*

When Aldo Moro was kidnapped, the Socialist leadership favourable to negotiations between the state and the Red Brigades distanced itself from the hard line. After the Turin conference (30 March– 2 April 1978), which took place during that period, the party went down the road of the so-called 'socialist alternative', which proved to be an ideological clash with the Communists. If I am not mistaken, the hostilities started with an article by Craxi published in *L'Espresso* during the summer, which put up Proudhon in opposition to Marx, as the basis for refounding socialist thought and doctrine.[27] I still held reservations about the Communists, even though I saw the progress they were making to free themselves from dogmas such as the dictatorship of the proletariat. My secular views could not agree with their totalizing vision of history and the prospect of a society without conflicts, where a new class exercised all power over everyone. However, I did not approve of an ideological polemic whose real target was Enrico Berlinguer's Communist Party. I told Craxi this in a letter dated 14 October 1978:

I must tell you that I look on the controversy between the party and the Italian Communist Party with a certain detachment and sometimes even with concern. It is becoming obsessive and now appears to be an obsession with *Avanti!*. I have never held myself back in defending the principles of democracy against the Communists, but I always preferred the method I would call maieutic, which tends to draw out a hidden truth from the adversary, to the opposite method which now appears prevalent, that of reproach, of scolding the ne'er-do-well and tirades against the scoundrel. No one willingly renounces their own past. Why should we expect it of the Italian Communist Party? Do none of the other parties have anything to renounce? The young are lucky because they have no past, but the past exists and each of us is carrying its burden. You cannot always start everything from scratch, and pretend that what has actually happened did not happen. Personally I prefer the kind of debate with the Communists that deals with the abiding value of principles and the correctness of certain proposals. It appeared to me that the party was on the right road with the 'project', which was after all the basis for the 41st Congress. This way forward could have allowed the party to attract many intellectuals of various

backgrounds who were interested in demonstrating their competence
in different fields. But in my opinion, the debate on Leninism has taken
us back to one of those ideological battles which, by creating a great
deal of hot air, always end up with a storm.

Two years later in February of 1980, the general secretary of the
Italian Socialist Party launched a programme of far-reaching constitutional and institutional reform. I thought it a tactical manoeuvre to
distract attention away from the crucial question of party alliances.
The party was squeezed between two titans, the Christian Democrats
and the Communist Party. As it was not able for historical reasons to
be the party of the left, it vacillated in the centre, while claiming an
independence that it was unable to turn into reality. In a political
system that was log-jammed, the Socialists were only the pendulum.

On that occasion, I was part of a dissident group that attempted
to oppose Bettino Craxi by supporting the candidature of Antonio
Giolitti. We were led by Giorgio Ruffolo, at whose house we used to
meet, and Federico Coen, the editor of *Mondoperaio*. Other members
were Giuliano Amato and Luciano Cafagna. At that time, I still hoped
that the Socialist Party could constitute a social-democratic force
capable of becoming an alternative government within our system,
instead of being the mediator between the Christian Democrats and
the Communist Party that held the balance of power.

However, our group was defeated without putting up a fight in a
memorable meeting of the Central Committee (14–18 June 1980).
The left of the party, led by De Martino, Lombardi, Mancini and
Signorile, had asked for the resignation of the party's general secretary and for the formation of a government with the Communists.
At the end of the deliberations, we witnessed a *coup de théâtre* that
delivered up the party to Craxi. Gianni de Michelis, who was on the
left of the party, allied himself with the general secretary. I remember
a long and depressing conversation with Claudio Signorile, and as we
left, we muttered, 'If this is meant to be the left, ...' We realized
that Craxi had not only won, he had won decisively.

*When interviewed by Giorgio Bocca on the eve of the Central Com-
mittee meeting, Bobbio confessed, 'I have never been so concerned
and anxious as I am at this moment.'*[28] *Craxi's Socialist Party had
become 'the party of neither . . . nor . . . : neither communist nor Christian democrat'. The intellectuals organized around the Socialist Party
who identified with* Mondoperaio *had signed a document critical of
Craxi's leadership, which was rejected by the general secretary as a
personal attack by an 'intellectual caste'. In an article in* La Stampa,
Vittorio Gorresio warned that the intellectuals of Mondoperaio *were*

the ones who were protecting the good name of the Socialist Party:
'they produce documents, carry out research, examine problems in
depth and are therefore to be respected for fulfilling the specific tasks
of a socialist party, as Julien Benda argued: a conservative party
defends vested interests; a socialist party also has an obligation to
fight for ideals'.[29] *The result of the Socialist Central Committee meeting*
was judged by political observers to be a compromise between Craxi
and the left of the party that kept the general secretary in control but
with reduced powers. Bobbio's pessimistic assessment was expressed
in an article published by Mondoperaio *(in March he resigned from*
the Central Committee):

There was a time when Socialist Party votes were not decisive for the formation of governments of the centre, not even when centre-left governments appeared on the scene. What is new today is that, following the drop in the electoral support for the Christian Democrats and their secular allies, the Socialist votes have become decisive. This is the key question for the centrist coalition but not for the left-wing alternative. In these conditions, the party cannot play one lot off against the other, as generally happens with a third-force party. It can only deal with one party, so its contractual strength is much diminished. Consider the bargaining strengths of these two different alternatives: one is 'You're either with us or against us', and the other 'You're either with us (the Christian Democrats) or you go to early elections'. The former is the ultimatum that the Socialist Party puts to the Christian Democrats, and the latter is the ultimatum that the Christian Democrats puts to the Socialist Party. In the first case, the adversary loses the opportunity to form a government by not accepting the ultimatum, and the second case the adversary gives an ultimatum whose alternative is not the formation of another government but taking responsibility for the unpopular measure (perhaps even a damaging one) of dissolving Parliament. It is the difference between playing one side off against the other, and being caught between two equally unpleasant alternatives. The situation in which the party currently finds itself is not that of controlling the game (and not even that of abandoning the game as it could do when its votes were not decisive), but that of being caught between a rock and a hard place.[30]

My political disagreement with Craxi manifested itself in various ways. This was especially true after his leadership became unchallenged within the party, which in practice was from the XLII Congress held in Palermo in 1981, where the direct election of the general secretary was approved (and therefore he could only be replaced by another congress). 'I don't like Craxi and his entourage', I wrote at the beginning of that year to an American friend, the political scientist Joseph

La Palombara who was a professor at Yale University, 'because I consider them a power group whose only aim is power and one that is willing to go to any lengths to secure it.' In his reply, La Palombara informed me that in America Craxi's star was rising, as the principal aim there was keeping the Communists out of power, which of course I had never doubted. Amongst my letters to socialists, I found one dated 20 August 1982, that is fifteen days after the PSI brought about the fall of Spadolini's first government, with the associated risk of early elections. It was addressed to Claudio Martelli, Craxi's deputy, but it was not sent, perhaps because of its overcritical tone:

> Don't you realize what early elections would mean for a country that is falling apart and has finally found in Spadolini a prime minister who is capable, authoritative and morally irreproachable? I very strongly disapprove of your way of conducting politics through *coups de théâtre* that involve personal attacks and always adopt a threatening tone. I am fearful about your unbridled ambitions (and I am not alone in this), and I am worried about your peevish behaviour.

Day by day, I could see a moral problem emerging in which the Socialists were mixed up: the enforcement of moral standards in public life was a question of good government, and the basis of democracy. I therefore rejected Craxi's invitation to contribute to the manifesto for the general election held on 26 June 1983. The conclusion to my letter was as follows:

> It is not that I am an unaware of the objective difficulties that the party faces, caught as it is between a rock and a hard place, and I therefore consider your concern over safeguarding the party's independence by not taking part in any preconceived electoral programme to be correct. But the problem is that your unscrupulous exercise of power has made you less and less credible. Even your good intentions seem increasingly the ones that pave the way to hell.
>
> As I consider this electoral contest to be the natural and ominous consequence of an odious and irresponsible policy, in which the current Socialist Party has played its part, I have no intention of taking part in any form. Besides I have never done so (except as an Action Party candidate in 1946). The only time I have taken a public stance in the context of the socialist formation was at the time of unification. And no good came of it. Since then I have told myself that political contests are not for me. Each to his own trade.

The most lively clash and the one that caused the greatest uproar was when Craxi was elected the party's general secretary by the amount of applause at the end of the Verona Congress (11–13 May

1984). I wrote an article for *La Stampa*, 'La democrazia dell'applauso' (16 May) in which I deplored what had happened:

> I cannot understand how the Socialist Party, which considers itself democratic and at the centre of Italy's democratic system, whose governments it has made possible in recent years, could have allowed its general secretary to be elected by acclamation. Election by acclamation is not democracy, it is the exact opposite of democratic election . . . In other words, acclamation is not an election, it is an investiture. A leader, who has undergone an investiture, is, at the very moment this occurs, released from all mandates and is accountable only to himself and his 'mission'.
> . . .
> Anyone who has the slightest knowledge of the so-called rules of the democratic game, knows very well that if an election is to be considered democratic, it must be the result of votes given by each of the electors *individually* and independently of each other. If at all possible, this should be done *secretly* when it is a matter of voting for a person. Acclamation expresses the opinion, or more correctly the sentiment, the mood, the immediate and purely emotional reaction not of the individual, but of a shapeless mass in which individuals no longer count as themselves, but as part of a whole that transcends them: that is of course what a mass is.
> In order for an election to be democratic, it must be regulated in a manner that allows for dissent, and that is why the golden rule of democratic decisions is majority and not unanimity, which would render any decision-making impossible in the case of voting by a large number of people, such as delegates to a party congress. Acclamation does not allow the expression of dissent, or rather it allows some people to keep their arms folded (I would imagine that some people were not applauding), but no one takes any notice. Election by acclamation is by definition a unanimous vote. By definition, I mean not on the basis of verifiable facts, such as the counting of votes.

Craxi got Carlo Tognoli, the mayor of Milan, and Francesco Forte to respond in *La Stampa*. Their main argument was that with a party firmly united around its leader, an election would have been a useless formality. My article met with a great deal of support, which included support from individual socialists. *Panorama* published a short article on 28 May 1984, which was inspired and blown up by I know not whom. It was entitled: 'Pertini says: Well done Bobbio!' It stated:

> Norberto Bobbio's lucid argument on the 'democracy of applause' launched at the Socialist Congress in Verona (the philosopher wrote that 'Acclamation is the exact opposite of democratic election') can include a particularly authoritative admirer amongst its many others:

Sandro Pertini. Indeed on Thursday 17 May, the president of the Republic lifted his phone and called Bobbio's home in Turin. The philosopher's wife, Valeria Cova, answered (Bobbio being in Milan at a political conference). Pertini asked her to congratulate her husband: 'I have always had the greatest respect for Bobbio. Now I have even more. Please tell him that I share his views. And tell him I want to see him.'

In 1984, Bobbio finally retired from university teaching at the age of seventy-five, and the Faculty of Political Science unanimously decided to make him professor emeritus. On 18 July, President Pertini appointed Bobbio a senator for life (with the Catholic writer Carlo Bo). This appointment provoked disagreement over the interpretation of article 59 of the Constitution, which states: 'The president of the Republic can appoint as senators for life five citizens who have brought honour to the country through their exceptional qualities in the social, scientific, artistic and literary fields.' Does this mean that there can be up to five senators appointed by presidents, or that each president is entitled to appoint up to five? At the time of Pertini's decision, there were in fact already five senators for life in Parliament (Amintore Fanfani, Cesare Merzagora, Leo Valiani, Eduardo De Filippo and Camilla Ravera). The latter interpretation was only upheld by one of Italy's constitutional experts, Giuseppe Ferrari, but his was an isolated voice. However, the appointment remained in force more as a fait accompli *than as the conclusion of any legal argument.*

I have never kept a diary. However, my appointment as senator was such an exceptional event that I could not resist the temptation to narrate what was happening to me. I had not even been a town councillor in the smallest Italian council. Suddenly, I had become a member of the upper chamber of the Italian Parliament. The diary started on 18 July 1984. It narrates that at 6.30 in the afternoon, I was at the Piero Gobetti Research Institute talking to Pietro Polito about his graduation thesis. I was called by Carla, the centre's director. The president's palace is on the phone: 'It's Doctor Maccanico, Pertini's adviser.' He tells me there's good news and passes me to the Senate leader, Francesco Cossiga, who greets me with words to this effect: 'Welcome, colleague, to the Italian Senate.' Then he gives me the news that the president of the Republic has signed the decree appointing myself and Carlo Bo as senators for life. I immediately asked him how they managed to overcome the more restricted interpretation of art. 59 of the Constitution, which, in my opinion, was the correct one, namely that there can only be five senators for life appointed by the president and there were already five sitting in Parliament. He told me to rest assured: the Senate Committee had already given a favourable ruling. He joked that the looser interpretation of article 59, that each president could appoint five, and the fact that Pertini who was nearly at the end of his seven-year term had only appointed three, meant that the incumbent senators, all well advanced in years (the youngest I think was Leo Valiani who was seventy-five like me), no longer had to fear that aspirants would wish them dead.

The news was shortly released on the evening news programmes. The telephone calls lasted the entire evening and started again in the morning at 7.30 with my old friend Vittorio Foa. Our bags were in the hall from the previous day, ready for our departure for Cervinia, but the phone kept ringing without a break and we could not leave. At about ten, the television people rang, and I begged them to come quickly because we wanted to leave. They came immediately for an interview lasting a few seconds, in which I expressed my concerns over not knowing my new profession. And at my age! I assured them that I would use the summer break for my senatorial studies. The various comments included a sonnet in Roman dialect by my friend Antonello Trombadori: 'President's sent two to the senate / Both buddies for many a year / Bo believes in Catholicism / and Bobbio in liberal-socialism.'[31]

Carlo Bo and I were to be introduced to the Senate on 31 July. At eleven in the morning, we were received by the Senate leader, Cossiga. We mainly talked about a mutual friend and teacher Giuseppe Capograssi, and I gave him my most recent book, *Maestri e compagni*. In exchange, he gave me a slim volume of poetry in Sardinian by an ancestor of his, which had been recently republished. We entered the chamber at exactly four o'clock in the afternoon. I was intimidated and looked around to find I knew almost no one. A communist was speaking against some amnesty or other for breaches of building regulations. When he saw me, he stopped to greet me and recalled our meeting at a conference in Bologna or Modena. Cossiga introduced us with a few words, followed by the ritual applause. We were required not to reply.

I registered with the socialist group as an independent. I have to admit that I felt like a fish out of water in Parliament, even though I did attend the Senate Legal Affairs Committee from 1984 to 1988 out of respect for Sandro Pertini and also because of a certain fascination that this new post exercised over me (I stayed as long as my health allowed me). However, when faced with the need to take crucial decisions, I always found myself to be unsure. I would ask myself who was really right? When there was the long, interminable discussion on the law against sexual violence, I was always assailed by doubts, especially over the delicate questions of rape between spouses and the age when you can be punished for your actions. Personally I always got on very well with the committee. There were some excellent jurists, including the eminent expert in criminal law from Turin, Marcello Gallo. But I was always doubtful when there was a decision to be taken. I am an indecisive person, even in the small things in life. I love to debate the pros and cons, rather than come to a conclusion, like Pascal's hunter: more interested in the hunt than the kill. A philosopher involved in the Spanish edition of my *In Praise of Meekness*[32] has described me as the philosopher 'de la indecisión'.

In the meantime, I had started a new public activity: writing for *La Stampa*. I had resisted repeated invitations from my friend Carlo Casalegno, as I feared that journalism might prove to be a waste of time. I was not sure of having the necessary attributes for being a good journalist. The only time I had written on a regular basis for a newspaper had been thirty years earlier, at the time of *Giustizia e Libertà*. However, in September 1976, I took part in a debate on democracy and pluralism organized by *L'Unità*'s National Festival which took place in Naples that year. The speakers were intellectuals like Aldo Tortorella, Nicola Badolini and Biagio De Giovanni. The editor of *La Stampa*, Arrigo Levi, sent Gaetano Scardocchia to Naples (later he was to be my editor), and devoted a front-page article to the debate that was published on 17 September, as 'Bobbio's three questions to the Italian Communist Party'.[33] I remember that after the debate, we all went to see *Mrs Carrar's Rifles*, at the Berliner Ensemble stand. It was an open-air theatre. The crowd was enormous, engrossed and generous in its applause, even though the play was in German. This could only be understood by those who have been to the National Festivals organized by the communists when they represented the only large opposition force to the Establishment.

How could I take part in a debate with a few hundred people, and then refuse to speak to millions of readers? On my return to Turin, Arrigo Levi telephoned to tell me that I could not refuse the offer: the newspaper wanted to use a debate on 'pluralism', seen as a precondition for democracy, to start a dialogue between intellectuals and politicians. In the end, I accepted. My contribution was published a few days later, having been condensed into two articles with rather didactic titles: 'What is pluralism?' (21 September) and 'How to interpret pluralism' (22 September).[34] I started from the assertion that everyone likes to declare themselves a pluralist. I asked whether we can be sure that we know what pluralism is? Are we sure that we all mean the same thing by pluralism? Articles appeared in the paper by Antonio Giolitti, Pietro Ingrao, Ugo La Malfa, Valerio

Zanone and Benigno Zaccagnini. The argument was taken up in other papers by philosophers, historians, sociologists and political scientists (Umberto Cerroni, Paolo Farneti, Franco Ferrarotti, Domenico Fisichella, Giuseppe Galasso, Lucio Lombardo Radice, Alessandro Passerin d'Entrèves, Pietro Rossi, Paolo Spriano and Carlo Tullio-Altan). I replied with two more articles: 'The pluralist Marx' (28 November) and 'All that glistens is not gold' (1 December),[35] in which I summarized the contradictions to which pluralism is exposed and the multiplicity of meanings it can take on. In the last of these articles, I wrote:

> Pluralism has always been two-sided: on the one side it is concerned with the totalizing power of the state and on the other with atomization caused by individualism. While from the state's point of view, the accusation that can be made against pluralism is that it weakens its cohesion and the necessary unifying force, from the individual's point of view, its danger is the natural tendency of each interest group to crystallize its structure as the number of its members gradually grows and it extends its area of activity, so that individuals who believe they have freed themselves from an overbearing state, end up being subject to various overbearing groups.
>
> It would be worth thinking about whether in our society, a feature of which is the presence of very large social groups and organizations, the demand for the traditional libertarian rights, such as the freedoms of thought, opinion and association, and even political freedom understood as the right to take part in the formation of the collective will, is not shifting from the traditional terrain of the state-apparatus to that of the large organizations that have grown within or even beyond the state (such as business enterprises). Art. 1 of the Workers' Statute which proclaims the right of workers to express freely their own thoughts at their workplaces, demonstrates that individual freedom is defended not only *against* the state, but also *within* the state, and that wherever power is constituted, sooner or later it will display its 'demonic' face.

The debate on pluralism was so far-reaching that, on New Year's Eve, I was invited to appear on television to comment on one of three words that summed up the year, which was of course 'pluralism' (another was 'comparison', and I cannot remember the third).

My first articles were too professorial in tone. I would write one a month at the most, and attempted to introduce the average reader to questions of political philosophy, and in particular to two very important themes: political ideologies and the organization of the state. In the early years, my writings for *La Stampa* revolved around four arguments (apart from pluralism): the nature of socialism, the relationship with violence, the third way and the institutional crisis. It was a question of serving up theoretical questions to the newspaper's readership, that were above all concerned with the nature of democracy. Giovanni Spadolini suggested to me that a selection of these articles should be put together in the series he was editing called 'Quaderni di Storia'. It was published by Le Monnier with the rather more academic than journalistic title of *The Crisis of Ideologies and Power*,[36] which reflected the nature of the writings it contained. After that, I began to adapt to the requirements of a great newspaper, as they were urging me to make topical comments on political events. However, I always found it very difficult to take on the guise of opinion-maker and leader-writer. This was mainly because writing does not come easily to me: I nearly always feel the need to rewrite an article before submitting it. In general, I avoid writing an article straight off, except in exceptional cases, such as when I was asked for obituaries (I remember those that I wrote for Karl Popper, Augusto Del Noce, Natalia Ginzburg and Franco Venturi). In 1990, *La Stampa* published a second collection of my articles in the series 'Terza Pagina' edited by Metella Rovero, this time with the decidedly journalistic title *Utopia Turned Upside Down*.[37] The title was taken from a leader on the fall of the communist regimes, published on 9 June 1989, which concluded as follows:

Are the democracies that govern the richest countries in the world capable of resolving the problems that communism has been unable to resolve? This is the problem. Historically communism has failed, I do not challenge that. Yet the problems remain, precisely the same problems that the communist utopia had pointed out and believed it could resolve, but now and in the near future, they are projected onto an international scale. This is why it is foolish to rejoice at this defeat and rub your hands together saying: 'I always told you so!' What self-delusion, do you really believe that the end of communism as a historical phenomenon (and I insist on the 'historical') has brought an end to the thirst for justice and the need for it? Wouldn't it be better to realize that while our world is ruled by the society of two-thirds, it is doing very well for itself and has nothing to fear from the impoverished, in the rest of the world the two-thirds, or even four-fifths or nine-tenths, is the impoverished part?

Democracy has defeated communism's historical challenge, on that we can agree. But what are to be the means and the ideals with which we will confront the problems that gave rise to the communist challenge?

As the poet said, 'Now that the barbarians are no more, what will happen to us without the barbarians.'[38]

My journalism naturally led me to express judgements on political life. I always tried to be even-handed in my approach, especially as far as individuals were concerned, but I could not avoid clashes with a few personalities, such as Bettino Craxi and Silvio Berlusconi.

Although Craxi's remarks about me were generally uncharitable, our personal relations when we met were always polite. There was one amusing episode. In 1985, I was interviewed by Andrea Marcenaro for *L'Europa* on the Craxi government.[39] I had told the interviewer that Craxi had displayed 'very considerable ability to govern' (although I do not think I said 'very'). For a year I had been a life senator. A few days after the weekly came out with the interview, I saw the prime minister in the Senate chamber calling an orderly and giving him a note for me: 'Dear professor, thanks for the high marks you gave me. I hope that I deserved them. Yours B. Craxi.'

However, he became decidedly hostile when I criticized the programme of reforms presented by the Socialist Party for the elections on 14 June 1987. The general sense of my criticisms was admirably summarized by the title *La Stampa* chose for my leader: 'A fog of words'.[40] Bettino Craxi responded with a letter to the newspaper in which he gave me a scolding:

> It is quite clear that Prof. Bobbio has not read the manifesto that will be the basis for debate at the Socialist Party conference, and if he did not read it, that is because he probably did not even know about its existence. I am referring to the last manifesto approved by the socialist executive at its meeting on 30 January and published in *Avanti!*'s Sunday edition of 1 February. It is a summary seventy pages long, made up of an introduction and sixteen chapters . . .
>
> Obviously anyone who wishes to make any constructive criticism of the nature and aims of modern socialist reformism must read this document. If not, any criticism becomes an abstract exercise based on prejudice and of little or no use. This also applies to Professor Bobbio, who, I'm sure, will want to devote another article on this document, which this time will be based on knowledge of what he wants to analyse and criticize, now that he knows of the existence of a document which is the product of a proper and methodical collective effort by scientists, leading figures in the arts, specialists, parliamentarians, civil servants and cabinet members, and represents the sum of and the authority of many forms of expertise.[41]

I decided to moderate the polemical tone, and limited myself in a brief reply to pointing out that my article evidently referred to a document published as a supplement to the Socialist Party's newspaper, *Avanti!*, at the beginning of February. I reminded him that my criticisms should not have sounded entirely new, as I had taken up ideas that I had already expressed at the Socialist Party conference held in February 1985 on the question of 'What kind of reformism?' My introductory paper on the theme 'Why we are reformists' concluded with these words: 'In order to survive and look to its future with confidence, a socialist party needs to have great ideals. It does not need to invent anything. It only has to remain faithful to its own history.'[42]

My subdued response upset my dear friend Luigi Firpo, who wrote to me complaining about my 'submissive mildness' in relation to what he considered a 'vulgar attack'. I replied: 'Following the scolding I received from Craxi, another scolding from you was all I needed. My response was supposed to be subdued and reasoned (the quip about the party "not being dogmatic and not being sectarian" was actually sarcastic), but you consider it mild and submissive. What a disaster!'

The last meeting occurred when he wrote me a polite letter inviting me to take part in the socialist conference on institutional reforms, organized in Rimini in March 1990:

> Dear Bobbio,
>   The conference on the PSI's programme will be held in Rimini from Thursday to Sunday. It will be a good opportunity to think aloud, debate ideas and bring forward proposals. The basic introductory paper, which Giuliano Amato will have sent you, is called 'Modern reformism, liberal socialism'. I would be very happy if you were there with us, even for a short while, to advise us, reproach us and encourage us.
>
>   Fraternal greetings,
>   Yours, B. Craxi.

I rang Giuliano Amato for some advice. The conference proceedings were to take place exactly a month after Sandro Pertini's death, and they were to be closed with a commemoration of the president, which I was supposed to conduct. That was what happened. Craxi was very happy about it, and we shook hands.

I wrote to him that same year concerning relations with the ex-communists. I was stunned that he did not understand that, after the Berlin Wall came down and Soviet communism fell, he should have adopted a policy of extending the victor's hand towards the vanquished, but instead he behaved like someone who went to the riverbank to wait for his enemy's body to float by. My letter remained unanswered.

12 November 1990

Dear Craxi,

I received your brief note asking me to renew my subscription to *Avanti!* It will of course be done, as I have had a subscription for years. Not only do I have a subscription, but I also read it. I suppose it would be pointless to say that I do not hold with its incessant, monotonous and peevish anti-communism. Nine times out of ten, the front-page leader is devoted to some polemical attack against the Communists, as though there were no other causes for indignation in our country or in the world. I have never been a communist, as you know, but now that traditional communism has collapsed, we have a wonderful opportunity for a great initiative to foster unity, while petty polemic on a daily basis seems to me completely sterile. It would not be enough, in my opinion, to change the party's name, put the word 'unity' in its title and wait for the prodigal son to return to his father's house. Without launching a significant initiative, I fear that he will not return. Indeed, constantly reproaching them for their past, which has been a large part of the Socialist Party's past, will drive them further away. As for this great initiative, I am the first to admit that it is a vague idea. But I am not a politician, only an observer. I am not so much expressing an opinion, and still less am I making proposals. I am giving you my impression. So with the authority that derives from your being prime minister for four years and now having a prestigious international post,[43] you could initiate a productive dialogue on the left in an attempt to assist the course of Italian history and bring to an end this Christian Democrat supremacy, which is becoming increasingly unbearable. Only you can do this. I am telling you this, because I despair at seeing the left so divided, so confused and in such disarray, while the Christian Democrats, always on the verge of division but always united in critical moments, are able to arrogantly assert 'L'état c'est moi'.

Thus the fall of the Berlin Wall, which should have swept the Italian Communist Party away and given renewed vigour to the Italian Socialist Party, ended causing exactly the opposite: the former managed to save itself, while the latter has almost completely dissolved. In the elections of 5 April 1992, not only did the PSI fail to draw any advantage from the downfall of its historical adversary, but actually received less votes than in any previous election.

I never had an untroubled relationship with Silvio Berlusconi, who I never met personally. There were many reasons for the disagreement, which were summarized in particular in three articles that appeared in *La Stampa* in 1994. Firstly, using Michael Walzer's definition of liberalism as the 'art of separation' (the separation of political power from economic power, and the separation of political and economic power from religious power and from cultural power), I argued that there had never been such a trend in democratic countries towards the integration of a great economic power and an equally great cultural power, through an extremely powerful instrument like television, with political power, as was occurring before our very eyes. This was the result of Berlusconi's 'entering the field', and, within the few months of an election campaign, becoming the prime minister of a government that even claimed to represent the quintessence of a liberal state. Secondly, I called attention to the inextricable link between a democratic regime and the rule of law, which the prime minister did not seem to care about, arguing that the 'majority takes all'. Reminding the readers of the older liberal theme of the 'tyranny of majorities', I explained that a democratic state is only the best or least bad form of government, if its actions take place within the rule of law, which should be understood as the government of laws rather than the government of people (even a majority is made up of people). On this point, Berlusconi had Giuliano Urbani give me a polite response.[44]

The more serious clash came on the question of his party. If the movement led by Berlusconi was not a party, I asked in my article entitled 'The phantom party',[45] what was it then supposed to be? It is difficult to know exactly what a party is, let alone a non-party. This time he responded in person with an article in *La Stampa*, 'What is Forza Italia?', and I came back with another article entitled 'The right to ask questions'.[46]

I had asked whether there was a statute for the movement or party. I have to thank a journalist working for *L'Europa* for the discovery that a statute did in fact exist, even though it was drawn up three months after the electoral victory and underwent an almost underground circulation.

> I save the readers from all the details concerning the odyssey of delays and excuses. Suffice it to say that on Friday the 8th, having tired of their beguilements, we threatened to write that (as far as we could see) there was no statute or Berlusconi had invented it. Then we were told that the document had been lodged with a notary in Rome. As it was a public document, the notary was required by law to provide us with an authenticated copy by midday on Monday. Two hours later, Forza Italia decided to send us the statute.
>
> Perhaps there was a certain reluctance to make the statute public, because it did not respond to any of the queries raised by Bobbio. Namely, what are the rules by which Forza Italia has been constituted? What is the division of duties and areas of competence? How is it financed? Are Berlusconi's powers limited or absolute? How long is his period of office as chairman? Is there a fixed term of office as in all other parties, or is it eternal as occurs in North Korea?[47]

Even though I wrote newspaper articles for many years (I have now stopped), I am convinced, indeed increasingly convinced, that opinion-makers do not have that influence over political events that they would like to think. Politics is carried out by professional politicians, not by journalists or intellectuals. Intellectuals are not capable of exercising concrete influence over matters that constitute the real political struggle. People are quite right when they compare an intellectual to a gadfly. It is important that we have debates like the one over whether a nation exists or not, which was instigated in particular by Ernesto Galli della Loggia in *Corriere della Sera* and Gian Enrico Rusconi in *La Stampa*, but are we going to deceive ourselves in thinking that this has even a minimal influence on the political world? At the end of the day, it is a discussion amongst intellectuals who are of little importance to politicians. The discussion on relations between politics and culture in the fifties, involving Galvano Della Volpe and Togliatti himself, had perhaps some influence on the battle of ideas. But these are completely different dimensions: the history of ideas is one thing, and real politics is another. These are two separate worlds, which do not cross and do not overlap, but proceed alongside each other without ever meeting. Of one thing I am quite certain: any power that intellectuals might have counts a great deal less than the power that people directly involved in political life can and do exercise. Perhaps it is no coincidence that my least successful book, in spite of the title *Doubt and Choice* given it by the publisher which I liked a great deal, is precisely the one that gathers together my writings on intellectuals.[48]

A balance sheet on my involvement in political life can be found in *The Future of Democracy*:

> I belong to a generation that lost its great hopes thirty years ago shortly after the Liberation, and never found them again except at a few rare and fleeting moments. They turned out to be indecisive and occurred about once a decade: the defeat of the *legge truffa* (1953), the advent of the centre-left government (1964), and the Communist Party's sudden growth (1975). If you wanted to trace this process, you could interpret these three stages as firstly the prevention of an untimely step backwards, secondly the shift by the dominant party from alliances with the right (including the fascist MSI party) to alliances with the left, and thirdly a signal of a left-wing alternative in the third. Those of us who have many years of dashed hopes behind us, are more resigned to our own powerlessness.[49]

Twelve years later, I confirmed this balance sheet when Giancarlo Bosetti interviewed me for *L'Unità* on 6 April 1996,[50] just before the elections in which Ulivo, the left-of-centre coalition, defeated Polo, the right-wing coalition:

> I am chronically disenchanted, I might even say disenchanted by temperament or by calling, but also partly because of the experiences I have gone through in the last half century of democratic life, not without a certain emotional involvement. In all that time, I managed to build up false hopes on only three or four occasions, but these periods of self-deception were short-lived. Once those hopes were dashed, it took some time before I could again abandon myself to new illusions.

7

Peace and War

On 27 September 1961, the writer Guido Piovene wrote a feature in *La Stampa* on the Peace March from Perugia to Assisi which had occurred three days earlier, on a glorious Sunday, involving nearly 3,000 people:

> It was the first demonstration of its kind in Italy and was brought about by the current international crisis. I cannot separate its meaning from the extraordinary serenity of its natural and human environment: the trip along the banks of Lake Trasimeno in the early morning, Perugia on a Sunday with its inhabitants filling Corso Vannucci between the cathedral and the terrace overlooking the countryside, the slow passage of the demonstration with its banners and slogans over the 24 miles of the route to Assisi, the pause at Santa Maria degli Angeli, where some young brides dressed in white looked on from the steps of the church, and an old man attempted to find a spot to throw birdseed to the pigeons amongst the enormous crowd of people and cars, and then the final sweaty climb up the slopes of Mount Subasio. We were surrounded by the most perfect views, typical of the Appenine Mountains, everywhere man had left his mark but never in an artificial manner: towers, castles and churches along the ridges of the hills, all was verve, lucid intelligence and gratifying physical vitality.

I also took part in the first Peace March, organized by Aldo Capitini, when the world lived through the nightmare of the balance of nuclear terror, and bombs were built by both sides that were capable of destroying humanity ten times over. I can remember the peaceful and well-ordered demonstration moving down to Ponte San Giovanni along an unsurfaced country road. It made you think of a stroll on a pleasant late summer's day. On the state-road, the procession began to fill out and lengthen because coaches and cars were arriving from all parts of Italy. We walked at a fairly brisk pace, and we stopped for lunch at Santa Maria degli Angeli. By the time we got to Rocca di Assisi, there were several thousand of us. A cheerful crowd filled the meadows. The speakers included Aldo Capitini, Arturo Carlo Jemolo, Ernesto Rossi and Renato Guttuso. The final resolution declared that peace was too important to be left in the hands of the powerful. Amongst my friends from Turin were Italo Calvino, Franco Fortini, Carla Gobetti and Fausto Amodei with his guitar, from which he was inseparable. Afterwards I wrote an article for *Resistenza*:

> There have been favourable and unfavourable interpretations of this march. I have to say that the majority of the unfavourable interpretations have come from people who did not take part and judged it with the rigorous criteria that one might use to judge the composition of, say, a government. There was a small altercation over banners, and my response to that would be to suggest that on future marches (which we must do everything to encourage) we should go without banners, each with their own likes and dislikes that no banner can ever express, and with our shared hopes that only active participation in the march can fully express. Peace today is far too important, as the resolution says, to be left in the hands of those who would rule over us: I would also like to add that it is also too important to be entrusted to parties for its organization. This is why Capitini's initiative is so timely, as it does not belong to any party and is not motivated by any political considerations but only by a moral ideal (but this does not mean it will not have political consequences). Today, in an age in which a nuclear catastrophe has become a possibility, the question of peace is a fundamental question: peace is an absolute good, the necessary condition for the implementation of all other values.
>
> We have to realize that we are now at a turning point as far as the question of peace is concerned: up until now we have been able to put peace on one side of the scale while putting other values such as justice, liberty and honour on the other side. But from the moment that war could mean a nuclear catastrophe, there no longer exists any possibility of proposing an alternative to peace. There is still some sense in human terms in declaring: either liberty or war. But what sense is there in human terms in the declaration: either liberty or the destruction of humankind? If there is an alternative, then it is not between peace and liberty, between peace and honour or between peace and justice, but, as Günther Anders correctly and bluntly points out, between being and not being. What I mean is that now peace concerns human beings in as much as they are human beings and part of the human race that is threatened by a sinister power struggle, and

not in as much as they are Italians or Chinese, communists or Christian democrats, Catholics or secularists. A demonstration such as the Peace March is an invitation to become aware of the gravity and the novelty of the situation, and to abandon our divisive tribal fixations when we need an increasingly wide alliance to challenge the will for power with the will to live. It is also an appeal to moral forces, which is the last resort when it appears that only a sense of responsibility on the part of decision-makers, and those who can influence them, is capable of shifting the course of events from the path of a complete rift to that of agreement and collaboration.[1]

For someone like me, who has lived under a despotic regime and through a five-year war while my ideas were maturing, the most urgent problems after the fall of that regime and the conclusion of the war, were democracy and peace, which were linked by the same aim: the elimination of violence as a means of resolving conflicts within the same state and in relations between nation-states. As far as the international problem was concerned, the first step was to create a federation of European states in order to avoid a repetition of the tragedy that has rightly been called the European Civil War, and lasted almost a century. The United States of Europe were perceived as the first step towards a universal federation that would achieve Kant's dream of 'perpetual peace'.

The unification of states goes through several phases: alliance, confederation, federal state. While a confederation is a society of states, a federal state is a state of states. The United Nations, whose statute came into force on 24 October 1945, represents an intermediate stage between the League of Nations, which was purely an association of nation-states, and the United States of the World, the ideal of a super-state. The super-state is a power situated above other states and in possession of a force as superior in relation to the individual states as the force available to the nation-state is in relation to the individual. Political union is required in order to achieve this objective, as it is the only kind of union that would allow the super-state to use force if necessary. Only the super-state can exercise the monopoly of force, transforming relations between equals into relations between a superior and an inferior.

There are two forms of pacifism, which are not mutually exclusive: one is institutional or juridical, and the other is ethical or religious. The former aims to eliminate war between sovereign states through the union of individual states into a super-state, while the latter attempts to do this by educating people in non-violence. My writings on peace and war mainly belong to the former category. The Peace March organized by Capitini was, on the other hand, a typical expression of the second category. The difference between the two forms of pacifism is clear: the super-state eliminates war, but not the use of force in the last resort (*extrema ratio*); educating people to non-violence tends towards the elimination of the use of force even in the last resort. The former is less effective but more realistic, while the latter is more effective but less realistic. Immediately after the war, I devoted a course to these questions and in particular to the history of the pacifist ideal from the post-Napoleonic Restoration to modern times. The course was run at the request of the Italian Society for International Integration, which was founded in Rome by Roberto Ago to support the UN's activities in Italy. Ago, an old friend, had given me the task of setting up a branch in Turin and of occasionally assisting with the society's activities in Rome, where it had an office at Palazzetto Venezia. These activities were aimed at young people who wished either to follow diplomatic careers or become officials in international organizations. I remember that the course I taught in 1948 was supposed to become a book and was prepared for publication. I cannot recall why publication never went ahead.

The majority of my writings on peace and war were gathered into two books: *Il problema della guerra e le vie della pace* (Bologna: Il Mulino, 1979) and *Il terzo assente* (Turin: Sonda, 1989). I started to concern myself with the question of war in the nuclear age when Einaudi asked me to write a preface for the diary of a visit to Hiroshima and Nagasaki (1961) by the German philosopher Günther Anders, who also produced his correspondence with Eatherly, the pilot who bombed Hiroshima (*Burning Conscience*, London: Weidenfeld and Nicolson, 1961). On visiting the Nagasaki Atomic Bomb Museum, the philosopher saw a hand that had been fused together with a bottle, and reflected that there is no longer any difference between the hand and the bottle if they are both material subject to destruction. From this he came to a new definition of nihilism: it is not that everything is nothing, but that everything can be annihilated. 'Everything *can be annihilated* in the same way.' I introduced the book at its launch in Turin, in the company of the author. Anders's proposal was a moral code, which was supposed to set out new duties in relation to the threat of humanity's annihilation, and these duties would be binding on all people. His vision sought the moral transformation of humanity and was to impose an absolute ban on the use of nuclear devices. Anders made a clear distinction between moral and institutional pacifism. He wrote: 'The task that we are facing . . . is not one of those that can be solved through purely political measures (and still less by purely administrative measures). The measures that need to be taken belong to a different category . . . This means that the transformation will have to be a moral transformation.' He was aware of the objection posed by realists, and replied that this objection arose from the eternal dispute between moralists and jurists. However the hope was that the awareness of the absolute prohibition would put down such deep roots that 'whoever considered the possibility of using these means [nuclear weapons] for their own political objectives would immediately find themselves facing the indignation of all humanity'.

How naive this hope was! With hindsight, we know that the reason why a nuclear war did not break out was essentially reciprocal fear, the so-called 'balance of terror', as Hobbes had correctly foreseen. According to Hobbes, only mutual fear could prevent the war of everyone against everyone else in the state of nature.

The idea of a moral code was to be taken up again by Gustavo Colonnetti (1886–1968). This old friend was a renowned scientist and professor of engineering at Turin Polytechnic and had been a deputy in the Constituent Assembly and chairman of the National Research Council following the Liberation. He was a profoundly devout Catholic, and was tormented by the heavy responsibilities that fell upon scientists. He wanted them to undertake a pledge not to work on the production of nuclear arms. It was to be a kind of Hippocratic Oath for scientists. I have very clear recollections of meetings with him at the demonstrations organized by the Turin Committee for Peace a few years later, just before his death. He had an enormous white beard and a solemn expression. Colleagues treated him with a little scepticism, but his sense of mission conferred on him an aura of religious nobility.[2]

In that same year, 1961, I became involved in the debate provoked by the French film *Tu ne tueras point* directed by Autant-Lara, which dealt with the question of conscientious objectors. If I am not mistaken, the controversy started at the Venice Film Festival before the film had even been released in French cinemas. I took part in an event at the Gallery of Modern Art in Turin, where for the first time I developed the idea that when faced with the threat of nuclear war, we should all be conscientious objectors:

> Conscientious objection means the refusal to bear arms. When the concept of arms includes a bomb that, as we read in the newspapers, has by itself the explosive power of all the bombs dropped in the last war, I wonder if bearing arms has not become a question of conscience not only for objectors who protest in the name of their religious faith, but for all of us, in the name of humanity. Conscientious objection literally means a situation in which the imperative of our conscience forbids us from carrying out an unjust act. If we examine our conscience, we cannot avoid acknowledging that today – and this is the conclusion that I wanted to draw – we are all potentially conscientious objectors.[3]

However this does not mean that I did not perceive and do not continue to perceive an insuperable difficulty with conscientious objection. In order for conscientious objection to achieve its own aim, it would really be necessary for all men to be objectors, because if they were all objectors except for one, then that one man would become lord of the entire world. The same reasoning could be applied to the question of disarmament: if all states in the world disarm except for one, then that state would dominate the earth. When you enter the political sphere, then you cannot cut yourself off from a minimal amount of realism. Unilateral disarmament favours the violent. The alternative of the war of everyone against everyone else is the despotism of the single individual. This is the problem that radical pacifists have to resolve: for as long as all men (and I mean all) are not non-violent, not only will non-violence not achieve its purpose, but it risks assisting the violent, for whom it is easier to dominate a world of non-violent people than a world of people as violent as themselves. The paradox of non-violence is that it encourages the violence of the violent. That is why I say: it would be terrible if there were no conscientious objectors, but it would also be terrible if there were only conscientious objectors.

In the following year, 1962, I wrote my first article on the philosophy of war, 'The nuclear conflict and the traditional justifications of war', which appeared in a special issue of *Il Verri* devoted to *The Nuclear Condition*, edited by the pacifist physician Giovan Battista Zorzoli.[4] I examined the four principal theories that traditionally have been used to justify warfare: the just war, war as the lesser evil, war as a necessary evil, and war as a good. I showed that in relation to a future thermonuclear war and its effects, these theories largely failed to hold together. I wanted to emphasize how the invention of nuclear weapons had radically changed the traditional meaning of war. Just to give one example, who could possibly still subscribe to the ravings of those worshippers of war from De Maistre ('War is divine in itself') to Papini ('The future has need of bloodshed'), when war means the destruction of humankind?

In 1963, Alberto Carocci asked me to write an article on this question for *Nuovi Argomenti*. He told me in his letter:

Another article in which I would be very interested would be a kind of introduction to the philosophy of peace and war. It is a question about which man has been meditating for millennia, but which underwent a sudden change with the invention of nuclear energy. Even at the time of the explosion of the Hiroshima bomb, which was 20 kilotons, Einstein said that a war fought with that bomb would have brought mankind back to the Stone Age. Nowadays, nuclear warheads are measured in megatons, and there are arsenals full of them. I have the impression that mankind would not just go back to the Stone Age, but that every biological form would be wiped from the face of the earth and several millions of years would have to pass before molluscs in the sea would be able to produce something similar to man. It is a radical change of circumstances that invalidates everything that human beings have thought up until now about the question of peace and war.

I accepted, but two years passed before I made up my mind to write the article. In the meantime, I had taught an entire course on this subject through the 1964–5 academic year,[5] and I wrote a radio lecture for the Third Programme, which the state broadcaster RAI put on the air in the second half of 1965.[6] The article for *Nuovi Argomenti* was published in issues no. 3–4 of 1966 and had the same title as my university course: 'The problem of war and the ways of peace' (this title was also used for a book; see note 7).

The article started with an explanation of the three possible inter-pretations of history through three metaphors: the fly in a bottle, the fish in a net and the labyrinth. The first comes from Wittgenstein's famous saying, according to which the task of philosophy is to teach a fly to escape from a bottle: this metaphor implies that there is a way out (evidently we are talking about an open bottle) and that, outside the bottle, there is a philosopher who knows where the way out lies. The interpretation is very different if we adopt the metaphor of the fish in a net, as it writhes around trying to find the way out, but, although it does not know it, there is no way out. When the net is drawn in to the bank and opened, but not by the fish, the way out will not be freedom but death.

I asked myself whether we human beings were flies in a bottle or fishes in a net. My reply was that we are neither of these. The human condition can be better represented by a third image, which I prefer: that of a labyrinth. We think we know that a way out exists, but we do not know where it is. As there is no one other than ourselves who can show it to us, we have to look for it ourselves:

Those who enter a labyrinth know that there is a way out, but they do not know which of the many paths that open up before them at different stages is the one that leads to it. They grope their way forward. When the way is blocked, they turn back and take another path. Sometimes the path that seems the simplest is not the right one; sometimes when they think they are close to their objective, they are further away, and just one false step is enough to end up back at the starting point. They need a great deal of patience, but they can never let themselves be deceived by appearances; they need to take one step at a time, and when confronted with a fork with no basis for a reasoned choice, they are obliged to take a risk while always being ready to retrace their footsteps. The nature of a labyrinthine situation is that no way out is absolutely assured. When the path is the right one in the sense that it leads to a way out, it is never the final way out. The only thing that a man in a labyrinth learns from experience (always supposing that he has reached the mental maturity to learn the lesson of experience) is that there are paths with no way out: the only lesson in the labyrinth is the lesson of the *dead end*.[7]

The labyrinth does not teach us where the way out is, but only which are the paths that go nowhere. Can we now consider nuclear war, unlike war in the past, to be a dead end? Once we have ascertained that the new bombs can kill both you and me, both my enemies and my friends, shouldn't we declare that nuclear war goes nowhere? 'Can we compare', I asked, 'nuclear warfare to warfare in the past?' I replied in the negative. I gave three reasons for this historic change. No war in the past, however long and cruel, endangered the whole of humanity. The majority of arguments used to justify war cannot be applied to nuclear warfare. A third utilitarian argument can be added to these two philosophical arguments. Nuclear war serves no purpose: 'The primary purpose of war is victory ... But as the power of weapons increases, it becomes more and more difficult to distinguish between victor and vanquished in the event of a war's unleashing its fullest horror. The only victors might be the non-belligerent, neutral, parties or more simply those lucky enough to be safe from the massacre.'[8] I added that there are two ways in which nuclear war could be considered a dead end: by regarding it as either impossible or unjustifiable. The first solution was that of the realists, who put their trust in the 'balance of terror'; the second was that of the idealists, who put their trust in the formation of nuclear awareness:

> If you don't ask me to prophesy, but just to give an opinion, I would reply that I am not optimistic. Around me I see only small groups of people who have finally been freed from the atavistic superstitions about the fertility of violence and regeneration through the spilling of blood. The ethics of politicians are still the ethics of power. Anyone who argues for the establishment of a single morality that applies equally to individuals and states, is still considered a visionary, a utopian and someone lacking a sense of history (the ultimate insult in the educated society he belongs to). I cannot shake off the sensation

that a society in which jurists, sociologists, philosophers and theologians have not rejected the idea of violence as a means of redeeming oneself or obtaining redress, will sooner or later end up with the most extreme test of violence that destroys everything. The ultimate weapon has come too early given the primitiveness of our customs, the superficiality of our moral judgements, the extravagance of our ambitions and the enormity of the injustices that the majority of humanity has to suffer, while having to choose between violence or oppression.

I am not an optimist, but that does not make me think that we should give up. It is one thing to forecast the future, and quite another to make your own decision. When I say that my decision is not to leave anything untried in order to create a nuclear awareness and that any philosophy that today does not commit itself to this undertaking is an idle waste of energies, I am not making any prediction about the future. I restrict myself to implying that I hope with all my being that it will not happen, even though at the very bottom of my heart I have a terrible foreboding that it will. However, the stakes are so high that everyone must adopt a position, in spite of the fact that the chances of success are so slight. It can happen that a grain of sand lifted by the wind brings a large machine grinding to a halt. Even if the probability of that grain of sand lifted by the wind landing up within the most delicate mechanisms and stopping the machine was just a billionth of a billionth, the machine that we are building is so monstrous that it is worthwhile for us to challenge our destiny.[9]

But the problem of war and peace is intimately related to the international protection of human rights. It is no coincidence that, since the middle of the sixties, movements for peace and movements for the protection of human rights have developed at the same pace. As I have often taken the opportunity to say, peace is the *sine qua non* for effective protection of human rights, and at the same time the protection of human rights in practice favours peace. Between 1964 and 1968, I had the opportunity to give lectures and write articles on such arguments. On these occasions, I tried above all to identify the philosophical criteria on which certain rights could claim to be fundamental and universal, but I did not deny that the philosophical problem could not be isolated from the examination of the historical, social, economic and psychological conditions relating to the implementation of human rights: 'The philosopher who insists on remaining pure, ends up condemning philosophy to a sterile existence.'[10] Thus the key problem is the difference between the content of the official declarations and the reality of international relations. As I emphasized in the conclusion to my speech to the National Congress on Human Rights held in Turin in December 1967:

You cannot pose the problem of human rights without taking into consideration the two other major problems of our times: those of war and poverty, the absurd contrast between the surfeit of *power*, which created the conditions for a war of annihilation and the surfeit of *impotence* that consigns great masses to hunger. This is the context in which we have to approach the problem of human rights – in a spirit of realism free from rhetoric . . . I would advise the following salutary exercise to anyone who wishes to make an impartial examination of the development of human rights since the Second World War: read the Universal Declaration and then look around. So many innocent victims of cruel wars, so much repugnant racism, so much degrading poverty, so much abuse of power, so much desire to oppress, so much unabashed arrogance, so much contempt for the weak and intense envy for the strong, and what fanaticism! So much for human dignity! Human history has lasted several millennia, but compared with our hopes, it has barely commenced.[11]

By distinguishing between the different activities carried out by international bodies to ensure the protection of human rights, the question of an authority *super partes* became increasingly prominent. It is possible through the declarations of human rights and the conventions that regulate them in practice to put pressure on individual states to introduce specific regulations and ad hoc procedures into their legal systems, where they do not have them. Secondly, international bodies can set up monitoring procedures within individual nation-states to verify if recommendations have been accepted and to what extent they are being respected. However, protection through a court at international level would be very different, if it had the power to impose itself on individual national jurisdictions, thus introducing a shift from 'guarantees *within* the state to guarantees *against* the state', as I have written elsewhere. This supranational authority, this universal super-state, whose task will be to regulate conflicts between states and guarantee the protection of human rights everywhere, is, at least for the moment, the *missing third entity*, which was used as the title of the second collection of my writings on these problems, published by Sonda in 1989.

The first attempt to create an international tribunal over and above national governments was the War Crimes Tribunal, which had been campaigned for by Bertrand Russell, the Nobel prizewinner for literature in 1950. Russell was involved in the civil-disobedience movements, and was famous for sit-ins and being arrested at one of them. In 1955, he was a signatory, along with Einstein, of the famous manifesto against nuclear weapons. The Russell Tribunal, founded in 1966 and based in Stockholm, brought charges against the United

States for the war in Vietnam. Its aim was to put governments on trial for the atrocities they commit and justify by reasons of state.

It was Joyce Lussu, Max Salvadori's sister and Emilio Lussu's widow, who got me involved in the Russell Tribunal. She was a spirited, courageous and wonderful woman, linked to the English political and cultural world through her mother. She had been given the task of setting up a section for the tribunal in Italy, and she invited me to take part. I received a letter of appointment from Russell himself, but I cannot remember what this Italian section actually did. We had a few meetings in Rome, not very many to be honest. In Italy, these initiatives appear and fade away with equal facility.

On Russell's death in 1970, Lelio Basso took over his commitment, and founded the Russell Tribunal II for Latin America in 1973 and later a foundation for the rights and liberation of peoples. I remember that two volumes of essays on internationalist themes were prepared for his seventy-fifth birthday. The launch was organized for the Capitol in Rome on 16 December 1978. When I entered the hall, I saw distressed faces. I was told that Basso would not be coming because he had died the previous night. We therefore celebrated and commemorated him on the same day.

Bobbio's papers contain a pile of letters, leaflets, newspaper cuttings and minutes of meetings concerning the Italian section of the Bertrand Russell Peace Foundation, which was set up in 1965 (with head office at Via del Babuino 9 in Rome). Bobbio, the scientist Adriano Buzzati Traverso and the economist Paolo Sylos Labini formed the board of management, with Joyce Lussu as secretary. An arts committee was set up and run by Carlo Levi, Giacomo Manzù and Cesare Zavattini. Twenty-three intellectuals from various backgrounds (writers, scientists, historians, publishers and politicians) made up the executive committee.[12] *The articles of association stated that the aims of the foundation were to resist the threat of nuclear warfare, campaign for comprehensive disarmament, promote research and organize meetings to mobilize Italian public opinion on the problems of peace. The first meeting took place on 2 October 1965. The minutes recorded messages of support from Italian pacifists such as Danilo Dolci, whose* Verso un mondo nuovo *was published in 1965 by Einaudi, Lucio Luzzatto, president of the World Peace Movement, and Aldo Capitini, president of the Italian Peace Council, and then continued as follows:*

Joyce Lussu then reads the report on the activities carried out by Bertrand Russell and the foundation over the preceding years in England and other parts of the world. She also reads Russell's message on the

Indo-Pakistani conflict, which provokes a lively debate amongst those present.

Norberto Bobbio considers Russell's condemnation of India in the Indo-Pakistani conflict to be a little one-sided, and he forcefully under-scores the importance, now more than ever, of defending peace without taking sides: otherwise you run the risk of deepening the divisions rather than contributing to peace.

. . .

On the other hand, Sylos Labini argues that, while a pacifist movement must support the need for negotiations to resolve international crises, and must condemn war in all cases, it is undoubtedly possible within such a movement to discuss the reasons for these kinds of crisis and to adopt positions on one of the parties to a dispute.

. . .

Enriquez Agnoletti insists upon the need for negotiations to resolve the crisis. He does not feel there is any contradiction between Russell's condemnation of Vietnam and his current statement: it is important to remember that Russell is speaking from London where the political divisions between parties are much less acute than here [in Italy], so expressing an opinion takes on a different tone.

. . .

Cesare Cases takes up the question of aggression which, in his opin-ion, is currently the greatest threat to peace. Occasionally you can understand the reasons that cause aggression, however it can have terrible consequences. Cases distinguishes between the question of a just or unjust war and the question of aggressor and the object of aggression. He considers the two questions to be different and believes that there is always a moral obligation to identify the aggressors and publicly condemn them.

Norberto Bobbio, rebutting the arguments in turn, again emphasizes that the question of aggression is closely linked to the question of justice: it can happen that a party attacks in order to defend itself. The question of peace comes first (justice comes later), partly because the lack of information and the complexity of the case could adversely affect the objectivity of our assessment. For this reason, he renews his reservations over Russell's judgement on the Indo-Pakistani conflict. Buzzati Traverso brings the debate to a close by asserting that the aims and objectives of the Italian Bertrand Russell Foundation are not the passive approval of Russell's declarations, but rather to enter into debate in the spirit of peace on the actual problems of the Italian and world communities, and to establish initiatives for this purpose.

The discussion then moves on to the action that has to be taken. Buzzati Traverso proposes campaigning for the 50,000 signatures required for a new law that would ban the construction and installa-tion of missiles of any kind on Italian soil, and would make the country open to inspection of any kind for verification. The new law would not demand the end of NATO. While remaining with NATO,

Italy would adopt a new and innovative position, commensurate with recent American studies which have shown that we already have the potential to destroy the entire planet.[13]

Does all this mean that institutional pacifism had made any decisive steps forward? I believe not. In recent years we have taken some steps backwards in the process of overcoming the sovereignty of the nation-state through a gradual intensification of international agreements, a process that started at the end of the eighteenth century. This process has not only come to a halt, but no attempts are being made to understand how to get it going again. Peace can be obtained between two belligerents, either by the victory and supremacy of one over the other, or by decisive interference from a third party, which is *super partes*. The first case is an imperial peace, and the second is a peace based on compromise, which Raymond Aron has defined as 'peace based on satisfaction'.[14] Within a single state, the first marks a despotic state, and the second is applied in democratic systems, where the state can be perceived as a third party that is above the other parties. However, the democratic system has not yet managed to prevail in international relations, and states continue to fight amongst themselves, resolving their conflicts on the basis of one party's supremacy over the other. In the current international system, the third party that acts as arbitrator, mediator or even holder of coercive power to prevent war or interrupt it in the event of its breaking out, exists only on paper. The third party *super partes*, or outside party, which acts for peace should be the United Nations. But how has it exercised this role?

In modern history, the international system has been sustained for centuries by the balance of power, which has been, however, an unstable form of equilibrium destined to evolve or break down according to the changes in alliances between states. Consequently, peace has always been a provisional state, and war has always been a possible result of the breakdown in relations. In the absence of international regulations backed up by penalties that can be imposed by force, peace has for centuries been at the mercy of this system. In a system that lacks 'a third party above all other parties' with powers of coercion, the only curb on the breach of a pact, is the principle of reciprocity. Neither of the two contracting parties violates the agreement, because they have an interest in the other party's keeping to the agreement. Hence the fragility of the principle of *pacta sunt servanda*, which in reality is always subject to the clause *rebus sic stantibus*, and this means that the pact lasts as long as the situation, in which the two contracting parties have an interest in maintaining the pact, does not change. The pact is all the more solid, the more the two contracting parties are equal in strength. Clearly a small state will be induced to observe a pact with a large state, while the opposite is not true. I have already pointed out that the balance of terror lasted as long as a certain degree of parity was maintained between the forces of the two superpowers.

During the eighteenth century, there was a proliferation of projects to overcome a system based solely on the balance of power, the most famous of which was Kant's *Perpetual Peace*. Following the stormy times of the Napoleonic Wars, the Holy Alliance could be considered the first attempt at a stable international order, which was not based exclusively on the balance of power or on partial and short-lived alliances. We had to go through the tragedy of the First World War to see the establishment of the League of Nations, the first permanent and tendentially universal association of states. But even the League of Nations did not challenge the sovereign power of states which, although not in itself the cause of wars, was always a sufficient condition for conflicts between states being resolved solely through war, albeit in the last resort.

Since then there have been those, like Luigi Einaudi, who highlighted the inadequacy of the new League of Nations for the task that it had been set, because it did not have the basis for overcoming the sovereign power of individual states. It was only a confederation, while it would have been necessary and more far-sighted, according to Einaudi, to have immediately attempted the formation of a federal state, at least initially for the European states, whose history had been blighted by continuous destructive wars. The principal argument used by Einaudi to justify his distrust of confederations was of a historical nature. He observed that in the past confederations had been set up with three principle aims, the maintenance of harmony between the associated states, their defence against attacks from other states, and the pursuit of civilization. However, they generally did not acquit themselves very well; this was true of the United Provinces in the eighteenth century, the Holy Alliance and, going back 2000 years, the League of Greek City States. The principal reason for the weakness of confederations arises from the fact that the power they are given is not the power of a state, which in essence is the ability to impose taxation and monopolize force. The United States of America are the first example of what Einaudi hoped for the European Community, the transition from a society of states to a state of states. The first of the articles he wrote on this subject concludes with these words: 'The current war is the rejection of European unity imposed by an overreaching empire, but it is also the struggle to develop a political structure of a higher order.'[15]

During the Cold War, the role of the United Nations was deprived of its authority by the balance of terror between the two great world powers: the United States and the Soviet Union. Peace was based solely on the fact that the two antagonists were in possession of such lethal weapons that a third world war would probably have led to the destruction of the assailant state as well as the state under assault. This strategy of mutual dissuasion proved effective in the Soviet missile crisis in Cuba in 1962, the only time when we got really close to a nuclear reprisal. In that case, the threatened state, the Soviet Union, preferred to withdraw. But the balance of terror was also an unstable form of equilibrium: the balance between the two great powers was continuously upset, only to find a new balance with a higher level of destructive weapons. Both in my writings on the subject of peace during the eighties and in the speech I gave in 1985 for the fortieth anniversary of the United Nations, I stressed that terror postponed the war, but made it increasingly destructive in the event of its breaking out. Opponents of the strategy of terror have proposed the solution of disarmament, in which I have never had a great deal of faith, because an agreement on weapons reduction will only achieve its purpose if the contracting parties are obliged to fulfil it. If there is no one to force them to maintain their undertakings, you return to a state of uncertainty in which no one is certain of the other's trustworthiness. As is well known, this uncertainty is, according to Hobbes's political philosophy, the state of nature, whereby men are in continual war against each other for as long as they remain in the state of nature: *homo homini lupus*. But as states are amongst themselves in the state of nature, according to Hobbes (*princeps principi lupus*), there can be no peace between either individuals or states, unless people and states create a power so superior to single entities, whether individuals or states, as to prevent either from winning. In my essay under the entry for 'Peace' (in volume VIII of the *Enciclopedia del Novecento*), I demonstrated the inherent weakness in the disarmament strategy through an allegory taken from a work by J. W. N. Watkins, a scholar who has studied Hobbes:

Tom and Harry are two Hobbesian men in a Hobbesian state of nature. Both are carrying lethal weapons. One afternoon, while they are searching for acorns, they come across each other in a small clearing in a wood. The thick undergrowth makes escape impossible. Tom shouts out, 'Wait! Let's not tear ourselves apart.' Harry replies, 'I am of the same mind. Let's count to ten and then throw our weapons over our shoulders into the trees.' Each of them then anxiously start to wonder whether or not they should actually throw the arms when they reach ten. They both think that if neither of them throws his weapons in the fear that the other won't, they will then have to fight to their last drop of blood and risk their lives. But each one also reflects that if he throws away his arms and the other doesn't, then his own death will certainly follow. There could be four outcomes: Tom throws them and not Harry, Harry throws them and not Tom, neither of them throws them away or both do. The last outcome constitutes fulfilment of the maxim *pacta sunt servanda*, but it is only one of the possible outcomes and not necessarily the most likely. If you consider the manner in which disarmament negotiations between the great powers are proceeding, it does not take long to realize the truth of the Hobbesian hypothesis. Is it not the case that the party that moves first in a situation where there can be no certainty that the other party will do likewise is putting itself in the hands of the other party? So no one takes the first move. The signing of a pact is one thing, but the fulfilment of its terms is quite another. Pacts that are not enforced by the sword of some superior body held over the contracting parties are, still according to Hobbes, simply a *flatus vocis* or so much hot air. We do not put enough emphasis on the importance of a third party in peace strategies.[16]

However something happened that I had not expected. I had not foreseen that the escalation could produce such a large imbalance between the antagonists that it would be impossible to re-establish a balance. When, in 1983, the American president Ronald Reagan announced the strategy of a defensive shield in space, officially called the Strategic Defence Initiative and polemically renamed 'Star Wars', he brought a decisive change in the conflict between the United States and the Soviet Union. To repeat an often-used metaphor, the Soviet Union was not KO'd but beaten on points. The Soviet president, Mikhail Gorbachev, realized that the power of the United States could not be equalled. The balance of terror had been thrown so much out of balance that it was no longer possible for balance between the parties to be re-established at a higher level.

It would have been reasonable at this stage to have expected a period of stable peace. This was not to happen. There was a sudden explosion of local wars which the United Nations sadly found itself powerless to stop. Intervention by the UN in the former Yugoslavia and Somalia proved to be disastrous. The result was that the ultimate power to settle disputes was entrusted to one of the parties: the United States. Indeed, parties to a dispute do not take their case to be heard at the United Nations; they take it to the White House. We are in a situation in which supreme international power is exercised by one of the parties, and the United Nations appears to have been completely deprived of its power, and therefore of its very reason for existence.

On 12 January 1991, a declaration by Bobbio appeared in the weekly Il Sabato on the failure of intellectuals to engage on the question of Kuwait's occupation by Iraq. He explained to the journalist who telephoned him that he had not yet found an answer to the question of whether the war was justified or not. However, on 15 January, the same day in which the UN's ultimatum expired, he issued a declaration on the Gulf War to the regional news on RAI's third channel, in which he resolved his doubts by arguing that the war was just, but it had yet to be seen whether it would be effective. On 17 January, Corriere della Sera published an interview in which Bobbio said: 'My worry is that pacifists could end up playing the game of the aggressor ... I am convinced that we should not and must not let aggression against a sovereign state go unpunished.' On 19 January, in a leader for La Stampa, he expressed his opinion that Saddam Hussein had made the war inevitable: 'However long the chain of "ifs" is, it always ultimately ends up at the door of the Iraqi dictator.' The adoption of this position opened a very difficult period for Bobbio, because he was bitterly opposed by his former students. These events were described in a small book called A Just War? put together by Carmine Donzelli and published by Marsilio in 1991:

There are two questions: is the war a just war? and if just, would it be effective? There can be no doubt as far as the first question is concerned: it is a just war, because it is based on a fundamental principle of international law, which justifies self-defence. As far as the second question on effectiveness is concerned, you need to take into account two conditions: war is effective above all if it is victorious; secondly, if it is rapid and limited in its geographical spread, which would mean restricted to the Iraqi theatre of war.

It is difficult to say what predictions are being made by the two antagonists. From Saddam Hussein's point of view, it could be said that if he accepts the war and rejects the ultimatum, this certainly means that the war could be victorious, irrespective of whether it is rapid or not, or whether it is contained or not. From the point of view of the Americans and their allies however, the war must not only be victorious, but it must also be rapid, with as little cruelty as possible, and as restricted as possible to relations between the Americans and their allies on the one side and the Iraqi government on the other.[17]

I received a polemical letter from Marco Revelli. I telephoned him immediately to tell him how much it had upset me. I told him that we should find a way to discuss the issue. I realized that our division reflected a split throughout Italian society involving both the left and the Catholics, in relation to a conflict between ethics of principle and ethics of responsibility. Besides, a day did not pass without the question being raised in the newspapers, or on the television and radio. In a way that had not occurred for a number of years, many Italian citizens were being unsettled by a moral question. A group of lecturers at Turin University, which included many of my former students, sent a letter of dissent to the newspapers with the overtly ironic title of 'Excuse me, teacher of peace': 'we believe in principle that there are no just wars, and this is the reason why we believe that the Gulf War must be avoided and must not be fought at any cost' (*L'Unità*, 19 January 1991). In my reply, I did not hide my surprise because the signatories were intellectuals inspired by the values of the Resistance, which has rightly been called a 'war of liberation'. As a war, was it then also to be considered unjust? In order to take some of the bad feeling out of the dispute, we organized a meeting at the Turin premises of the Gramsci Institute, and accurate reports by the journalist Loris Campetti appeared in the *Manifesto* on 30 January and by the sociologist Franco Ferraresi in *Corriere della Sera* on 31 January. I recall that the meeting was very civil, in spite of the difference of opinions, and I defended my ideas from attacks which were mild to a greater or lesser extent. One of my more severe critics was my old friend Gastone Cottino.

> The meeting took place at the Gramsci Institute, without the press and with a restricted audience. Bobbio laid out his position again: the concept of a just war is a technical and legal one, which should not be charged with values outside legal use. It simply implies that in certain cases force is legitimate: if there has been a breach of international law and the breach occurred with the use of force, then the use of force is legitimate. It is an analogous concept to that of self-defence and necessity, both situations in which it is justified to commit acts which otherwise would be unlawful. Just, therefore, in the sense of being legitimate and necessary. However, this is not enough by itself, the war must be appropriate to the purpose and must not be excessive in its effects: it would be completely unjustifiable if righting a wrong turned into a massacre. There can be recourse to war only after all other means of settling the dispute have been exhausted. Bobbio argues that in the current situation, these are far from having been resolved in a satisfactory manner.
>
> The speakers concentrated precisely on these aspects: doubts over the concept of a just war in a period in which the terrifying technology of weapons of mass destruction makes it impossible for the effects of war to be proportional to their causes (Gian Enrico Rusconi); the loss of heart in political alternatives to war, and the effectiveness of embargoes and economic pressure (Gian Giacomo Migone); the nobility of the rejection of war and any nationalistic appeal (Gastone

Cottino). Some of these contributions were composed and some were passionate, but they were all argued in a reasoned manner with the clear intention of entering into a dialogue with the other speaker without attempting to crush him, and of maintaining a good-natured debate amongst people who were however divided by a profound disagreement.[18]

The question of a just war provoked a wide-ranging debate with many more contributions, amongst which I can remember ones from Massimo Cacciari, Cesare Luporini and Danilo Zolo. They argued that the distinction between just and unjust wars needed to be considered obsolete: 'Restricted to those textbooks on moral theology', wrote Zolo in his article 'Una guerra giusta', 'which for centuries have offered excellent arguments to all sides to a dispute in order to justify every kind of war as a religious war.'[19] In my reply, which appeared in *L'Unità* on the same day, I upheld the distinction between the lawful and unlawful use of force, but confessed that I had many doubts over whether all the peaceful solutions had been explored and whether the war could have been delayed:

> I confess that, after the first few days, I too am uneasy. But would we be resting easier in the case of the opposite scenario? At the moment, it is difficult to give a reply, because it is not yet possible to predict whether the necessary conditions will be applied for the use of force to be commensurate to the purpose, and therefore justifiable – the lesser evil: restricted in space and time.
>
> However, one point remains valid: the renunciation of force in some cases does not mean removing force from the equation, but only means favouring the force used by a despot.[20]

These were days of intense activity. Following the firing of Iraqi missiles into Israeli territory, I was invited to address the Turin Synagogue along with Alessandro Galante Garrone and the mayor, Valerio Zanone. I wrote several articles in *La Stampa*, and in one of the last ones, I quoted from an Amnesty International report on the treatment of children under the dictatorship of Saddam Hussein (*Iraq: Children, Innocent Victims of Political Repression*, 1989). I wanted to explain that, once the ultimatum had expired, war was a tragic decision, but the tragedy had started a long time before for the Iraqi people. My article was followed by a magnificent letter on human rights from Ennio De Giorgi, an eminent mathematician at the Scuola Normale of Pisa and a member of the Accademia dei Lincei: 'We should treat as friends to be saved and not enemies to be destroyed those peoples who, due to their misfortune (and perhaps also to our past negligence and complicity), are subject to regimes that do not respect human rights.' In my reply, I pointed out that the question of human rights is linked to that of peace: '*Inter arma silent leges. During war, law is silenced.*' I wondered whether we should not invoke a moral limit, so that whoever chose war as the ultimate resort did not pursue it with such ruthlessness.

My last contribution to the peace debate was a lecture I gave on the UN's current situation, which was organized in Turin on 18 September 1995 by Ernesto Olivero.[21] The fundamental question I posed concerned the reform of the UN on the fiftieth anniversary of its foundation. I started from the obvious comment that the Security Council, the institution's executive body, is still made up of the five victors of the Second World War: the United States, the Soviet Union, Britain, France and China, while the Soviet Union no longer exists, and the China of 1945 has now been reduced to Taiwan. At the same time, two of the current major world powers, Germany and Japan, were on the losing side. I stated that the fundamental reforms that are now required could be summed up in the following formula: more power and more democracy. They are contradictory require-ments, but the processes of greater power and greater democracy should be developed alongside each other. More power means that the United Nations should possess the instruments of authority avail-able to any state: military force and the ability to raise taxes. As far as the former is concerned, the UN's powers, far from having been increased, have been diminished in recent years, following the failures of UN peacekeeping forces in Somalia and Yugoslavia, as have the resources made available to the UN for carrying out its duties.

More democracy means two things: more democratic states within the international system as a whole and a greater democratization of the rules by which the final decisions are taken by the executive bodies. To date, the number of non-democratic states has been higher than the number of democratic ones, although there has been a favourable trend towards a reduction in the imbalance between them. Besides, the degree of democracy in a state is not a criterion for membership of the United Nations, as it is sufficient to be a state in the legal and formal sense of the word, following the principle of effectiveness: the ability to exercise power over a nation successfully and on a continuous basis, irrespective of whether that power is exercised demo-cratically or autocratically.

The democratization of the entire system will never be carried out until the right of veto by great powers is abolished. There is still an enormous difference between the decision-making powers of the Security Council, made up of an extremely limited number of states (even after recent increases), and the power of the assembly of all member-states, which has become increasingly unmanageable with their increasing numbers (there were fifty-one member-states at the time of the UN's foundation, and this has now nearly quadrupled).

I concluded that my preference for institutional pacificism did not prevent me from perceiving its inherent difficulties, which have been particularly highlighted in Danilo Zolo's *The Prospect of World Government*,[22] and I have therefore acknowledged that we should not abandon ethical and religious pacifism. This is not at all incompatible with institutional pacifism; indeed, it is its moral foundation, as becomes clear to anyone who reads the introduction to the UN statute, in which the deliverance of future generations from the scourge of war is entrusted to a reaffirmation of faith 'in fundamental human rights and the dignity and value of human beings'.

8

Taking My Leave

I am now an old man. At the end of April 1993, Valeria and I celebrated our golden wedding anniversary as guests at the beautiful house and large garden that Marco and Cia own in Pino Torinese. All thirteen of us were there: Luigi and Patrizia, Andrea and Nicoletta, Marco and Cia, and five grandchildren, Andrea's Marco and Tommaso, and Marco's Simone, Emanuele and Federico. We only invited our closest relations and a few old friends: around fifty people. Our children surprised us by giving us two portraits painted by Stefano Levi della Torre. I was given the task of pulling the cord that would remove the cloth that covered them. I then said something that I have often had occasion to repeat: 'When you grow old, emotional attachments become more important than ideas.'

The last book that I had published by Einaudi was called *Old Age and Other Essays.*[1] Every day that passes, I feel more detached, distant, bewildered and rootless. I have become old in the fullest sense of the word. An old man loves to reflect on the past and attempt to draw up a balance sheet before the end, which cannot be far off, rather than continuously getting involved in political battles, as I have over the last thirty years. This explains why *Old Age* is not a political book, but a random selection of autobiographical writings, preceded by the essay that gives its name to the book, which I wrote for the Faculty of Political Science at Sassari University when they decided to inaugurate their first academic year by awarding me with an honorary degree. I replied to the dean, Virgilio Mura, that I intended to give a lecture on a non-academic subject: a reflection on old age, which we called *De senectute.* I had in fact passed my eightieth year, and I felt it was time to reflect on a condition of life that I had never dreamed of reaching. Since then, reflecting on the condition of old age has become for me almost a daily exercise, almost a habit, so the Sassari lecture has now been followed by other writings, which form the original nucleus of the book and in which I emphasize that old age is in the past tense:

> And the past is relived through recollections. The great wealth possessed by the old is the marvellous world of the memory, an inexhaustible source of reflections on ourselves, the universe in which we have lived, and the persons and events that have caught our attention along the way. The wonder of this world is the unsuspected quantity and immeasurable variety of things that it contains: the images of faces that have long since disappeared, places visited in the distant past and never revisited, characters from novels read in adolescence, fragments of poetry memorized at school and never forgotten, and many, many scenes from films and plays. It contains the faces of actors and actresses who have long been forgotten but are ready to reappear whenever you wish to see them, and when you see them again, you feel the same emotions as you did the very first time. It contains endless popular songs, arias from operas, excerpts from recitals and concerts that you replay within your mind.[2]

I realize, however, that I need to put this wealth of memories in order. I constantly fail to put persons and events in the right place, even though I still have a reasonably good memory, not so much for recent things, which I forget from one day to the next, but for things from the past. I regret that I never kept a diary except for my notes on my first years in the Senate. It would be very useful if I could now consult such a diary. However I have kept cards, autobiographical pages, quotations from books, work notes, newspaper cuttings and, above all, part of my correspondence, including rough copies of many letters, because I have written and continue to write letters. As I cannot avoid writing about myself in letters, they end up being a kind of involuntary diary.

Reflection on the past arises from the awareness that we have reached the end of the journey: the metaphorical journey, within which many real spatial journeys have taken place. I have spoken of some of these: in England, China and the countries of Eastern Europe. I cannot end the story of my life without at least some reference to the journeys that I have made over the last twenty years to Spain and such Latin American countries as Brazil, Argentina, Chile and Columbia, where many of my works have been translated and commented upon.[3] My peregrinations through the world of

Iberian culture started with a memorable occasion, a speech I gave on 25 October 1978 at the Cortes in Madrid, at the invitation of the leader of the PSOE [Spanish Socialist Workers' Party] parliamentary group, Gregorio Peces-Barba Martinez, at the time that the new Spanish Constitution was being approved. I talked about a subject that was very dear to me at the time and was topical in the country to which I had been invited: the question of democracy and socialism. I have to thank my friend Gregorio, who was to become the speaker of the Cortes and is now the rector of Charles III University in Madrid, for having opened up new horizons, just as I would also like to thank Elias Diaz and Alfonso Ruiz Miguel, both from the Autonomous University of Madrid for the warmth and cheerfulness with which they greeted me and Valeria on the many trips that followed that first one.

Old age cannot be separated from a sense of coming to the end, the feeling that you too have reached that appointment with death. You realize that you no longer have much time in which to assess your life. Your interest in the future fades. The future no longer belongs to you. On the other hand, you feel the need to understand whether your life has had any sense, and if so, what. This was the question that concluded a long interview published in *Nuova Antologia*, at the time the bibliography of my writings came out.[4] At the end of the interview, Pietro Polito, who was conducting it, asked me if there was a single thread running through and connecting the myriad of apparently fragmented events. I replied that I did not know:

> I really couldn't say whether you could find an underlying structure. The bibliography certainly would not help you to find one. The order in which the items are organized in this bibliography is purely formal and extrinsic: chronological for the entries as a whole, and alphabetical within the chronological periods of one year. These two criteria work perfectly for finding a book or pamphlet, but they are not of any use for finding out the relationship between a book or pamphlet with others as far as their content is concerned, that is, to be able to pass from a purely formal and extrinsic order to a substantive and intrinsic one. A useful analogy would be a large library. There is usually a subject catalogue next to the alphabetical catalogue on authors' names. Anyone who wished to discover the thread running through my writings held in a large library, would have to start with the subject catalogue. But you have to understand that the bibliography in itself is only the *sine qua non* for any further classification. Anyone who is looking for this hypothetical thread would have to undertake the enormous task not only of cataloguing the items by argument, as has been successfully done by Michelangelo Bovero and Luigi Bonanate at the end of the volume, but also of finding amongst these arguments an order that is substantially different to the alphabetical one in which they are laid

out in this appendix. Would it be worthwhile? I can only say what would be the surest way of finding this thread, but I cannot guarantee that you would find one.[5]

Bobbio's curiosity over the past was reflected in the interest he showed in books of memoirs. In 1992 and 1993, he wrote prefaces for three autobiographical works by self-taught writers which were published by small publishing houses. They were Cucire un motore, *a collection of short stories by Mario Macagno, a mechanic from Turin who had fought in the Resistance and was a keen palaeontologist and mountaineer;[6]* Domani chissà, *memoirs of a retired worker from Turin between 1931 and 1952, with a dramatic section in the middle which is set in the Mauthausen concentration camp;[7] and* Dall'abisso alla vetta, *the life of Antonio Ruju, a Sardinian born in 1911 who fought courageously as a partisan in Piedmont and survived the most terrible periods of poverty until finally achieving affluence.[8] The final lines of the preface to Ruju's work demonstrate why Bobbio had concerned himself with these texts and had agreed to write the introductions: 'Whoever picks up this book should read the last pages in which the author, having nearly reached the end of his life, carries out a brief assessment of his entire life, and uncovers his peasant roots and the moral teachings of his own father, a poor peasant who never bowed his head when persecuted by fascism for being a subversive.'*

Nor should we forget the more recent preface (1994), written for the Memoirs *of his grandfather Antonio Bobbio, which was edited by Cesare Manganelli and published by Piccolo in Alessandria (referred to at the beginning of this book). Through the grandfather, throughout his life an author of detailed diaries, diligently noted down every day in small exercise books, Bobbio sketched an image of old people:*

Grandfather was very different. As we knew him, he belonged to another time. He was severe, austere, stiff and self-controlled, with a perennial propensity to be pedagogic that meant using even the minutest daily event to draw out universal teachings . . . From what I can recall, he was an intimidating figure, one who instilled respect: more of a character from literature than from a cheap novel. They said he was profoundly religious; his were those traditional religious beliefs of which our family had completely lost any understanding.[9]

In his preface, Bobbio evoked family episodes from the past, including an exchange of letters with his brother Antonio throughout 1964, in which they amused themselves by recalling events and minor incidents mainly linked to Alessandria. Before his death, Antonio had these letters transcribed and brought together in two large and attractively bound volumes with an extremely detailed index of names, a few copies of which were handed out within the family.

The growing lack of interest in daily political events is also due to the fact that I have found myself increasingly absorbed by reflections on the great questions of life and death, and good and evil. It is now a few years since a collection of my articles was published on moral problems in a volume called *In Praise of Meekness*, in which the virtue of meekness is interpreted as the quintessentially non-political virtue. I said that the choice of this virtue was a reaction to the violent society in which we are forced to live and added:

> Not that I am so unsophisticated as to believe that human history has always been an idyll: Hegel once called it 'an immense slaughter'. But today there are these 'megatons' and they represent something totally new in the *destiny of the earth* (to quote the title of Jonathan Schell's well-known book). . . . What terrifies me are these damned megatons together with a will for power which remains undiminished, indeed it seems to have increased and to have been revered in this century. But there isn't just the will for power amongst the powerful, there is also the will for power amongst the little people, the isolated bomber, the tiny group of terrorists, the kind of person who throws a bomb into the crowd so that the greatest number of innocent people dies . . . You have understood: I identify the meek with non-violence, and meekness with the refusal to use violence against anyone at all. Meekness is a non-political virtue. Or you could even say that, in this world bloodied by the hatreds of those with great or little power, it is the antithesis of politics.[10]

My favourite essay in this collection, from a biographical point of view, is a reflection on the question of evil which has accompanied me throughout my life:

> Evil has two aspects which, although often and not always correctly associated with each other, should be kept quite distinct. These are active evil and passive evil. The former is inflicted, and the latter is endured. Inflicted evil and evil suffered. The general concept of evil includes two opposing human realities: wickedness and suffering. The paradigmatic figures of these two faces of evil are Cain and Job. When we pose the question of evil in general, as we are doing now, our mind indiscriminately turns to an episode of violence or pain: we might conjure up the image of a brutal murderer or just as easily the image of a mother crying. When we think of Sarajevo, we are presented with images of soldiers shooting and of men and women running away in panic: we think of butchers and victims. These images alternate, are superimposed and are continuously confused with each other.

I tried to correct the mental habit that tends to associate the inflicted evil with the evil suffered, as if there were a relationship of interdependence, by which suffering can be interpreted as the consequence of a wrongdoing. In reality suffering can arise from an infinity of causes, which have nothing to do with either our voluntary or our involuntary actions. Establishing a link between suffering and guilt is a convenient solution for the questions raised by the presence of evil, whether in connection with diseases, catastrophes, Auschwitz or Sarajevo:

> Not only is it not possible in any manner to prove that suffering implies a wrongdoing, it is not even possible to prove that in the general economy of the universe, the evil suffer more. The events of human history demonstrate exactly the opposite to any impartial observer: the tyrant Stalin died in his bed, while Anna Frank, the image of innocence, died in a concentration camp. The afflicted have always directed Job's question towards the heavens: 'Why?' Is there a reason for the evil person being saved while the innocent one is lost?
>
> Is there any point in posing the question, which at the time we found so disturbing? Why did an officer in Hitler's entourage unwittingly shift the case containing a bomb which Colonel von Stauffenberg had carried with him to kill Hitler, thus saving Hitler? Not only was he saved, but he could carry out his brutal vendettas. No, it has no sense. This too is a question which cannot be answered. But simple people have always had their answer: 'There is no justice in this world.'[11]

The end of the philosopher 'activist' was what you might call sanctioned by the decision after many years to end my journalistic activity for that great newspaper, *La Stampa*. I wrote my last political article to mark the fiftieth anniversary of the Italian Republic on 2 June 1996. I consider myself to be in every sense a product of the First Republic. Even though I was against the political system that held it up (I never voted Christian Democrat), I belong to a period that has now passed. I do not have much faith in the novelty just for the sake of it. Besides, this novelty is made up of the Lega Nord[12] and Forza Italia, as well as the rebirth of a party which considers itself to be the legitimate heir to fascism: all movements which I find disagreeable. The system is still unstable. Indeed the government led by Silvio Berlusconi only lasted seven months. I will not make any predictions about the duration of Prodi's government which emerged from the last elections. But is there anyone who seriously believes that it will last the full five-year term of the legislature? I should add that politics have become increasingly difficult to disentangle, especially for an old person whose ideas have become ossified, as

I repeat in all my laments. I understand less and less, or, perhaps more precisely, I have less desire to understand.

Finally, my unease is also due to the fact that one of the problems on the agenda is the constitutional question. It is a question that does not excite me, because I am sentimentally attached to the current Constitution, which was the first decisive step towards the rebirth of the country following its collapse. There is a fundamental reason for my lack of interest in constitutional questions: I do not believe that the principal and long-standing problems that Italy now has to confront are of a constitutional order. They are, in reality, questions that have nothing to do with the constitution.

One of the most serious problems is the administration of justice, starting with civil law. Even the most insignificant legal proceedings go on for so long that citizens cannot feel protected – not to speak of the criminal law. We have before us the spectacle, which I believe is unprecedented in the civilized world, of judges trying each other.

A second example is our education system. For years we have been waiting for a reform of the secondary schools, which still use the curricula introduced by Gentile. The inability of our political class to bring in the necessary reforms is incredible. If it is not able to reform the schools, why should we believe that it is capable of reforming the constitution? My grandson, who is at university, is studying three courses, and all three are held in cinemas in the area. Here again, this has nothing to do with the constitution.

As a third example, we all know the difficulties that the civil service finds itself in. For the most part, it is incapable of providing citizens with efficient services and making the machinery of state work as it should. We have discussed it endlessly. I think back to the inaction that greeted the reforms planned by that great legal mind, Massimo Severo Giannini, and in more recent times, by the brilliant Sabino Cassese. Is there any need to change the fundamental law in order to improve the state of public services?

The only real constitutional problem is the stability of government, in relation to which increasing currency is being given to the strange idea that the only solution is to set up a presidential republic as in America or France. But this is *a* problem, it is not *the* problem. You could also add the problem of decentralization, which was already supposed to have been dealt with by the establishment of regions, a spectacular failure precisely in relation to the restrictions placed on the central power of the state. I have always been of the conviction, which I have often repeated but which was said long before by Montesquieu, that the foundation of a good republic is the virtue of its citizens, more so than the justness of its laws. Let's be clear, I am not against reforming the Constitution in principle. I challenge the constitutionalist illusion whereby Italians will live happily ever after, once the old Constitution has been destroyed and the brand new one ushered in.

I am a child of a century that will perhaps be remembered as the most cruel in history. My most distant memories go back to the First World War, which has rightly been called 'the pointless massacre'. All three world wars of this century, the one against the central powers, the one against Nazism and fascism, and the Cold War against communism, were fought out between democratic and autocratic countries, and victory always went to democracy.

Democracy might have won, but its victory has not been definitive. In a secular (not mythical or religious), liberal and realistic (not universalizing or utopian) view of history, nothing is ever definitive. Not only has history not ended, as an American historian announced a few years ago, but perhaps it has hardly begun, judging from the technical and scientific progress that has radically transformed the possibilities of communication between all living people. The difficulty is in telling which direction it will take. Is the form of democratic government, whose victory I have just celebrated, destined to expand further or to die out gradually? According to the Eurocentric vision of history, Asia has always been considered a despotic world in opposition to Greek liberty, as extolled in Pericles' famous epitaph. Forms of government are now appearing and gaining strength and consensus in Asia, which remind us of the enlightened despotism of eighteenth-century absolute monarchies, whose dominion in Europe was disrupted by the American and French revolutions and the recognition of human rights, when the ancient primacy in the relationship between rights and duties which had characterized previous eras was overturned. Human beings have duties, but as individuals with value in themselves, they have rights irrespective of circumstances of time and place in which they live, such as the right to life, liberty (the various forms of liberty) and equality (at least equality as a starting point). They may be assigned duties, either to other individuals or to the community to which they belong, only in as much as they are primarily recipients of fundamental rights. In enlightened despotism past and present, the image of the subjugated and yet contented individual replaces the one we are more familiar with through the tradition of Greek and Christian thought, whereby the individual is anguished but free. Which of the two forms of society is destined to prevail in the near future, no one can say.

The current age, as I have said, is distinguished by increasingly rapid technological and scientific progress: so rapid as to give an old man a feeling of vertigo. It is both irresistible and unstoppable. According to the general opinion of the scientists who are responsible for it, it has been, until now, irreversible because the new appliance drives out the old appliance, which quickly becomes a museum piece, be it a washing machine, a motor car, a computer or any implement of war. In relation to the ongoing creation of increasingly efficient new appliances (i.e. capable of achieving their required purposes), one could with good reason speak of a 'permanent revolution', using 'revolution' in its proper sense of a transformation so radical as to leave no possibility of a return to the previous state of affairs.

On the other hand, you cannot talk so confidently of permanent revolution in relation to costumes, social relations and rules of behaviour, where revolutions are almost always followed by periods of restoration. Restorations should be understood as the re-emergence of the old state of affairs following the exhaustion or flagging of the spirit of renewal. In the case of human history, it seems more appropriate to apply the dialectic concept of development that proceeds through affirmation and negation, rather than the concept generally accepted by the scientific community of revolutionary transition from one paradigm to another.

In my speech in April 1995 to mark the Agnelli Prize for Ethics in Contemporary Society, I said that the attributes of acceleration, relentlessness and irreversibility that apply to technological and scientific progress, are not appropriate for moral progress. Having been obliged to live in a hostile world both in terms of natural hazards and the harms inflicted by their fellow creatures, human beings have attempted to make it more habitable by, on the one hand, inventing the productive capabilities of instruments designed to transform the surrounding world and make survival possible, and on the other hand, by inventing rules to regulate behaviour that make society possible. I observed that the invention of instruments to control and subdue nature has progressed much more rapidly and with more dramatic effects than the establishment of rules to control and subdue the human world. Compare a tribal village with a modern metropolis, with its skyscrapers, its streets which run parallel or intersect, its thousands of motor cars which drive along them, and its complicated systems of illumination and communication. Then compare the moral code of that tribe, which regulates its births, marriages and deaths, the main events in community life, as well as relationships between individuals for the formation, conservation and distribution of power, with our codes, constitutions, incentives to do good and not to do bad, rewards and punishments, which still include the death penalty. The comparison provides, I believe, a historical demonstration of the level of development between the two systems: not only that the former is more rapid and the latter slower, but that the former is inexorable to the point of continuously destroying the power of the rule that nature has attempted to impose on innovators, while the latter has been much more resistant to change. Clearly nature has been much more submissive to mankind's dominion than mankind itself.

In relation to irreversibility, human history has always been represented as a series of advances and retreats, of civilization and barbarism, of change and stagnation, of revolution and restoration, and of progress and decline. The Industrial Revolution, with all its subsequent phases which lead us to talk of a first, second and third Industrial Revolution, one linked into the other, could be compared with a continuous stream. Institutional change, on the other hand, is intermittent. While technological and scientific progress never ceases to arouse our wonder and enthusiasm, albeit mixed with anguish over the perverse effects it sometimes produces, we continue to interrogate ourselves over the question of moral progress just as we did one thousand or two thousand years ago, repeating the same arguments ad infinitum and posing the same questions with no answers or with unsatisfactory answers. It is as though we are constantly immersed in what believers call the *mystery* and non-believers call the *problem* of evil, in its two aspects I have already referred to: those of active evil (wickedness) and passive evil (suffering).

I would not hesitate in defining as dramatic the problem of the contradiction between the development of science and the great ethical questions provoked by that development, and between our wisdom as investigators of the cosmos and our moral illiteracy. But the problem is one thing, its solution is quite another. The science of good and evil has yet to be invented. There is not a moral or legal question, there is not a question of behavioural rules or discipline of the way we act that does not give rise to different and opposite solutions. Just to give the first examples that come into my head, there is the legitimacy of abortion, the death penalty, organ transplants and surrogate mothers. Scientific development in all fields of human activity is increasingly confronting us with new problems that involve choosing between different solutions, none of which can be answered by this new knowledge. It does not provide answers because scientific discoveries and technological innovations provide us with increasingly perfect instruments for achieving ends that were previously unknown, but they tell us nothing about the intrinsic good or evil in those ends. This depends on moral judgements that are often in conflict with each other, according to the historical circumstances, the social status of

A Political Life

the persons debating them, the interests at work amongst the parties, and the philosophies and ideologies that motivate them. I concluded my speech by saying:

> We have to realize yet again that our moral sense develops, always supposing it does develop, much more slowly than economic power, political power and technological power. All our declarations of rights belong to an ideal world, to the world of what should be, of that which would be good. But let us look around (every day our always improving mass media with the hundred eyes of Argus take us round the world several times over), and we see our streets covered in blood, piles of abandoned bodies, entire populations driven from their homes, ragged and starving, and emaciated children with bulging eyes who have never smiled and will not smile before meeting a premature death. It would be nice, perhaps even encouraging to call human rights a great invention of our civilization, as an analogy with the creation of increasingly sophisticated appliances, but compared with technological inventions, human rights are merely an invention whose creation has been loudly proclaimed but whose machinery has never been made to work. The *new world ethos of human rights* shines out from grandiose international declarations and world conferences that celebrate and comment upon them in a learned manner, but the response to these grand occasions and their learned comments is in reality their systematic violation in nearly all the countries of the world (perhaps we could say *all* the countries, without fear of being mistaken), in relations between the powerful and the weak, the rich and the poor, and those who know and those who do not.[13]

It is difficult to say what all this will mean for the 'future of democracy'. The nineteenth century has been called with good reason the century of faith in indefinite progress. Belief in the certainty of progress arose from the conviction that scientific progress and moral progress were intimately connected, that moral progress depended on an ever greater distribution of knowledge, and that the advancement of wisdom and the advancement of behavioural patterns would go at the same pace. Today no one can believe that.

Today we no longer have that certainty. This affirmation, even if only a hypothesis, could be the reason for the reawakening of religion in all its forms, both noble and ignoble. The religious preacher offers a hope and attempts to resuscitate the God whose death was announced by Nietzsche. The defeat of the Enlightenment? Yes and no. According to the new religious converts, secularization has resulted in nihilism or, in other words, the destruction of all values. However, the exasperated reaction of those who wish to restore religion has degenerated into fundamentalism, which transforms a criminal act into a lawful one, indeed into a duty, and a negative value into a value, because 'God desires it'. Within the same few days, some youngsters threw rocks from a motorway bridge for fun and killed a young woman, and a group of Islamic fanatics cut the throats of five young girls to punish a village for having opposed their resistance movement.

Democracy eschews both these extremes. Approaching the question in terms of rule, democracy is often contrasted with anarchy or an absence of rules at the bottom of society, and with despotism or an absence of rules at the top of society. Approaching the question in terms of values, democracy is based on the strong value of the human individual as a person against nihilism, and on mutual respect between individuals against all forms of ideological fanaticism.

It is equally uncertain whether technological progress will exercise a beneficial or a harmful influence on democracy, as it puts into men's hands instruments for transforming and manipulating nature and the human world which were hitherto unthought of. It could either favour the will for power or encourage unrealistic projects to solve problems that humanity has suffered from the beginning of history. Besides, as I have said many times, human history is ambiguous over salvation and perdition. We do not even know if we are in control of our own destiny.

Chronology of Events

1909   Norberto Bobbio is born in Turin, the son of Luigi, a surgeon, and Rosa Caviglia.

1915   Following the Treaty of London, Italy enters the First World War on the side of the Allies in exchange for territorial promises.

1919   The Fascist Movement is founded by Mussolini and the myth of the 'mutilated victory' is fostered (based on the idea that Italy had not been sufficiently rewarded in territorial terms. Italy enters a period of serious industrial unrest).

1921   The Italian Communist Party is founded.

1922   Following the March on Rome in October, Mussolini takes and begins to consolidate power and build a totalitarian state, a process that is completed by 1929 at the latest.

1927   Norberto Bobbio enrolls as a law student at Turin University.

1929   Giustizia e Libertà ['Justice and Freedom'] the dynamic anti-fascist organization, is founded abroad by exiles. It has important Turin connections and is to have a significant role in preparing the Resistance.

1931   Norberto Bobbio graduates in philosophy of law.

1932–3   He travels in Germany with Renato Treves and Ludovico Geymonat, and studies at Marburg University.

1933   He graduates for a second time in philosophy.

1934   He starts to teach at the Law Faculty at Camerino University.

1935   He is arrested on 15 May for anti-fascist activities, along with his friends in the Justice and Freedom group. He starts to edit the magazine *Rivista di Filosofia*. Italy invades Ethiopia in October.

1936   The conquest of Ethiopia is completed by May in a brutal and costly campaign. Mussolini proclaims the Empire. Italy sends troops to assist Franco in the Spanish Civil War.

1939   Norberto Bobbio is appointed to Siena University. Italy invades Albania, and Mussolini enters the so-called Pact of Steel with Hitler.

1940   Italy declares war on Britain and France, whose defeat is imminent. Bobbio obtains the chair of philosophy of law at Padua University.

1942   Norberto Bobbio joins the Action Party, as part of the Liberal-Socialist Movement, both being clandestine anti-fascist organizations.

1943   Norberto Bobbio marries Valeria Cova. The Allies land in Sicily. Following a vote by the Fascist Grand Council on 25 July, King Victor Emmanuel III dismisses Mussolini from government and has him arrested. On 8 September the armistice is declared and the Germans invade Italy. The Badoglio government and the royal family abandon Rome. On 12 September Mussolini is freed by SS commandos. In the same month, the Italian Social Republic is declared and joins the number of Nazi puppet-states around Europe. On 6 December, Bobbio is arrested in Padua for anti-fascist activities.

1944   Norberto Bobbio's first son, Luigi, is born on 16 March. A congress of anti-fascist parties held in Bari calls for the abdication of the king and the establishment of a constituent assembly once the war is over. In June Badoglio resigns as head of government in favour of Bonomi, who represents the parties in the Committee of National Liberation (CLN). Patriotic Action Groups (GAPs) are set up in the cities to organize partisan activities. In November, General Alexander, on behalf of the Allies, appeals to the partisans to lay down their arms as victory was supposedly assured. His request is ignored and partisans continue to liberate areas from Nazi–fascist control.

1945   In April the German army is routed. The Allies find many of the northern cities have been already liberated when they arrive. With an insurrectionary situation in the North and the Italian economy in a catastrophic state, Bonomi is replaced by Parri as prime minister. Parri is a leading member of the Action Party. However, his party only lasts until December, when he is replaced by the Christian Democrat leader Alcide De Gasperi, marking the beginning of that party's 45-year dominance of Italian politics.

1946   On 2 June, a referendum favours the Republic and the elections are dominated by the three mass parties: the Socialists (20.7 per cent), the Communists (19 per cent) and the Christian Democrats (35.2 per cent). The Action Party is unable to make its mark and Norberto Bobbio fails to be elected in its list. His second son, Andrea, is born on 24 February.

1947   Luigi Einaudi, as the liberal budget minister in De Gasperi's government, applies rigorous deflationary policy to stabilize the lira.

1948   Norberto Bobbio takes over the chair of philosophy of law at Turin University. In April the Christian Democrats win an absolute majority defeating the Popular Front of Socialists and Communists. Einaudi is elected president of the Republic, and an attempt on Togliatti's life causes a general strike and violence throughout Italy.

1949   Italy joins NATO.

1951   Mario, Bobbio's third son, born.

1953   The attempt to introduce the so-called *legge truffa*, which would have allocated extra seats to the party with an absolute majority, fails to get through parliament after a sustained campaign by the left. De Gasperi resigns.

1955   Einaudi publishes Bobbio's *Politica e cultura*, which reflects his contribution to the debate with the Communists on libertarian rights. He leaves for China as part of a cultural delegation.

1957   The Socialist Party's alliance with the Communists comes to an end following the events in Hungary. The Treaty of Rome establishes the European Economic Community.

1962   The Christian democrat Fanfani forms the first centre-left government with the support of the Social-Democrats and Republicans, and the external support of the Socialists. Norberto Bobbio moves to the chair of political science.

1963   The post-war boom is beginning to cause structural problems in the Italian economy. The South is left behind and excessive expansion of credit causes inflationary pressures.

1964   The left wing of the Socialist Party splits away and forms the Italian Socialist Party of Proletarian Unity (PSIUP). Norberto Bobbio publishes *Italia civile*, a collection of memoirs.

1965 The economic situation starts to improve again, owing to an increase in exports and better monetary control.

1966 Following lengthy negotiations, the Socialists and Social-Democrats agree to reunite.

1968 Student unrest commences at Turin University, before spreading to the rest of the country.

1969 The 'hot autumn' or *autunno caldo* involves the protests spreading from the universities to the factories. On 12 December a bomb explodes in Piazza Fontana, the first of many atrocities which were to mark the post-1969 period. Garzanti publishes Bobbio's *Il profilo ideologico del '900*.

1976 Einaudi publishes Bobbio's *Quale socialismo?* [*Which Socialism?*, trans. R. Griffin, Cambridge: Polity, 1988].

1981 Spadolini, a republican, becomes prime minister. For the first time, a non-Christian democrat leads the coalition, in which the Christian Democrats still remain by far the largest party.

1983 Craxi, the leader of the Socialist Party, becomes prime minister, and remains the head of government until 1987.

1984 Einaudi publishes Bobbio's *Il futuro della democrazia* [*The Future of Democracy*, ed. R. Bellamy, trans. R. Griffin, Cambridge: Polity, 1987]. He is made a senator for life by the president of the Republic, Sandro Pertini.

1985 Einaudi publishes *Stato, governo e società*.

1992 Scalfaro is elected president of the Republic. His presidency is to witness sudden changes in the Italian political landscape, as the Christian Democrats and Socialists begin to break up under the weight of scandals and the changed reality in the post-Soviet era.

1994 The Christian Democrats attempt to re-form under the new name of Italian Popular Party, a name that goes back to Don Sturzo's party in the pre-fascist era. The Communists have already changed their name to the Democratic Party of the Left, and a new force has appeared on the right Forza Italia, a semi-party led by the media mogul Silvio Berlusconi. His coalition, which also includes the fascist National Alliance and Bossi's xenophobic separatist movement in the north, Lega Nord. The coalition only manages to survive until December. Donzelli publishes Bobbio's *Destra e sinistra* [*Left and Right*, trans. A. Cameron, Cambridge: Polity, 1996]. The book, which analyses the left–right distinction and defends its relevance in modern politics, is an enormous publishing success and sells a third of a million copies around Europe.

List of Bobbio's principal published books mentioned in this work

La filosofia del decadentismo (Turin: Chiantore, 1944)
The Philosophy of Decadentism: A Study in Existentialism, trans. D. Moore (Oxford: Basil Blackwell, 1948)

Lezioni di filosofia del diritto: Ad uso degli studenti [*Lessons on Legal Philosophy*] (Turin: Giappichelli, 1946)

Teoria della scienza giuridica [*Theory of the Science of Law*] (Turin: Giappichelli, 1950)

Politica e cultura [*Politics and Culture*] (Turin: Einaudi, 1955)

Diritto e stato nel pensiero di Emanuele Kant [*Law and the State in the Thought of Immanuel Kant*] (Turin: Giappichelli, 1957)

Il positivismo giuridico [*Legal Positivism*] (Turin: Editrice Co-operativa Universitaria, 1961)

Italia civile [*Civilized Italy*] (Bari: Lacaita, 1964; Florence: Passigli, 1986)

La teoria delle forme di governo nella storia del pensiero politico [*The Theory of Governmental Forms in the History of Political Thought*] (Turin: Giappichelli, 1976)

Quale socialismo? (Turin: Einaudi, 1976)
Which Socialism?, trans. R. Griffin (Cambridge: Polity, 1998)

Il problema della guerra e le vie della pace [*The Problem of War and the Paths to Peace*] (Bologna: Il Mulino, 1979)

Le ideologie e il potere in crisi [*The Crisis of Ideologies and Power*] (Florence: Le Monnier, 1981)

L'analogia nella logica del diritto [*Analogy in Legal Logic*] (Turin: Law Institute of the University of Turin, 1938)

Maestri e compagni [*Mentors and Comrades*] (Florence: Passigli, 1984)

Il futuro della democrazia (Turin: Einaudi, 1984)
The Future of Democracy: A Defence of the Rules of the Game, ed. R. Bellamy, trans. R. Griffin (Cambridge: Polity, 1987)

Stato, governo e società [*State, Government and Society*] (Turin: Einaudi, 1985)

Italia fedele: Il mondo di Gobetti [*Loyal Italy: The World of Gobetti*] (Florence: Passigli, 1986)

Teoría general del derecho [*The General Theory of Law*] (Bogotá: Editorial Temis, 1987)

Il terzo assente [*The Absent Third*], ed. P. Polito (Milan: Sonda, 1989)

Il profilo ideologico del '900 (Turin: CLUT, 1972; Milan: Garzanti, 1990)
Ideological Profile of Twentieth-Century Italy, trans. L. Cochrane (Princeton: Princeton University Press, 1995)

L'età dei diritti (Turin: Einaudi, 1990)
The Age of Rights, trans. A. Cameron (Cambridge: Polity, 1996)

L'utopia capovolta [*Utopia Turned Upside Down*] (Turin: La Stampa, 1990)

Una guerra giusta? [*A Just War?*] (Venice: Marsilio, 1991)

Diritto e potere: Saggi su Kelsen [*Law and Power: Essays on Kelsen*] (Naples: Edizioni Scientifiche Italiane, 1992)

Il dubbio e la scelta: Intellettuali e potere nella società contemporanea [*Doubt and Choice: Intellectuals and Power in Contemporary Society*] (Rome: NIS, 1993)

Elogio della mitezza e altri scritti morali (Milan: Linea d'Ombra, 1994)
In Praise of Meekness: Essays on Ethics and Politics, trans. T. Chataway (Cambridge: Polity, 2000)

Destra e sinistra (Rome: Donzelli Editore, 1995)
Left and Right, trans. A. Cameron (Cambridge: Polity, 1996)

De senectute e altri scritti autobiografici (Turin: Einaudi, 1996)
Old Age and Other Essays, trans. A. Cameron (Cambridge: Polity, 2001)

Tra due repubbliche [*The Passage from One Republic to the Next*] (Rome: Donzelli, 1996)

Notes

Introduction

1 See N. Bobbio, *Il dubbio e la scelta: Intellettuali e potere nella società contemporanea* [*Doubt and Choice: Intellectuals and Power in Contemporary Society*] (Rome: La Nuova Italia Scientifica, 1993).

2 The Action Party was formed in 1942 by anti-fascist intellectuals from the Justice and Freedom group and the Liberal-Socialist Movement. It played an important role in the Resistance, as well as in the formation of the first government after Liberation. Due to the Christian Democrats' dominance and the Action Party's own lack of a mass base, the party was routed in the 1948 elections.

3 N. Bobbio, 'Scienza del diritto e analisi del linguaggio', *Rivista Trimestrale di Diritto e Procedura Civile* (1950), IV, 2 June, pp. 242–67.

4 N. Bobbio, *Diritto e potere: Saggi su Kelsen* [*Law and Power: Essays on Kelsen*] (Naples: Edizioni Scientifiche Italiane, 1992).

5 N. Bobbio, 'Intorno all'analisi funzionale del diritto' ['On the functional analysis of law'], in *Sociologia del diritto* (1975), vol. 1, pp. 1–25.

6 G. Calogero, *La scuola dell'uomo* (Florence: Sansoni, 1939).

7 A. Capitini, *Elementi di un'esperienza religiosa* (Bari: Laterza, 1937).

8 N. Bobbio, 'Democrazia e pace: la calamita di una vita di studi' ['Democracy and peace: the magnet of a lifetime of research'], *La Stampa*, 7 June 1996.

9 See N. Bobbio, *The Future of Democracy: A Defence of the Rules of the Game*, ed. R. Bellamy, trans. R. Griffin (Cambridge: Polity, 1987); original title: *Il futuro della democrazia* (Turin: Einaudi, 1984).

10 H. Kelsen, *General Theory of Norms* (Oxford: Clarendon Press, 1991), chapter 26. Bobbio devotes three chapters to Kelsen and the question of legal power in his *Diritto e potere*, pp. 103–55.

11 N. Bobbio, 'L'alternanza sblocca la democrazia' ['Alternation unlocks democracy'], *La Stampa*, 23 April 1996. The report in *Le Monde* is cited in this article.

12 Ibid.

13 See Bobbio, *The Future of Democracy*.

14 N. Bobbio, 'An autobiographical aperçu of legal philosophy' in *Ratio Juris*, nos. 9–12 (1996), p. 123.

15 N. Bobbio, *The Age of Rights*, trans. A. Cameron (Cambridge: Polity, 1996), p. vii; original title: *L'età dei diritti* (Turin: Einaudi, 1990).

16 N. Bobbio and D. Zolo, 'Hans Kelsen. The theory of law and the international legal system: A talk', *European Journal of International Law*, 2 (1998), pp. 355–67.

17 Bobbio's modern refinement of 'cosmopolitical right' has a long history. He first mentioned the concept in an early Kantian writing, *Diritto e stato nel pensiero di Emanuele Kant* (Turin: Giappichelli, 1957), pp. 278–80. He addressed the concept again in *Il problema della guerra e le vie della pace* (Turin: CLUT, 1965), pp. 208–10. A concise summary integrating the concept with Kant's legal and political philosophy is found in his 'Introduzione' to N. Merker, ed., *Per la pace perpetua* (Rome: Editori Riuniti, 1989), pp. vii–xxi. Bobbio restated the concept in *The Age of Rights*, pp. 120–2.

18 N. Bobbio, 'Democracy and the international system' in D. Archibugi and D. Held, eds, *Cosmopolitan Democracy* (Cambridge: Polity, 1995), pp. 17–41.

19 The term is found in I. Kant, *The Philosophy of Law*, trans. W. Hastie (Edinburgh: Clark, 1887) in his discussion of 'Nature and conditions of cosmopolitical right', pp. 226–8.

20 See N. Bobbio, *Il problema della guerra e le vie della pace* (Bologna: Il Mulino, 1979) and Bobbio, *Il terzo assente* [*The Absent Third*] (Milan: Sonda, 1989) for Bobbio's extended reflections on war and peace.

Chapter 1 Before the Conflagration

1 Actual title: *Il Vero, il Bello e il Ponano nei 'Promessi Sposi'*

2 Actual title: *Memorie*.

3 N. Bobbio, *De senectute e altri scritti autobiografici* (Turin: Einaudi, 1996), pp. 53–4.

4 In the Italian education system, *liceo*, here translated as 'senior secondary school', is the school which prepares pupils for university and is attended by pupils aged 14–19 [*translator's note*].

5 In the Italian education system, *ginnasio*, here translated as 'junior secondary school', covers the last two years of the *scuola media* before the possibility of going on to *liceo* or senior secondary school [*translator's note*].

6 '*Crepuscolarismo*' (literally, 'twilightism') was an Italian twentieth-century literary movement [*translator's note*].

7 The list of books comprised: G. B. Angioletti, *Il giorno del giudizio* [*Judgement Day*]; C. Formichi, *Il Buddhismo* [*Buddhism*]; B. Croce, *Elementi di politica* [*Basic Politics*]; P. B. Shelley, *Liriche* [*Poetry*]; G. B. Shaw, *Uomo e superuomo* [*Man and Superman*]; P. Géraldy, *Le prélude*; G. Baretti, *La Rivista Letteraria*, vol. II; A. de Musset, *Poésies nouvelles*; L. Chiarelli, *La maschera e il volto* [*The Mask and the Face*]; G. Carle, *La vita del diritto* [*Legal Life*]; I. Valetta, *Chopin: La vita. Le opere* [*Chopin: His Life and Works*]; D. Lattes, *Ebraismo* [*Jewish Studies*]; P. Géraldy, *La guerre, madame*; P. Géraldy, *Aimer*; Stendhal, *La Chartreuse de Parme* [*The Charterhouse of Parma*]; Sun-Sun-Ku, *Il Confucianesimo* [*Confucianism*]; G. Rensi, *L'ateismo* [*Atheism*]; and B. Croce, *Teoria e storia della storiografia* [*Theory and History of Historiography*].

8 See *L'Indice dei Libri del Mese*, XII, no. 8, September 1995, p. 19.

9 N. Bobbio, *Left and Right*, trans. A. Cameron (Cambridge: Polity, 1996), pp. 83; original title: *Destra e Sinistra* (Rome: Donzelli, 1995).

10 See P. P. Brescacin, *Umberto Cosmo e la pratica della libertà* (Susegana: Arti Grafiche Conegliano, 1995), pp. 88ff.

11 *Ordine Nuovo*: an historically important political newspaper founded by Antonio Gramsci [*translator's note*].

12 See G. Bergami's comment on Zini's *Diario* published as *La tragedia del proletariato in Italia: Diario 1914–1926* (Milan: Feltrinelli, 1973), vol. I, p. 35, n. 28. See also the diary itself which was edited by Bergami, *Pagine di vita torinese: Note del Diario (1894–1937)* (Turin: Centro Studi Piemontesi, 1981). 'Il soldato di Lambessa', was the name of a series of radio conversations held by Franco Antonicelli. In one of them, he referred to Zini and his cursed book 'which has become so rare, and deserves to be republished' (Rome: ERI, 1956), p. 112.

13 Leone Ginzburg, *Scritti giovanile inediti*, published as an appendix to *Da Odessa a Torino: Conversazioni con Marussia Ginzburg*, with a preface by Norberto Bobbio (Turin: Albert Meynier, 1989).

14 Giustizia e Libertà: an anti-fascist movement founded in Paris in 1929 by exiles mainly living in Paris. The founders included Carlo Rosselli, the author of *Socialismo liberale* [*Liberal Socialism*], later tragically murdered with his brother Nello by fascist assassins, Emilio Lussu and Gaetano Salveruini. The aims of the organization were liberal, democratic and republican. It continued as an effective movement, right up until the Resistance, during which it merged with other anti-fascist organizations to form the Action Party [*translator's note*].

15 A. Monti, *I miei conti con la scuola* (Turin: Einaudi, 1965), pp. 232 and 243.

16 OVRA: the secret police force established under fascism [*translator's note*].

17 N. Bobbio, *Maestri e compagni* (Florence: Passigli, 1984), pp. 162–3.

18 Ibid., pp. 174–5.

19 'L'insegnamento di Gioele Solari', in N. Bobbio, *Italia civile* (Florence: Passigli, 1986).

20 Daughter of General Ugo Allason and mother of the physicist Giancarlo Wick, Barbara Allason died in 1968 at the age of ninety-one.

21 'L'indirizzo fenomenologico nella filosofia sociale e giuridica', published by the Institute of Law at the University of Turin in 1934. In the same year, Bobbio also published 'Aspetti odierni della filosofia giuridica in Germania (F. Kaufmann e Schreier)' in *Rivista Internazionale di Filosofia del Diritto*, XIV, series 4–5, July–October 1934.

22 N. Bobbio, 'La filosofia di Husserl e la tendenza fenomenologica', *Rivista di Filosofia*, XXVI, no. 1, January–March 1935.

23 M. Mila, *Scritti civili* (Turin: Einaudi, 1995).

24 This incident is narrated in detail using the police papers in G. De Luna, 'Una cospirazione alla luce del sole: Giustizia e Libertà a Torino negli anni trenta', in *L'itinerario di Leone Ginzburg*, ed. N. Tranfaglia (Turin: Bollati Boringhieri, 1996), pp. 12–39.

25 The inconsistency of the numbers appeared in the original text.

26 See State Archive, Ministry of Internal Affairs, Police General Management, AA.GG.RR. Division, Cat. G1, Envelope 281, Files 756024, Sub-Section 3.

27 See L. Salvatorelli and G. Mira, *Storia d'Italia nel periodo fascista* (Turin: Einaudi, 1964). The quote was taken from the later edition (Milan: Mondadori, 1969), p. 218.

28 N. Bobbio, 'L'arresto di Martinetti in casa Solari il 15 maggio 1935', *Rivista di Filosofia*, LXXXIV, no. 3, December 1993, p. 372.

29 P. Martinetti, 'Riflessioni sul soggiorno nelle carceri "Nuove" di Torino', *Rivista di Filosofia*, LXXIV, no. 3, December 1993, p. 373.

30 Salvatorelli and Mira, *Storia d'Italia*, p. 316.

31 G. De Luna, 'Giorgio e Livio', introduction to G. Agosti and L. Bianco, *Un'amicizia partigiana* (Turin: Albert Meynier, 1990), p. 13.

32 F. Antonicelli, *Ci fu un tempo. Ricordi fotografici di Franco Antonicelli* (Turin: Regione Piemonte, 1977), p. 24.

33 The text which is published here is the copy held in the State Archives, Ministry of Internal Affairs, General Management of the Police Force, Division AA.GG.RR., Sect. 1, Enforced Residence, recorded on 18 July 1935, File reference no. 710–11647, entitled 'Statement by Norberto Bobbio to His Excellency the Head of the Government'.

34 N. Ajello, 'Macché scandolo, è un pezzo di storia', *La Repubblica*, 16 June 1992.

35 G. Bocca, 'Strategia, compromesso o eccesso di zelo?', *Corriere della Sera*, 16 June 1992.

36 See A. Papuzzi, 'Bobbio, il diritto di difendersi', *La Stampa*, 16 June 1992.

37 G. De Luna, 'Quella caduta di Bobbio', *L'Unità*, 16 June 1992.

38 M. Revelli, 'Gli archivi del ricatto', *Il Manifesto*, 17 June 1992.

39 State Archives, Ministry of Internal Affairs, General Management of the Police Force, Political Police Division, Cat. K7, G. 118, File K7/15.

40 A member of the Quadrumvirate that directed the fascist seizure of power, and therefore a close associate of Mussolini, although in the end he was to be tried and executed by the latter in the short-lived Republic of Salò [*translator's note*].

41 Bobbio, *Left and Right*.

204 Notes

42 M. Veneziani, *Sinistra e destra: Risposta a Norberto Bobbio* (Florence: Vallecchi, 1995), p. 36.
43 B. Gatta, 'Così il Quadrumviro raccomandava Bobbio', in *Il Tempo*, 17 June 1992. For the whole affair, see Bobbio's essay in *Mezzo secolo: Materiali di ricerca storica*, XI, Annals 1994–6, published by Piero Gobetti Research Institute, the Piedmontese Historical Society or nice Resistance, and the National Film Archive of the Resistance in Turin.
44 See 'Destra e sinistra. Bobbio contro Veneziani', *Corriere della Sera*, 13 August 1995.
45 Ministry of Education, extract from the *Bollettino Ufficiale*, part II, 16 March 1939, XVII, no. 11.

Chapter 2 The Resistance

1 R. Zangrandi, *Il lungo viaggio attraverso il fascismo* (Milan: Feltrinelli, 1962), pp. 193–4.
2 Ibid., p. 483.
3 Ibid., p. 484.
4 N. Bobbio, *Maestri e compagni* (Florence: Passigli, 1984), pp. 279–80.
5 N. Bobbio, 'Cinquant'anni dopo', preface to A. Capitini, *Elementi di un'esperienza religiosa* (Bologna: Cappelli, 1990), pp. xiii–xiv.
6 Giovanni Gentile (1875–1944), both philosopher and dedicated fascist intellectual who supported Mussolini throughout his life. He was shot by partisans.
7 G. Calogero, *La logica del giudice e il suo controllo in cassazione* (1937).
8 For Bobbio's relationship with Calogero, see F. Sbarberi, 'Liberté et égalité. La formation de la théorie démocratique chez Bobbio', *Archives de Philosophie*, vol. 57 (Paris: Beuchesne Éditeur, 1994). For Calogero's political thought, see the most complete collection of his political writings: *Difesa del liberalsocialismo ed altri scritti politici*, new edn ed. M. Schiavone and D. Cofrancesco (Milan: Marzorati, 1972).
9 N. Bobbio, 'Introduzione: Tradizione ed eredità del liberalsocialismo', in N. Bobbio et al., *I dilemmi del liberalsocialismo*, ed. M. Bovero, V. Mura and F. Sbarberi (Rome: La Nuova Italia Scientifica, 1994), p. 59.
10 'Bobbio racconta quegli anni bui rischiarati da Croce', *Nuova Antologia*, no. 2172, October–December 1989, p. 194.
11 G. De Luna, *Storia del Partito d'Azione* (Milan: Feltrinelli, 1982), p. 17.
12 Zangrandi, *Il lungo viaggio*, p. 195.
13 *Badoglio a Caporetto* (1923), *Fissazioni liberali* (1924) and *Da Caporetto a Vittorio Veneto* (1925). For further information, see N. Bobbio, *Italia fedele: Il mondo di Gobetti* (Florence: Passigli, 1986).
14 *Resistenza*, XVIII, no. 1, January 1964, p. 5.
15 See the commemoration of Egidio Meneghetti in *Annuario dell'Università di Padova per l'anno academico 1984–85*.
16 Ibid. Meneghetti died in 1961. A collection of his prose works and poems in dialect has been published under the title *Poesie e prose* (Vicenza: Neri Pozza, 1963).

17 The originals of the minister's letters and the draft copy of Bobbio's reply have been preserved along with other documents concerning this episode in Bobbio's personal archive.

18 See L. Garibaldi, *Vita e diari di Carlo Alberto Biggini* (Milan: Mursia, 1983).

19 For further details, see Bobbio's account 'Una vecchia amicizia', in *Le virtù del politico*, ed. G. Carbone (Venice: Marsilio, 1996), pp. 31–6. This volume marked Antonio Giolitti's eightieth birthday.

20 G. Amendola, *Lettere a Milano* (Rome: Editori Riuniti, 1973), pp. 115–16.

21 V. Foa, *Il cavallo e la torre* (Turin: Einaudi, 1991), p. 128.

22 A copy of this letter was sent to Bobbio in 1993 by Angelo Ventura of Padua University, who found the document by chance when carrying out research at the Central State Archive in Rome.

23 Interview with G. De Bosio in *Memoria, mito, storia* (Turin: National Cinematographic Archive of the Resistance and the Piedmont Region, 1994), p. 70.

24 Bobbio gave a detailed account of this episode in a supplement produced on its fiftieth anniversary: 'Per la libertà. A 50 anni dall'appello del rettore Concetto Marchesi', published by the Paduan newspaper *Il Mattino*, 9 November 1993. The supplement contains Marchesi's inaugural address for the academic year 1943–4 and his famous appeal to the students.

25 N. Bobbio, *Italia civile* (Florence: Passigli, 1986), pp. 275–81.

26 Ibid., pp. 286–96.

27 See *Torino in guerra tra cronaca e memoria*, ed. R. Roccia and G. Vaccarino (Turin: Archivio Storico della Città di Torino, 1995), which includes the full text of the 'Diario di Carlo Chevallard 1942–45', ed. R. Marchis.

28 For further information, see Bobbio 'Il Comitato di liberazione della Scuola a Torino', in the collection of essays *Scuola e Resistenza*, ed. N. Raponi (Parma: La Pilota Ed., 1978).

29 'Non solo "anti"', *L'Unità*, 21 April 1995, pp. 2–3. The discussion was edited by Giancarlo Bosetti for *L'Unità*, and by Pasquale Chessa for *Panorama*. A fuller version of the discussion can be found in N. Bobbio, R. De Felice and G. Rusconi, *Italiani, amici nemici* (Milan: Reset, 1996), pp. 9–54. The most important study on the complexity of the partisan war is Claudio Pavone, *Una guerra civile* (Turin: Bollati Boringhieri, 1991).

30 P. Greco, 'Cronaca del Comitato piemontese di liberazione nazionale, 8 settembre 1943–9 maggio 1945', in *Aspetti della Resistenza in Piemonte* (Turin: Books Store, 1977), pp. 245–54.

31 A. Gobetti, *Diario partigiano* (Turin: Einaudi, 1956), p. 409.

32 The '*x-mas*' motor launches were something of which the Fascists were inordinately proud and their seamen were something of an elite [*translator's note*].

33 Roccia and Vaccarino, eds, *Torino in guerra*, p. 502. Nicola Abbagnano taught history of philosophy and Augusto Guzo was professor of philosophical theory.

34 Ibid. The diary's final entry is also evocative. Immediately below 20 May: 'End of the chronicle of partisan activity, but not of my memory of them.'

Chapter 3 Finding Out About Democracy

1 'L'opera civile di Egidio Meneghetti', in E. Meneghetti, *Poesie e prose* (Vicenza: Neri Pozza, 1963), p. 198.
2 N. Bobbio, *Tra due repubbliche* (Rome: Donzelli, 1996), p. 42.
3 G. De Luna, *Storia del Partito d'Azione* (Milan: Feltrinelli, 1982), p. 353.
4 P. Ginsborg, *Storia d'Italia dal dopoguerra a oggi* (Turin: Einaudi, 1989), vol. I, p. 117.
5 P. Scoppola, *La repubblica dei partiti* (Bologna: Il Mulino, 1982), p. 353.
6 E. Di Nolfo, *La repubblica delle speranze e degli inganni* (Florence: Ponte alle Grazie, 1996), p. 245.
7 V. Foa, *Questo Novecento* (Turin: Einaudi, 1996), p. 80.
8 The *biennio rosso* [the 'two red years'] was a period of industrial unrest which lasted from 1919 to 1921, and was one of the destabilizing factors that contributed to the advent of fascism [*translator's note*].
9 C. Cattaneo, *Stati Uniti d'Italia*, ed. N. Bobbio (Turin: Chiantore, 1945).
10 'I partiti politici in Inghilterra', a lecture given in Rome on 7 April 1946 and organized by the Italo-British Association. Now in Bobbio, *Tra due repubbliche*, p. 55.
11 G. Ryle, *Lo spirito come comportamento*, trans. N. Bobbio (Turin: Einaudi, 1955).
12 Bobbio, *Tra due repubbliche*, p. 85.
13 N. Bobbio, 'Società chiusa e società aperta', *Il Ponte*, II, no. 12, December 1946. Popper's work was translated by Armando in 1973.
14 Bobbio, *Tra due repubbliche*, p. 96.
15 *Rivista di Filosofia*, XXXVII, no. 3–4, July–December 1946, pp. 204–6.
16 N. Bobbio, 'Il pensiero politico di Luigi Einaudi', in *Annali della Fondazione Luigi Einaudi*, later reprinted in *Luigi Einaudi: Ricordi e testimonianze* (Florence: Le Monnier, 1983).
17 Actual title: *Liberismo e liberalismo*. P. Solari's edition was published by Ricciardi in 1957.
18 The Italian Social Movement (Movimento Sociale Italiano) or MSI marked the return of fascism to the Italian political scene. Although fascism was theoretically illegal, the name purposely mirrored the name of Mussolini's brutal Nazi-fascist puppet-state in the final part of the Second World War, the Repubblica Sociale Italiano (also known as the Repubblica di Salò). One of the partners in the current (2002) Italian government, Alleanza Nazionale, is a continuation of the MSI [*translator's note*].
19 Actual title: *Storia d'Europa nel secolo decimonono*.
20 Actual title: 'Politica culturale e politica della cultura'.

Chapter 4 Dealings with the Communists

1 In Italian political terminology, 'real communism' or 'real socialism' imply socialism as it actually occurred in practice, as opposed to ideal socialism [*translator's note*].

2 *The Autobiography of Bertrand Russell. II, 1914–1944* (London: George Allen and Unwin, 1968), pp. 109–10.

3 C. Rosselli, 'Per l'unificazione politica del proletariato italiano. III. Il partito comunista' (1937), in *Scritti dell'esilio*, ed. C. Casucci (Turin: Einaudi, 1992), p. 490.

4 N. Bobbio, 'Né con loro, né senza di loro', *Nuvole*, II, no. 3, March–April 1992. The article was later published in the book *Il dubbio e la scelta* (Rome: NIS, 1993).

5 Palmiro Togliatti (1893–1964) was a founder member of the Italian Communist Party in 1921 and fled the country in 1926. After the war, his leadership saw the party grow into the largest party of the left and the largest communist organization in the West [*translator's note*].

6 Actual titles: *Lettere di condannati a morte della Resistenza italiana* and *Lettere di condannati a morte della Resistenza europea*.

7 'Un centro di studi sulla cultura popolare', *Letture per tutti*, IV, no. 5, July 1952; 'Necessità della lettura', ibid., IV, no. 10, December 1952 (an issue devoted to the centre's Second National Conference held in Bologna on 9–10 January 1952); 'Sei mesi di attività del Centro popolare di Torino', ibid., V, nos 7–8, July–August 1953.

8 F. Fortini, *Asia Maggiore* (Turin: Einaudi, 1956), pp. 121–3.

9 Ibid., pp. 172–4.

10 See 'Né con loro, né senza di loro', now in Bobbio, *Il dubbio e la scelta*, p. 222.

11 'Utopia turned on its head' [L'utopia capovolta'] was the title Bobbio gave to his article commenting on the Tienanmen Square Massacre, which appeared in *La Stampa* on 9 June 1984.

12 From the article 'Né con loro, né senza di loro', in Bobbio, *Il dubbio e la scelta*, p. 223.

13 N. Bobbio, 'Ancora dello stalinismo: alcune questioni di teoria', *Nuovi Argomenti*, nos 21–2, July–October 1956, pp. 1–30; later partially republished with the title 'Stalin e la crisi del marxismo', in the collection of essays by Bobbio et al., *Ripensare il 1956* (Rome: Lerici, 1987), p. 253.

14 Bobbio, 'Stalin e la crisidee marxismo', pp. 256–7.

15 N. Bobbio, *Which Socialism?*, trans. R. Griffin (Cambridge: Polity, 1998); original title: *Quale socialismo?* (Turin: Einaudi, 1976).

16 Actual title: 'I conti non tornano', *Rinascita*, 17 October 1964.

17 Actual title: 'Ipotesi sulla riunificazione', *Rinascita*, 28 November 1964.

18 Bobbio's articles on this subject have been published together in *Le ideologie e il potere in crisi* (Florence: Le Monnier, 1981), pp. 123–54. The first article, 'La terza via non esiste', was published on 1 September 1978 and the last, 'Vita difficile per la terza forza', on 2 January 1979.

19 Strictly speaking, *liocorno* in Italian means 'unicorn' from the old French *licorne*, but also suggests a false etymology based on *lione* or lion. In this second instance, Giorgio Napolitano is probably referring to the unicorn.

20 G. Napolitano et al., *La giraffa e il liocorno. Il PCI dagli anni '70 al nuovo decennio* (Milan: Franco Angeli, 1983).

21 N. Ajello, 'I miei dubbi sulla destra', *La Repubblica*, 10 February 1995.

Chapter 5 My Teaching Experience

1 Actual title: *Lezioni della filosofia del diritto 1940–41*; published by the Faculty of Law at Padua University and La Grafolito.

2 G. Chiesura, *La zona immobile* (Forte dei Marmi: Galleria Pegaso, 1994), and *Sicilia 1943* (Palermo: Sellerio, 1993), p. 101.

3 For the text of these lectures, see N. Bobbio, *Lezioni di filosofia del diritto: Ad uso degli studenti*, as given in Padua in the 1942–3 academic year, reprint (Turin: Giappichelli, 1946), pp. 113–14.

4 See A. Papuzzi, 'Se questo è un tedesco', *La Stampa*, 14 April 1995, and *Il mondo contro* (Turin: Libri della Stampa, 1996), p. 102.

5 Bobbio, *Lezioni di filosofia*, pp. 219–20.

6 See A. Papuzzi, 'I fiori di Bobbio', *Alp*, XII, no. 137, September 1996, pp. 56–7.

7 Actual titles: *Teoria della norma giuridica* and *Teoria dell'ordinamento giuridico*.

8 N. Bobbio, *Teoría general del derecho* (Bogotá: Editorial Temis, 1987).

9 Coursebooks printed by Giappichelli: *Diritto e stato nel pensiero di Emanuele Kant* (lecture notes put together by Bobbio's student G. Sciorati, 1957) and *Locke e il diritto naturale* (1963).

10 Actual title: *Il positivismo giuridico* (Turin: Editrice Cooperativa Universitaria, 1961).

11 Actual title: 'Scienza e tecnica del diritto'.

12 Actual title: *Teoria della scienza giuridica* (Turin: Giappichelli, 1950).

13 'The majority of the reasons for the world's troubles are grammatical.'

14 'Alongside the need to define, you find the danger of becoming confused.'

15 A. Conte, *Filosofia del linguaggio normativo. II, Studi 1982–1994* (Turin: Giappichelli, 1995).

16 Ibid., p. xv.

17 Ibid., pp. xxv–xxvi.

18 Ibid., pp. xix–xx.

19 Actual titles: *L'idea individuale nel diritto privato* and *Storicismo e diritto privato*.

20 Actual title: *Studi storici di filosofia del diritto*.

21 Actual title: *L'analogia nella logica del diritto*.

22 Actual titles: *Studi sulla teoria generale del diritto*, *Giusnaturalismo e positivismo giuridico*, *Studi per una teoria generale del diritto*, and *Saggi sulla scienza politica in Italia*.

23 N. Bobbio, 'La teoria pura del diritto e i suoi critici', *Rivista Trimestrale dei Diritto e Procedure Civile*, VIII, no. 2, June 1954; republished in Bobbio, *Studi sulla teoria generale del diritto* (Turin: Giappichelli, 1955).

24 N. Bobbio, *Diritto e potere. Saggi su Kelsen* (Naples: Edizioni Scientifiche Italiane, 1992).

25 J. A. Schumpeter, *Capitalism, Socialism and Democracy* (New York: Harper & Brothers, 1942; 3rd revised and enlarged edn, 1950).

26 See also A. Papuzzi's interview with Bobbio, 'Democrazia minima', in A. Papuzzi et al., *Che leggere? Lo scaffale del buon democratico* (Rome–Naples: Theoria, 1995).

27 T. Hobbes, *Elementi filosofici del cittadino*, ed. N. Bobbio (Turin: UTET, 1948). Another edition came out in the same series in 1959, with the addition of a rare text written towards the end of Hobbes's life and published posthumously: *Dialogue Between a Philosopher and a Student of the Common Laws of England* (1681).

28 S. von Pufendorf, *Principi di diritto naturale*, ed. N. Bobbio (Turin: Paravia, 1943).

29 N. Bobbio, 'Le repliche di un ottuagenario', *Notiziario*, University of Turin, VI, no. 6 (November 1989).

30 A. Gnoli, 'Bobbio racconta Schmitt', *La Repubblica*, 19 December 1995. The interview followed an article also by Gnoli on the correspondence between Bobbio and Schmitt: 'Quel breve incontro', *La Repubblica*, 8 December 1995.

31 The Bobbio–Schmitt correspondence is held in Norberto Bobbio's private archive. The translation of Schmitt's letters is by Geminello Preterossi.

32 A reference to Schmitt's short work *Donoso Cortés* (1950) which Bobbio received with *Ex captivitate salus*. A Spanish scholar and politician, Donoso Cortés (1809–53) rejected liberal ideas in favour of the supremacy of the Church.

33 P. P. Portinaro, *La crisi dello jus publicum europaeum: Saggio su Carl Schmitt* (Milan: Edizioni di Comunità, 1982).

34 G. Martinoli, *L'università come impresa* (Florence: La Nuova Italia, 1967).

35 'Un dialogo difficile ma necessaria', 'Il potere accademico: una definizione', 'Arte di arrangiarsi e libertà del docente' and 'Arduo il dialogo con gli studenti', in *Resistenza*, XXII, no. 1 January 1968, no. 2 February 1968, no. 3 March 1968 and no. 6 June 1968, respectively.

36 The committee was appointed by the Ministry of Education on 14 February 1968, when student agitation was already spreading to the whole of Italy.

37 P. Ginsborg, *Storia d'Italia dal dopoguerra a oggi* (Turin: Einaudi, 1989), vol. II, pp. 463–4.

38 Given that the Katanga Succession (1960) was generally seen as an attempt by Belgium to reimpose its influence on part of its former colony, the Congo, it is perhaps surprising that left-wing extremists should adopt this name. The choice seems most likely to have been a reference to the

viciousness of the ensuing civil war and brutal execution of Lumumba than to any political affinity [*translator's note*].

39 'Giovinezza', meaning 'Youth', was a fascist song.

40 N. Bobbio, *Old Age and Other Essays*, trans. A. Cameron (Cambridge: Polity, 2001); original title: *De senectute* (Turin: Einaudi, 1996).

41 *Ideological Profile of Twentieth-Century Italy*, trans. Lydia Cochrane (Princeton: Princeton University Press, 1995). Original title: *Il profilo ideologico del '900*, now published separately (Milan: Garzanti, 1990). Garzanti originally published the text as part of the volume *Il Novecento* in the series 'Storia della Letteratura Italiana', ed. Cecchi and Sapegno (1969). A separate edition was published by Cooperativa Libraria Universitaria Torinese in 1972, and another by Einaudi in 1986. An English translation was published with assistance from the Giovanni Agnelli Foundation in 1995 (with an introduction by M. L. Salvadori).

42 'Quale giustizia o quale politica?', *Il Ponte*, XXVII, 1971, pp. 1437–46.

43 This article, based on a lecture that Bobbio gave at the University of Venice at the invitation of Emanuele Severino, was published in *Rivista Italiana di Scienza Politica*, X (1980), pp. 182–203, and then included in the collection of essays *Il futuro della democrazia* (Turin: Einaudi, 1984), where the above quotation appears on p. 98.

44 N. Bobbio, 'Lettera ai compagni', XIII, May 1981, p. 1.

45 F. Ferraresi, *Minacce alla democrazia. La destra radicale e la strategia della tensione in Italia nel dopoguerra* (Milan: Feltrinelli, 1995).

46 'Strategia e terrorismo: Carteggio tra Norberto Bobbio e Falco Accame (1993–94)', supplement to *Agorà 92*, no. 7.

47 *La strage: L'atto di accusa dei giudici di Bologna 2 agosto 1980*, ed. G. De Lutiis (Rome: Editori Riuniti, 1981).

48 N. Bobbio, 'Un paese tragico', in *Verso la seconda Repubblica* (Turin: La Stampa, 1997), p. 45.

49 N. Bobbio, 'La violenza oscura', *La Stampa*, 27 December 1984; now in Bobbio, *L'utopia capovolta* (Turin: La Stampa, 1990), p. 83.

50 'Uomini come cose', *La Stampa*, 29 November 1978, now in N. Bobbio, *Ideologie e potere in crisi* (Florence: Le Monnier, 1981), p. 94.

51 Ibid., p. 94.

52 *La Stampa*, 15 May 1977. Translated into French in the short volume entitled *Italie '77: Le Mouvement et les intellectuels* (Paris: Seuil, 1977), pp. 153–9.

53 Bobbio wrote Farneti's obituary, 'Ha avvicinato i due grandi nemici: storici e sociologi', in *Avanti!*, 19 August 1980. See also Bobbio's prefaces to Farneti's books: *La democrazia in Italia tra crisi e rivoluzione* (Turin: Fondazione Agnelli, 1978), *Diario italiano* (Milan: Rizzoli, 1983), and Farneti et al., *Il sistema politico italiano tra crisi e innovazione* (Milan: Franco Angeli, 1984), with an introduction by Bobbio dedicated to Farneti.

54 N. Bobbio, *La teoria delle forme di governo nella storia del pensiero politico* (Turin: Giappichelli, 1976); later translated into Spanish and Portuguese.

55 R. Rizzo, 'Un alfiere in libertà', *La Stampa*, 20 May 1979.

Chapter 6 Political Battles

1 E. Pugno and S. Garavini, *Gli anni duri alla Fiat* (Turin: Einaudi, 1974), p. 3.
2 CISL, Confederazione Italiana Sindacati Lavoratori, traditionally closest to the Christian Democrats: CGIL, Confederazione Generale del Lavoro, traditionally closest to the Communist Party [*translator's note*].
3 P. Bairati, *Valletta* (Turin: UTET, 1983).
4 FIOM, Federazione Impiegati e Operai Metallurgici, an industry-based union as in Britain representing blue- and white-collar workers in the engineering sector [*translator's note*].
5 Later published as G. Carocci, *Inchiesta alla FIAT* (Florence: Parenti, 1959).
6 Ibid., p. 60.
7 See A. Papuzzi, *Il provocatore* (Turin: Einaudi, 1976), p. 47.
8 *Risorgimento*, VIII, no. 1, January 1958, p. 19.
9 See the political column by M. Pinzauti in *La Stampa*, 31 October 1966.
10 See *Pannunzio e 'Il Mondo'* (Turin: Albert Meynier, 1988).
11 The PSI (Partito Socialista Italiano) was the Italian Socialist Party and the PSDI (Partito Social-Democratico Italiano) was the Italian Social-Democratic Party. They briefly merged to form the United Socialist Party (Partito Socialista Unificato) [*translator's note*].
12 V. Foa, *Questo Novecento* (Turin: Einaudi, 1996), p. 301.
13 See *Avanti!*, 1 November 1966.
14 See N. Bobbio, 'Dopo l'unificazione', *Resistenza*, January 1967.
15 The Italian Socialist Party of Proletarian Unity was established on 12–13 January 1964 at the end of a conference held by the socialist left. The general secretary was Tullio Vecchietti, and leading figures in the Central Committee were Lelio Basso, Vittorio Foa, Emilio Lussi and Cesare Musatti.
16 The United Socialist Party obtained 14.5 per cent in the elections for the Chamber of Deputies and 15.2 per cent in the Senate elections, losing over 5 per cent in relation to the sum of the votes obtained by PSI and PSDI in the 1963 elections: 19.9 per cent for the Chamber and 20.3 per cent for the Senate.
17 The ex-social-democrats and a group of autonomists left the reunified party, which reverted to the name of Italian Socialist Party, in July 1969.
18 See *Socialismo e democrazia rileggendo Lelio Basso*, ed. F. Pedone (Concorezzo: Ronchi Editore, 1988); for the acts of the conference see *Rileggendo Lelio Basso: socialismo e democrazia oggi*, pp. 13 and 15.
19 Speech given on 18 April 1984 at Palazzo Vecchio. See *Nuova Antologia*, no. 2151, July–September 1984.
20 N. Bobbio, 'Democrazia socialista?', in Bobbio et al., *Omaggio a Nenni* (Rome: Quaderni di Mondoperaio, n.d.).
21 N. Bobbio, *Which Socialism?*, trans. R. Griffin (Cambridge: Polity, 1998).
22 See G. Galli, *Ma l'idea non muore: Storia orgogliosa del socialismo italiano* (Milan: Marco Tropea Editore, 1996), pp. 279–80.

23 *L'Espresso*, XIII, no. 31, 1 August 1976, and *Mondoperaio*, 29, no. 9, September 1976.

24 G. Scardocchia, 'Il fiato dei comunisti sul collo del PSI', *La Stampa*, 21 July 1976.

25 G. Goria, 'Le verità di Bobbio', *Paese Sera*, 23 July 1976.

26 A. Pa., 'Che cosa può fare il PSI tra la DC e i comunisti', *Corriere della Sera*, 22 July 1976.

27 B. Craxi, 'Il Vangelo socialista', *L'Espresso*, 24 August 1978.

28 G. Bocca, 'Questo PSI che sta dietro solo ai giochi di potere', *La Repubblica*, 11 January 1980.

29 V. Gorresio, 'I rissosi orfani di Nenni', *Stampa Sera*, 14 January 1980.

30 N. Bobbio, 'Un partito fra due fuochi', *Mondoperaio*, no. 2, February 1980. Bobbio's article was part of a series on socialist policy, which included: 'Le due anime del PSI', a discussion between G. Amato, L. Colletti, L. Pintor and M. L. Salvadori; 'Gli equivoci dell'alternativa', by C. Ripa di Meana and P. Craveri; 'Sulla politica del PCI' by G. Calchi Novati and M. L. Salvadori; and 'La Costituzione dimezzata' by G. Zagrebelsky.

31 Original text: 'Du' senatori ha ffatto er Presidente / Du' cari amichi de tant'anni fa. / Carlino Bbo, cattolico credente, / e Bbobbio de "Ggiustizia e Llibertà".'

32 N. Bobbio, *In Praise of Meekness: Essays on Ethics and Politics*, trans. T. Chataway (Cambridge: Polity, 2000); original title: *Elogio della mitezza e altri scritti morali* (Milan: Linea d'Ombra, 1994).

33 Actual title: *The domende di Bobbio.*

34 Actual titles: 'Che cosa è il pluralismo?' and 'Come intendere il pluralismo?'

35 Actual titles: 'Marx pluralista' and 'Non è tutto oro quel che luccica'.

36 Actual title: *Le ideologie e il potere in crisi.*

37 Actual title: *L'utopia capovolta.*

38 The article was used with the title 'The upturned utopia' in *New Left Review*, no. 177, September–October 1989, with the title 'Utopia Overturned' in *The European Journal of International Affairs*, Autumn 1989, and with the title 'Utopia dada la vuelta' in *El Sol*, I, no. 34, 24 June 1989. It was criticized by E. Galli della Loggia in 'Caro Bobbio, mi rallegro se crolla il comunismo', *La Repubblica*, 11 June 1989, with a reply from Bobbio in 'Chi si contenta', *La Stampa*, 13 June 1989.

39 A. Marcenaro, 'Che cantonata ha preso il PCI', *L'Espresso*, 16 November 1985.

40 Actual title: 'Parole nella nebbia', *La Stampa*, 8 February 1987, front page.

41 B. Craxi, 'Se Bobbio leggesse il programma del PSI', *La Stampa*, 11 February 1987.

42 The speech, with the title 'Riformismo, socialismo, uguaglianza' ['Reformism, socialism and equality'] was published in *Mondoperaio*, no. 38, May 1985, pp. 64–71, with a reply by Claudio Martelli, which gave a rather unfavourable verdict on Bobbio's paper. For Bobbio's

reply to Craxi, see 'Riformismo: Bobbio risponde a Craxi', *La Stampa*, 12 February 1987.
43 The general secretary of the UN, Pérez de Cuellar, had announced that the Hon. Bettino Craxi, general secretary of PSI, would be appointed his personal representative for the debt problem in developing countries. The appointment was confirmed in December 1989.
44 The articles in *La Stampa* in 1994: 'Separazione come arte liberale', 10 February, and 'I poteri e le leggi', 15 August (G. Urbani's article in reply: 'Ci vuole un clima costituente', 17 August).
45 'Il partito fantasma', *La Stampa*, 3 July 1994.
46 S. Berlusconi, 'Che cosa è Forza Italia?', *La Stampa*, 5 July 1994, and N. Bobbio, 'Il diritto di fare domande', *La Stampa*, 9 July 1994. Forza Italia was entirely the creation of the media mogul Silvio Berlusconi and was the dominant party within the right-wing coalition that was briefly in power in the 1990s and returned to power in 2001 [*translator's note*].
47 A. Gilioli, 'Che partito leggero! É' tutto un mistero', *L'Europa*, 28 July 1994. The article included an extract from Forza Italia's statute.
48 N. Bobbio, *Il dubbio e la scelta* (Rome: NIS, 1993).
49 N. Bobbio, *Il futuro della democrazia* (Turin: Einaudi, 1984), 1991^2, p. 74.
50 G. Bosetti, 'Io elettore tra dubbi e speranze' ['As a voter assailed by doubts and hopes'], *L'Unità*, 6 April 1996.

Chapter 7 Peace and War

1 N. Bobbio, 'La marcia della pace', *Resistenza*, XV, no. 10, October 1961.
2 Colonnetti organized a conference on 'The responsibility of scientists and technicians in the modern world', which took place at the Turin Academy of Science between 13 and 14 June 1967. He was particularly worried about the military use which would certainly have occurred in emergency situations and which he defined as 'terrifying'. As he could not take part in the conference, Bobbio sent a message of support, as can be seen from the conference acts.
3 See 'Non uccidere', speech read on 4 December 1961 and published in *Resistenza*, XV, no. 12, December 1961. Reprinted in N. Bobbio, *Il terzo assente* (Turin: Sonda, 1989), pp. 129–42.
4 See N. Bobbio, 'Il conflitto termonucleare e le tradizionali giustificazioni della guerra', *Il Verri*, VII, no. 6, 1962. The article was republished in Bobbio, *Il terzo assente*.
5 The lectures were gathered into coursebooks edited by Bobbio's students, Nadia Betti and Marina Vaciago, and were published in 1965 by the Turin University Library Co-operative, with the title *Il problema della guerra e le vie della pace*.
6 'Filosofia della guerra nell'era atomica'. The text was published by the magazine *Terza Programma*, no. 3, 1965, and republished in Bobbio, *Il terzo assente*.

7 N. Bobbio, *Il problema della guerra e le vie della pace* (Bologna: Il Mulino, 1979), pp. 22–3.

8 Ibid., pp. 22–3.

9 Ibid., pp. 96–7.

10 From the lecture given at the conference on 'Le Fondement des droits de l'homme', organized by the Institut International de Philosophie (L'Aquila, 14–19 September 1964). The text appeared in the conference acts, under the title 'L'Illusion du fondement absolu', and was republished under the title 'Sul fondamento dei diritti dell'uomo' in *Rivista Internazionale di Filosofia del Diritto*, XLII, no. 2, April–June 1965, and in the volume already referred to, *Il problema della guerra e le vie della pace*.

11 N. Bobbio, 'Solo una società più libera e avanzata potrà rispettare i diritti dell'uomo', *Resistenza*, XXI, no. 12, December 1967. With a few changes, this text was used in a speech to the Italian Society for International Integration, on the occasion of the opening of the International Year of Human Rights, Rome, 28 January 1968 (see Bobbio, *Il problema della guerra*, p. 156).

12 They were M. L. Astaldi, L. Basso, L. Bigiaretti, R. Bonazzi, D. Carpitella, C. Cases, L. Cavalieri, T. Codignola, G. Colonnetti, L. Del Fra, A. Donini, E. Enriquez Agnoletti, A. Galante Garrone, B. Giacci, G. La Pira, V. Laterza, C. Luporini, G. Manzù, T. Maselli, A. Mondadori, G. Savelli, G. Tofano and G. Toraldo di Francia.

13 The proposal subsequently took the following form: 'In relation to Art. 11 of the Constitution, the Italian Republic forgoes the manufacture and use of nuclear weapons or other arms of equal or greater destructive power, and undertakes to prevent the introduction, storage or transit of the said weapons on its soil, whatever the provenance'. However the proposed law was never put before Parliament.

14 R. Aron, *Pace e guerra tra le nazioni* (Milan: Edizioni di Comunità, 1970).

15 N. Bobbio, 'Luigi Einaudi federalista' in C. Malandrino, ed., *Alle origini dell'europeismo in Piemonte: La crisi del primo dopoguerra, la cultura politica piemontese e il problema dell'unità europea* (Turin: Fondazione Einaudi, 1993). Bobbio returned to this argument in a round-table discussion on 5 February 1996 on the United States of Europe as it is represented in the thought of Giovanni Agnelli and Attilio Cabiati. See 'Il senatore Giovanni Agnelli e l'unità europea', *Nuova Antologia*, no. 2197, January–March 1996, pp. 292–7.

16 N. Bobbio, 'Pace, concetti, problemi e ideali', in *Enciclopedia del Novecento*, vol. VIII (Rome: Istituto della Enciclopedia Italiana, 1989), pp. 812–24.

17 Declaration to Tg3 del Piemonte [the regional television news] on 15 January 1991; see N. Bobbio, *Una guerra giusta?* (Venice: Marsilio, 1991), pp. 39–40.

18 F. Ferraresi, 'Guerra "giusta", incontro tra intellettuali e Bobbio', *Corriere della Sera*, 31 January 1991.

19 See *L'Unità*, 22 January 1991.

20 N. Bobbio, 'Ci sono ancora guerre giuste?', *L'Unità*, 22 January 1991.
21 Bobbio's lecture was the first of a series organized by Sermig [Servizio Missionario Giovani] in conjunction with an anti-war campaign called 'Contro l'urlo della guerra, grida pace con noi' (see *La Stampa*, 19 September 1995).
22 D. Zolo, *La prospettiva del governo mondiale* (Milan: Feltrinelli, 1995).

Chapter 8 Taking My Leave

1 N. Bobbio, *Old Age and Other Essays*, trans. A. Cameron (Cambridge: Polity, 2001).
2 Ibid., pp. 30–1.
3 For further information, see J. De Lucas, 'La influencia de Bobbio en España' and A. Stella Narducci, 'La influencia de Bobbio en IberoAmerica', in *La figura y el pensamiento de Norberto Bobbio* (Madrid: Instituto de Derechos Humanos Bartolomé De Las Casas, 1994), pp. 259–82 and 283–308.
4 N. Bobbio and P. Polito, 'Dialogo su una vita di studi', *Nuova Antologia*, no. 2200, October–December, 1996.
5 Ibid., p. 63.
6 M. Macagno, *Cucire un motore* (Pollone: Leone & Griffa, 1992).
7 F. Malgaroli, *Domani chissà* (Cuneo: L'Arciere, 1992).
8 A. Ruju, *Dall'abisso alla vetta* (Turin: Genesi Editrice, 1993).
9 A. Bobbio, *Memorie*, ed. C. Manganelli, with preface by N. Bobbio (Alessandria: Edizioni Il Piccolo, 1994), p. 9.
10 N. Bobbio, *In Praise of Meekness: Essays on Ethics and Politics*, trans. T. Chataway (Cambridge: Polity, 2000).
11 Ibid.
12 Lega Nord is a right-wing nationalist party, which is currently (2002) in government with Berlusconi's Forza Italia and the renamed Fascist Party, Alleanza Nazionale. Its erratic leader, Umberto Bossi, wishes to create a new state called Padania in the north of Italy without any historical basis [*translator's note*].
13 From the speech 'Progresso scientifico e progresso morale', Turin, 7 April 1995, unpublished.

Index